Praise for *The Software Developer's Career Handbook*

Perhaps you're lucky enough to have Michael Lopp as a friend or even as your boss. For the rest of us, there's this book. It's pure gold, and it will repay you many times over for the time you spend with it.

—*Seth Godin, Author,* This Is Marketing

Michael Lopp is that rare beast: the completely honest manager who uses plain language. You want to know how to cultivate a thriving career in this industry? Listen to Lopp.

—*John Gruber, Daring Fireball*

Michael Lopp's *The Software Developer's Career Handbook* is full of personal stories that come across like a relaxed conversation with a thoughtful, funny, friend. It's so engaging and entertaining, you won't realize you're gaining valuable advice along the way.

—*Jim Coudal, Field Notes Brand*

This book is a must-read for aspiring software developers, those transitioning into a leadership role, and even seasoned managers. Michael Lopp's advice will inspire you to achieve the impossible.

—*Gina Bianchini, Founder & CEO, Mighty*

A tech career is a chess match where each move sets up the next move. However, unlike a chess match, you don't know what the new square will hold when you move there. How can you intelligently and confidently play such a game? Read this book.

—*Kent Beck, Chief Scientist, Mechanical Orchard*

The Software Developer's Career Handbook

A Guide to Navigating the Unpredictable

Michael Lopp

Beijing · Boston · Farnham · Sebastopol · Tokyo

The Software Developer's Career Handbook

by Michael Lopp

Copyright © 2023 Michael Lopp. All rights reserved.

Published by O'Reilly Media, Inc., 1005 Gravenstein Highway North, Sebastopol, CA 95472.

O'Reilly books may be purchased for educational, business, or sales promotional use. Online editions are also available for most titles (*http://oreilly.com*). For more information, contact our corporate/institutional sales department: 800-998-9938 or *corporate@oreilly.com*.

Acquisitions Editor: Melissa Duffield
Development Editor: Jill Leonard
Production Editor: Christopher Faucher
Copyeditor: nSight, Inc.
Proofreader: Piper Editorial Consulting, LLC

Indexer: BIM Creatives, LLC
Interior Designer: Monica Kamsvaag
Cover Designer: Susan Thompson
Illustrator: Kate Dullea

August 2023:   First Edition

Revision History for the First Edition

2023-08-09:   First Release

See *http://oreilly.com/catalog/errata.csp?isbn=9781098116675* for release details.

978-1-098-11667-5

[LSI]

Contents

Preface

For years, any work related to artificial intelligence or machine learning I've called work done by robots. For example, if I'm asking, "Is this list generated by humans or robots?" I'm asking whether machine learning was done to generate this list. I'm distilling a complex ecosystem down to the most basic elements by asking, "Is this work done by humans or robots?"

I like labeling things. It makes the world easier to understand.

The title I chose for my first book was *Managing Humans.* That book arrived long before the AI fever that gripped the mid-2020s when this book was published but is another example of my predilection of finding a descriptive label. It's a handy way to say more with fewer words.

This book was originally published as *Being Geek,* which you will notice is no longer the title. At the time of its writing, 2010, the buzz around nerds and geeks was strong. I did a lot of public speaking, where I was describing the nerd and geek mindset. The idea of swerving away from my leadership roots was an exciting detour.

As I wrote the book, I became increasingly frustrated by the title. Much of my writing is focused on leadership, and as I wrote each next chapter, I was forcing "geek"—somehow, anyhow—in the book. By the time I was finishing the book, I'd fully returned to my leadership roots. I was writing another book on leadership.

This dissonance stuck with me long after its publication. Compared to the first book, my impression was that this book was a dud, but it wasn't. Like *Managing Humans,* the original text continued to sell. I continued to get asked about it. It wasn't a best seller, but it had legs.

One inbound comment came from Philip Sharp at the Rands Leadership Slack community: "What about a second edition?" Revision was on my mind as I was finishing the fourth edition of the first book, so I grabbed it and skimmed it. *Oh, there's some good writing here.*

A few weeks later, I pitched O'Reilly on a revision, and we discussed my unease with the first book and found a new title, the subtitle of the first book: *The Software Developer's Career Handbook*. It's a mouthful but a stronger description of this work.

In addition to adding eight new chapters to this book, I've mostly cauterized the term *geek* from this book. This was easier than expected because, as a person who mostly wanted to write about leadership, I could replace the word *geek* with *engineer* or, in other cases, *leader* with no further edits. Through the editing process, we've also dropped a few chapters that did not age well and modernized chapters where aging technology dated a chapter.

Finally, this book still starts and finishes with a consideration of your current job and then your next job. Still, the middle contains helpful advice about understanding humans, leaders, culture, and communication. For the careful observers of my career, you'll notice the leadership portions are focused on the mindset of a first-time leader. This book was originally written before I attempted the role of an executive, and I stayed true to this voice as I revised it. I think there's an important place for the voice of a first-time leader in the rapid growth world of technology.

A final label. The narrator throughout this book is Rands. This is a pseudonym I've been using for decades. The comfortable anonymity of Rands provides a professional distance from the topics I cover. Similarly, just about every proper name and situation described in this book is fake. They've been deliberately constructed in order to tell a tale.

And that tale starts now.

O'Reilly Online Learning

O'REILLY®   For more than 40 years, *O'Reilly Media* has provided technology and business training, knowledge, and insight to help companies succeed.

Our unique network of experts and innovators share their knowledge and expertise through books, articles, and our online learning platform. O'Reilly's online learning platform gives you on-demand access to live training courses, in-depth learning paths, interactive coding environments, and a vast collection of text and video from O'Reilly and 200+ other publishers. For more information, visit *https://oreilly.com*.

How to Contact Us

Please address comments and questions concerning this book to the publisher:

O'Reilly Media, Inc.

1005 Gravenstein Highway North

Sebastopol, CA 95472

800-889-8969 (in the United States or Canada)

707-829-7019 (international or local)

707-829-0104 (fax)

support@oreilly.com

https://www.oreilly.com/about/contact.html

We have a web page for this book, where we list errata, examples, and any additional information. You can access this page at *https://oreil.ly/software-dev-handbook*.

For news and information about our books and courses, visit *https://oreilly.com*.

Find us on LinkedIn: *https://linkedin.com/company/oreilly-media*

Follow us on Twitter: *https://twitter.com/oreillymedia*

Watch us on YouTube: *https://youtube.com/oreillymedia*

Acknowledgments

I would like to acknowledge and thank:

The Rands Leadership Slack community. You asked for a second edition of this book, so it happened.

Lyle Troxell, my podcast cohost, who asks the best questions that lead to the best conversations.

Tom, Jeff, David, Mark, Justin, Laura, Tony, JG, Joshua, Jon, Julia, Matt, Ross, Ali, Richard, and Cal. Working with you made me a better leader. I wish we hung out more.

42. You remain the answer to life, the universe, and everything.

PART I

Building a Career Playbook

For each new job, I can remember the moment I decided to leap. The consideration that went into these decisions was epic. There were pro and con lists, spreadsheets, and endless conversations with trusted people that started with support and finished with, "Enough talking. When are you going to decide?"

This first section of *The Software Developer's Career Handbook* walks you through the endless list of decisions and tasks you can perform as you consider and search for your next gig. From early warning signs in the current gig to figuring out how to constructively stalk your future employer, these chapters document the various plays you can make as you consider the next move in your career.

These chapters leave the most complicated part to you—making the decision.

How to Win

You've had a small number of career-defining moments.

Small decisions cross your desk and inbox all day, but this isn't a small decision. It's massive, and once you've made this decision, there is absolutely no going back. At this moment, you make a painful discovery—*Crap, I'm an engineer.*

You don't have an MBA. You know there is a People Team in the building somewhere, but you've no idea what to do with them. You want to hide in the comforting structure of code, but you know that this decision will significantly affect your career at this moment...if only you knew how.

Can I argue for more money after I receive an offer? OK, how? What do I do when my boss lies to me? What do I need to do to resign? Should I apply for a management gig? What's a program manager? They make more money doing less, right? Can I get a promotion without talking to a single human being? Why can't I work from home all the time? There isn't a class in college that teaches any of this. Wikipedia can define it, but it can't help a social introvert who sees much of the world through a keyboard.

This is the hand you've been dealt. Let's embrace your situation.

A System Thinker

We engineers are different, and understanding these differences is an excellent place to start. I believe engineers are system thinkers. The world is like a computer. After years of successful use of the computer, we've come to follow a specific ideology:

We seek *definition* to understand

the *system* so that we can discern

the *rules* so that we

know what to do next so that

we *win*.

Definition, system, and rules go back to our ever-favorite tool, the computer. Our success has tweaked our perspective of the planet. Given enough time and effort, you can totally understand the system. *A solid-state drive has these attributes and will make these operations faster. More memory will improve these types of operations. When my boss tells me I'm passive-aggressive, I should...*

Wait, what? Passive what?

A crisis occurs when a situation appears that doesn't follow the rules, doesn't fit in the system, and is inherently indefinable. We go on high alert when we see a flaw in the system because the system is what we tell ourselves to get through the day. Unfortunately, this structure is a comfortable illusion full of certain flaws that I like to call people.

People Are Messy

People screw things up. They are the sources of bugs. They ask odd questions, and their logic is flawed. In the pleasant mental flowchart we have in our engineering heads, a single person causes us to frustratingly ask, "Who are these people, and why the hell don't they follow the rules? Can't they see the system? *Don't they want to win?*"

Yes, they do.

No one wants a reminder that life is a crapshoot. That we're all making it up as we go based on reacting to whatever random strangeness occurs in our corner of the world. The lack of control is especially discomforting to the engineer, so we construct imaginary structured versions of our world to make the chaos a bit more palatable and predictable.

I'm an engineer, and while I'm just as ambiguous and emotionally slippery as that comic book enthusiast in the cube next door, I've been staring at engineers struggling with messy parts of high tech for two decades. I believe I can improve our chances to win, even with all these people stumbling around and touching our stuff.

The advice and this book begin with a contradiction: prepare for the unpredictable.

The unpredictable shows up on your doorstep in two forms: simple unpredictability, which you can assess and act on immediately, and world-changing unpredictability, which rocks your world and requires serious work. In *The Software Developer's Career Handbook*, I hope to equip you with a system of improvisation that will help you act on the simple unpredictability and, second, to encourage you to develop a blueprint for your career to prepare for when the sky really falls.

A System of Improvisation

In my head, a handbook is a book with curled pages, a beaten cover, and folded pages that are never far away. It's achieved this state by being repeatedly and tactically useful. *The Software Developer's Career Handbook*'s chapters are structured to your job, understanding leadership, the tools you'll need, and then, well, your next job. The idea is not the arc; the idea is that as you're going through a tiny bit of unpredictability, you can flip to Chapter 39 and read about how to interpret your yearly review so you can make a decision: *Am I or am I not going to get fussy about this poorly written review?*

The chapters of *The Software Developer's Career Handbook* are standalone, meaning minimal threads tie one chapter to the next. This is partially a function of where some of the chapters originated—my weblog, *Rands in Repose*—but also a function of the engineer's attention span, which can be...limited. My hope is these fully contained, easily consumable chapters are useful when small decisions show up in that they help you take apart your decisions. They aren't prescriptive because whatever decisions you have on your plate are yours to make, and the best I can offer is to tell you the story of when I made that decision, what I thought, and how I moved forward.

It's satisfying: completing a task, making a decision, getting a thing done. These small bits of motion you apply to your day make up most of the decisions you make in your life, and they happen with little pomp and circumstance. Making these decisions and seeing what happens to make up the bulk of your experience and how you continue your endless search for rules that define your system. The better you get at them, the more success you have, and the quicker you make them the next time they show up.

Still, these are tiny bits of unpredictability, and you must know what to do when massive unpredictability appears.

A Career Blueprint

You read a book. From beginning to end. While the chapters of *The Software Developer's Career Handbook* can stand alone, the book is intended to tell a long story about your job, your manager, the way you work, and how you'll eventually search for a new role. The time it takes to read this book will, hopefully, give you some distance from the day-to-day work of your job and remind you that you're working toward something more significant. Your job is not just what you're doing; it should prepare you for what you want next.

As you read this book, you need to keep three classes of questions in your head:

- What am I doing?

- What do I do?

- What matters to me? What do I care about?

Your workday is deviously designed around focusing you on the first question. Think about your state of mind when you get in the car to drive home, when you're barely pulling yourself out of the sea of things to do. You're not dreaming about your next gig; you're not thinking strategically about your career; you are recovering from a day of tactical tasks. That's what you're doing, but is that what you do?

Maybe you're lucky. You're the software architect. You're the director of design. You're the guy who cares more about databases than anything else on the planet Earth. You've discovered a more significant theme to what you're doing. It's your career, which is much bigger than a job.

That's what the People Team will do for me, right? My boss has that covered, right?

Wrong.

As an avid watcher of management in Silicon Valley for almost three decades, I know the good intentions of the People Team and the partial attention of your boss do not a career make.

Whether you know what you do or don't, reading this book from cover to cover is a few hours of your time when you get to ask, What matters to me? What do I care about? Does this management gig float my boat? Am I a developer for life? Is the fact that I spend the entire subway trip home cursing my gig a bad sign? It's professionally fashionable to bitch about your company and your inept manager, but when you start bitching about your career, I call bullshit. The idea that anyone besides you is responsible for your career is flawed. Your boss is only your boss while he's your boss. Your career is yours forever.

You choose your career, and the choice makes life easy when massive unpredictability arrives. Think about it like this: How much easier would it be to make that big decision if you knew exactly what you wanted to do? Is it easier or harder to argue for that new project at work when you know it's perfect for your career goals? How would the review conversation with your boss go when you're completely sure you want to get into management?

All decisions are easier when you're clear about where you're headed.

A Collection of Moments

Your career is a collection of moments when you make a decision. PC or Mac? Answering that recruiting email or not? Confront or retreat? Even with this book in hand, you're going to screw up as many decisions as you make correctly, which is a troubling thought for the system-searching engineer who is simply trying to win, but there are still rules to discern.

With time and experience, you'll learn there is a finite set of personalities walking the halls. Yes, they have nuances, but these personalities and motivations can be understood. Your boss and his motivation will vary from company to company, but it's a knowable set of motivations varying from "hiding until I retire" to "driving everyone crazy as I attempt to conquer the world." It's OK to quit a job with people you like because there are many people to like out there. You can make most meetings useful. You can dig yourself out from underneath the endless list of things to do.

The Software Developer's Career Handbook is a distillation of 25 years in Silicon Valley working at large and small companies. I've had equal parts of calm and chaos, and I've been keeping notes the entire time because I believe I'm always one rule away from figuring it all out, and that's how you win.

2

A List of Three

The number three has been mystically bouncing around in my life for years. First, there was the VP of marketing who was obsessed with it. "Triangles, Rands, I see them everywhere. There's power in there." She kept three pieces of polished obsidian on her desk in a triangle formation at all times. Then there was the director of engineering. All of his advice was dispensed in digestible lists of three. It was a handy, lightweight way of distributing bright ideas.

As a means of simplifying the infinite, I see no reason why three can't help. Three is everywhere. Yes, no, maybe. Socialism, communism, capitalism. Memory, understanding, will. Of the people, by the people, for the people. I'm a fan.

This is why it comes as no surprise that I can pack both career development and management philosophy into a list of three items:

1. Technical direction

2. Growth

3. Delivery

Conveniently, the list applies to managers and individuals, but let's talk about it from the individual career perspective. Let's turn the list into questions:

1. Are you actively defining the technical direction for your product, feature, or task?

2. Do you understand what you need to do in order to grow?

3. Are you hitting your dates? Are you meeting your commitments? Are you doing what you say you're going to do?

That's it. That's all. There are shelves full of management and career development books that are going to explain in excruciating detail the 27 aspects of a good manager or 42 habits of effective developers, and I'm certain there are gems in those books. It is the nature of experts to dive deep, to explain in detail, and God bless 'em, but I've got work to do, so let's keep it brief.

Technical Direction

Whether you're a manager or an individual in software development, you own code, and that code is in—wait for it—one of three states: you're writing it, you're fixing it, or you're maintaining it. When you're writing the code for the first time, technical direction as a goal isn't hard to keep in the front of your mind. What am I building? What tools am I using? Is it going to perform? I don't know what you're building, I don't know what company you work for or your development culture, but I do know that for the code you own, you set the technical direction, not your manager.

A manager's job is to forget. That's what they do. They get promoted and begin the long process of forgetting everything that got them promoted in the first place. I'm not joking. Manager amnesia will be the source of much professional consternation throughout your career.

Now, in defense of my brethren managers, we don't forget everything. During all that forgetting, we're learning other useful things like organization politics, meeting etiquette, and the art of talking for 10 minutes without saying a thing. The things that we do remember are the painful scars of being an engineer. The scars of experience pop up as random inspiration and make it look like we're keeping track of everything, but we aren't. We don't. This is why my management strategy is to assume those closest to the problem can make the best decisions. That's how I scale.

There are those managers who are desperately trying not to forget. They believe that given enough time and effort, they have the same degree of visibility they had when they owned the code. These people are called micromanagers, and they are going to fail because they're not learning how to forget.

It's not just micromanagers driving their teams up the wall with their weekly status reports, 1:1 code reviews, and a complete disregard for the management structure. It's their quest to know it all that is destroying trust on their team. *Why did you hire these people?* To get more done. They're not extensions of you; they're entirely themselves. Deal with it. Again, those who are closest to the code are eminently qualified to set the technical direction of the work.

Rands, he's not a micromanager. He fashions himself a visionary and he won't shut up about Scala. How the hell can I get things done when I'm being Scala-beaten?

That's the beauty of my list of three. Your manager, micromanager or not, has the same goal with a slightly different lens. It's his job to set technical direction—just like you. So, yeah, he's going to do research at the technical edges; he's going to think about radical re-architecture. Hopefully, he's competent and has the ability to do so, but he's working at a higher level and you own the bits.

It's easy to forget with micromanagers and visionaries cluttering your day with their agenda, but as the owner of the code, it's your job to care—daily. Whether during the joy of writing the code, the annoying days of bug fixing, or the seemingly endless maintenance tasks, it's your call where the code will go next. Are we spending too much time on maintenance? Is it time to throw it away and start over? Sure, it's not necessarily your decision to make, but it's absolutely your responsibility to raise the issue, to have an opinion, and to affect the plan.

This code is crap. We need to start over.

::A strong defensible opinion::

Growth

Early in my career at Borland, I was baffled by the stock. What is it? Who sets it? What's an option? How do I spend it? Borland was in its heyday, so during all of the stock confusion, the price just went up...for two years. My thought was, *That's what stocks do. They grow.* Then we missed our number. The earnings we had predicted were missed and the stock took a beating.

More confusion.

Everything in the building looked exactly the same. Everyone was working hard, but we were suddenly worth 25% less? This was my first lesson in perception being reality. The market sees growth as a leading indicator, and the panicky mob that is the stock market equates a lack of growth with death.

And they're right.

As the second item in my career philosophy, growth represents the strategy by which you are learning, doing more, getting promoted, getting the shit kicked out of you, and garnering more responsibility. There's a simple rule designed to grab your attention: *if you're not growing, you're dying.*

Let's see if you're dying. Ask yourself the following:

- Have you failed recently?

- Is there someone within throwing distance who challenges you daily?

- Have you learned something significant in the last week?

Any answer of no is a troubling sign. You're coasting. Sure, it's comfortable, but while you're sitting there in your mediocrity, your industry is aggressively attempting to make you irrelevant. It's not personal; it's a function of all of those other bright people who aren't scared of failure, who have surrounded themselves with catalytic personalities, and who thrive on understanding.

Rands, isn't it my manager's job to grow me?

There are two parties responsible for your growth. You and your manager. Now, this isn't actually true, but early in your career, it's a convenient illusion. It is allegedly your manager's responsibility to care more about your growth than you. They do have more experience and are able to identify and assign opportunities suitable for that growth. *She's ready to be a tech lead. I can feel it.*

Unfortunately, you're always second in line regarding growth with your manager. I pessimistically believe that your manager will consider their interests before they consider yours. It sounds devious, but the same rule that applies to you applies to your manager: *grow or die.*

Perhaps a healthier way to think of it is that your manager is responsible for your job, but you're the manager of your career. The primary goal of both jobs is to identify and act on opportunities inside the company that will challenge you, force you to learn, and push you to the edge of discomfort. These opportunities are going to confuse you because it's unfamiliar territory and you don't have a map...which is the point. A good manager creates opportunity, but it's your responsibility to take it.

However, your boss is not going to discover opportunities outside of the company. They're likely never going to say, "Yeah, we're doomed. Get the hell out." There is no one more qualified and informed to make decisions regarding your larger future than you.

I am ready for more.

Delivery

It's an unfortunate necessity that in our industry, the sky falls—frequently. With over two decades of experience in Silicon Valley working at companies big and small, I can confirm that random disasters are a constant.

Let's assume that you're a responsible person in the next disaster. Let's assume it's of a deeply technical nature, and let's assume you're not capable of handling this disaster. Who do you call?

Got a name? I bet you do. It's the guy who can do anything. He's probably got an office in a company where only managers have offices. He probably wears very strange T-shirts and has odd eating habits, but what's important about this guy is he delivers—like a machine. There's nothing that you can't ask this fellow to do that he doesn't leap on, can't explain, or can't argue about.

My guess is this guy is deeply technical—maybe an architect, perhaps a free electron—but going back to the question, why'd you call him to help with the disaster?

He delivers. It's not even a question. You don't consider for a moment that he won't be able to help. Even if the technical expertise you require has absolutely zero intersection with his experience, you know he'll be able to help.

It's a skill, yes, but it's not the skill that everyone admires; it's the reputation. It's the expression you'll see on your boss's face when you tell him, "Yeah, I know it's a disaster, but Ryan's helping." *Oh good, it's handled.*

If technical direction is your ability, and growth is the refinement and shaping of that ability, then delivery is the reputation you construct around that ability, and the rule is also simple: *do what you say you're going to do.*

Quips, quotes, tweets, and clever names are littered all over my writing, but don't let their simplicity imply they are easy to apply. Doing what you say you're going to do is hard. Let's do the math:

- How many requests were made of you today? Let's call that X.

- How many of those requests have you completed or plan to complete to the satisfaction of the requestor? Let's call that Y.

If X is ever larger than Y, then your reputation is suffering. Any task, big or small, that has landed on your plate and you failed to complete is eroding your reputation. Here's why:

It wasn't a big deal. They didn't even notice. Yeah, they did. Maybe they didn't follow up, and maybe it wasn't that big of a deal, but there was a brief moment when they internally measured you: *Didn't follow up. Didn't complete. Doesn't care.* That's what they remembered.

I couldn't say no. It was my boss. When you accept a task from your boss, whether you can complete it or not, the assumption is that you'll do it. Saying no to the person who signs the checks is tricky, but again, consider your reputation. Are you going to lose more points for saying no to a task or for failing at that task?

But I want to be a team player. Yeah, good teams don't fail.

In the words of Bayard Rustin, a Quaker and civil rights leader, *Speak truth to power.* When the boss is signing you up for failure, your move isn't laying down the no; your move is to tell the truth. *Hey, I have no idea how to be successful here. I care about being successful, and so should you. Help.*

You need to be maniacal about your reputation. Yes, a single failure to deliver isn't a disaster. Mistakes happen. X is sometimes bigger than Y, but some misses are vastly bigger than you expect. That one offhanded request from your VP that sounded like it wasn't a big deal? Well, by itself, it wasn't a big deal, but the three tasks after that were a big deal, and when she reverse engineers where the failure originated, she's not going to remember that the request was offhanded. She'll think, *Right. Unreliable.*

A reputation is a community-based opinion that you don't control. It takes years of work to develop and a single missed key responsibility to destroy.

Simplifying the Infinite

I use the word *rule* a lot in this chapter, but I'm not a rule guy—I'm a direction guy. If you're looking for the definitive 38 ways to manage your career effectively, I'm sure there's a book for that. The list of three is intended to give a semblance of structure and a sense of direction.

For me, technical direction reminds me to care daily about my work. Growth is actively watching my career and ensuring that today is not a dull repetition of yesterday. Finally, delivery is my daily investment in my reputation. Keeping this list in my head keeps me asking questions and, more importantly, keeps me growing.

The fundamental unit of growth is knowledge. Knowledge isn't facts, and knowledge isn't data. It's your consumption of facts, data, situations, and personalities; and the consumption yields a discovery. It's when you mentally build something new. This knowledge may not be novel, but what makes it unique is that you built it for yourself.

The act of creation makes knowledge yours. It grows your mental arsenal—giving you a new experience to reflect upon forever.

3

The Itch

My expiration date for a gig has, historically, been three years. Strangely, this mirrors what I believe is the development cycle to get a product right—three releases before it's real. One release per year, the product is done...and so am I.

I say this as if there's a plan that I know after three years it's time to move on, but this is not a science. This is a historical observation. When I look at my résumé, it's obvious. In fact, I often start leaving before I even notice I'm leaving.

Leaving starts with an itch.

Are You Answering the Email?

I have a script to answer all inbound recruiter requests via email. It reads:

Hi {first_name},

Thanks for thinking of me. I am not currently looking for the next thing, and, no, I don't have any referrals in mind for this fine position.

Best of luck in your search,

Lopp.

Your first question is, Why even respond? It's an efficiency thing combined with a smidge of politeness. I want them to know I received the email so they can keep sending such queries, and I also want them to know that I'm not interested in an ongoing conversation.

The rare times that I do respond are because it is incredibly clear they aren't just cold emailing. They've done their research and they truly believe I might be a fit. This is exceedingly rare because even at the executive level, recruiting is a numbers game: *the more emails you send, the more likely you get a response.*

In these exceptional cases, I do some instant mental analysis that sounds like this: *Recruiter. Meh. Well, at least they are trying. I wonder if it's something interesting? More interesting than what I'm doing right now? More potential? More learning? I like learning.*

I'm making it sound like this inner dialog is complex and drawn out, but it's not. It's a gut check. *Am I happy in my job?* Yes? OK, ignore the email. No? Well, let's see what they have to say.

As I respond to the email, a silent alarm goes off in my head because it's likely I haven't admitted to myself that there's a chance I'd consider another gig, but here I am typing a response and wondering what the world has to offer.

I've never ended up in a gig that started with a cold call. Still, I have ended up in a new gig because a random recruiter email knocked me out of professional lethargy and created a professional itch I needed to scratch.

THE PISSED ITCH

Before we figure out whether you're ready for a new gig, let's first figure out your mindset because it will dictate whether or not we proceed. Are you pissed off at your boss? Did you just get a really bad review? Did you just learn you weren't included in the next fancy project? Are you seething?

Right, stop reading.

The rest of the chapter assumes you're in control of your temper and your current gig. You are driving. If you're pissed, you're not in the mindset to make solid strategic decisions about your next gig. You're motivated by a single thought: *I. Am. Out of here.* There's a litany of good reasons to be angry with your boss, company, or team, but you don't want to start a job change being pissed off. Nothing taints common sense more than being pissed off.

EARLY WARNING SIGNS OF DOOM

Deciding to engage with a recruiter is just one sign that cracks are forming in your job satisfaction. There are others...

Engagement

How engaged are you in your work? I know you love working on that new feature in the product—you'll always love doing new things—but how about the busywork? How engaged are you in the work that is necessary but tedious? Remember when you joined the company and everyone was bright, and you had no clue the boring work was, well, boring? Now that it's boring, can you crank through it, or are you finding excuses not to do it? I'm not talking about a lull of interest; I'm talking about a complete lack of interest in the inane but essential work that moves the company forward.

It's a warning sign when the onerous busywork drops off my plate. I'm not doing it, because I've got a new gig in mind, though I'm months away from that realization. It's an early sign that the core satisfaction in my job has begun to erode when I'm unable to charge through the work I hate.

Wanderlust

How much are you thinking about your job when you're not working? Are you thinking of it when you go to sleep? My question is, How much are you thinking about your job when you don't have to?

There's a larger job satisfaction analysis going on inside of wanderlust. In tech, 9-to-5 jobs are dead. I'm a fervent supporter of maintaining a work-life balance that allows you to explore as much of the planet Earth as possible, but I'm also the guy who thinks if you're going to do this job, you should be absolutely crazy about it. This doesn't mean that you're obsessively working 24 hours a day on the product, but it does mean that the work you are doing is part of you.

If your work isn't finding you in the car or on the bus, if you're not thinking about the things you build when your mind is wandering, it might be a sign that you're going through the motions with your work.

Why? Software development is puzzle solving. *Given this esoteric set of problems, people, and code, how am I going to build the best possible thing I can?* You don't always solve these problems sitting at your desk. You solve them in the bar, in the shower, in the places you let your mind wander.

If my mind isn't always passively chewing on the things I need to build, again, it's a sign that I might not care about what I'm doing.

Whether your engagement is fading or you are lost in wanderlust, both mental states are hurting your current gig more than you think. When your engagement fades, you stop doing busywork. When you are mentally wandering outside of your gig, again, you're decreasing your daily investment in your gig.

It's not all bad news. Your big projects are getting attention. The people who stand at your door yelling get your time, but the quiet work isn't being touched. A decent percent of the day is busywork, and when you choose not to do that work one day, no one notices because it's not high-priority work. When you don't do that work for three weeks, the busywork becomes an untended garden where the low-priority work slowly grows into reputation-affecting mistakes.

You can go months giving the boring work half of your attention, but it's just a matter of time before you ignore a task that really matters. Now you're the person who's looking for a gig not only because you're bored but also because you're screwing up.

You need to consider your new gig from a place of confidence. You don't want to be running from a mistake but rather walking toward a new opportunity.

THE CONTRADICTION LIST

Before you answer that tempting recruiting email, there are a couple of questions I want you to ask yourself, and then, with these answers in hand, I'll explain why you should ignore them.

Who are you leaving behind?

I have a Rolodex. It's not actually a Rolodex; it's a list, and on that list is everyone I'll call when I do the startup thing. In each company I've worked, I've had the Rolodex moment when I realize that someone I'm working with belongs on this list. It's a rare, wonderful moment.

There's a risk when you leave a gig that you're leaving people behind who you're going to need at a later date, who aren't going to survive the transition to your new gig. There's also a chance that you've missed an obvious Rolodex candidate.

The reality is this Inclusion on the Rolodex is defined by the ability to survive job changes, although, paradoxically, you won't actually know that for sure until you leave. Part of my inclusion criteria is that I see my relationship with this person as larger than the current gig. If they're on the Rolodex, I believe the current job no longer defines our relationship, and there's no better way to test this hypothesis other than by switching gigs.

Are you done?

In your current gig, are you close to a state where all of your major commitments are complete or won't come crumbling down if you leave? I'm not saying every single task has been crossed off; I'm saying that the work you can uniquely do can either be completed or handed off to a competent person. My real question here is, What's the story that will be told about you when you leave? Will it be, He's the guy who bailed when it got tough, or He left us at a tough time but left us in good shape?

The reality is this. You're never done. There's never a good time to go. If you're a key player in the organization, everyone will likely freak out when they hear you're leaving, meetings will be held to brainstorm backup plans, you'll leave, and things will pretty much proceed as they did when you were there.

Nature abhors a vacuum, and while your absence will be visually obvious, culturally, one or more people will start jockeying for your gig the moment the departure rumor starts wandering the hallways.

What itch are you trying to scratch?

This is the last question, but it should be first. You're still reading, so your motivation isn't "I hate this company." What is your motivation? Do you want a raise? That's great, a place to start, but you know you can get a raise just doing a good job where you're sitting right now, with people you know, in familiar surroundings. Switching gigs strikes me as a pretty radical change, given all you want is more money.

Is your motivation bigger than that? Dumping all your current responsibilities and everyone you professionally know is a shock to the system. You're in for months of confusion sitting in a place you don't know with people who speak in strange acronyms. Your motivation around looking for a new gig should be commensurate with the confidence beating you're about to take.

The reality is this. Take the beating. Every job is a fascinating new collection of people and responsibilities. You must carefully consider whether you'll fit into this potential new gig, but even with that due diligence, it's a crapshoot. You'll never know exactly what you'll learn, but I guarantee in the chaotic flurry of new, there is an invaluable experience to discover.

Bright and Shiny

Once you have telemetry on the potential new gig, my last questions are: Is it just new or is it unique? and Is it progress?

A new job is not like a new car. The morning after you buy the car, you walk into the garage and think, *Crap, a new car. I can't believe...all the new.* Then, you get in the car and start your drive to work, swimming in the new car scent, and halfway to work, you realize, hey...it's just a car.

In analyzing a potential new gig, you must separate the new from the unique. What is genuinely unique about this new job? For me, answers are varied: it's a startup, it's shrink-wrap, it's not another fucking database product, or it's a step back, but it's a company I've wanted to work at since I was a kid.

Once you've defined what's unique about the potential gig, you've got a bigger question: Is it what you want to do? This is the career question. This is when you figure out whether or not you know what you want to be when you grow up.

It's OK not to have a solid answer to that question. I'm still working on it, but just because you don't have an answer to a very hard question doesn't mean you shouldn't ask it. Does this new gig fit into whatever hazy goals you have for yourself? If you want to stand in front of a thousand people talking about changing the world, does this gig feel like a step in that direction?

The place to start thinking about a new job, about figuring out what itch you need to scratch, isn't whether or not you want the job; it's considering, *Do I know what I want to do?*

4

The Sanity Check

The amount of infrastructure sitting between you and your next gig is impressive.

Ironically, this infrastructure was purchased and configured to get you as close to this job as quickly as possible, but it doesn't. Corporate job sites are usually outsourced affairs because HR departments traditionally have neither the budgets nor the expertise to build the system they'd actually use. They shouldn't; it's not the core competency.

With half-baked solutions manned by contract recruiters, it's almost a miracle when an email shows up with a recruiter wanting to set up a phone screen. Someone, somewhere in the organization has successfully mapped you to an open position. This is a really big deal because, in my experience, the chance that you'll get this job has improved logarithmically. It's not 50/50, but it's vastly better than when you were a random résumé sitting on a desk.

There's a sense of relief when you have an actual conversation with a human being, and as soon as you hang up the phone with the recruiter, you're going to call your best friend and say, "Hey, I got an interview with The Company!"

No, you didn't. You got a phone screen, and a phone screen has little to do with an interview. While your situation isn't as tenuous as the 30 seconds you have to make an impression with your résumé, you're still not in the building, and nothing real is happening until you're in the building.

Here's the precise mental process I use as I walk through the phone screen; but before I do that, you've got homework.

Stalk Your Future Job

Before you even talk to me, you're on a fact-finding mission. You've got a job description, and after the phone screen has been set up, you've got my name. You might also have an idea of the product or technology associated with this gig or you might not, but even without a product name, you've got plenty of information to start with.

Do your research. Google me. Find out anything you can about what I do and what I care about. This isn't stalking, this is your career, and if I happen to be an engineering manager who writes a weblog, well, you can start to learn how I think. Maybe I don't have a weblog, but I post to LinkedIn. That's data, too.

How is this going to help you during the phone screen? Well, I don't know what you're going to find, but anything you can gather is going to start to build context around this job that you know nothing about. This helps with phone screen nerves as well. See, I have your résumé, and you have nothing. Aren't you going to feel better about talking with a total stranger when you figure out from staring at my Instagram that I absolutely love Weimaraners (*https://oreil.ly/DPqWg*)? Isn't it going to be reassuring to know I swear in my tweets (*http://twitter.com/rands*)? A bit of research into who you are talking to is going to level the information playing field.

Similarly, if you have a product name or technology, repeat the same process. What is the product? Is it selling well? What do other people think about it? I'm not talking about a weekend of research here. I'm talking about an hour or so of background research so that you can do one thing when the phone screen shows up: ask great questions.

That's right. In your research, you want to find a couple of compelling questions, because at some point during the phone screen I'm going to ask you, "Do you have any questions for me?" And that is the most important question I'm going to ask.

Initial Tuning

Before I ask you the most important question, I need to figure out a couple of things early in our chat. What I need to learn are the following.

CAN WE COMMUNICATE?

I'm going to lead off with something simple and disarming. It's either going to be the weather or something I picked up from your extracurricular activities. "Do you really surf? So do I! Where do you surf?" These pleasantries appear trivial, but they're a big deal to me because I want to see if we can communicate. It's nowhere near a deal killer if the pacing of our conversation is awkward—I'll adjust, but how off is it? Are we five minutes in and we still haven't said anything? OK, maybe we have a problem.

ONE MORE SOFTBALL

My follow-up questions will now start to focus on whatever questions your résumé left me with. I have no idea what I'm going to ask because it varies with every single résumé, so my thought is that you should have your résumé sitting in front of you because it's sitting in front of me as well. It's my only source material.

Whatever these follow-up questions are, I'm still figuring out how we communicate. This means you need to focus on answering the questions. It sounds stupid, but if it's not absolutely clear to you what I'm asking, it's better to get early clarification rather than letting me jump in five minutes into your answer to say, "Uh, that's not what I was asking."

See, you and I are still tuning to each other. It's been 10 minutes now, and if we're still not adjusted to each other's different communication styles, I'm going to start mentally waving my internal yellow flag. It doesn't need to be eloquent communication, but we should be making progress.

NO MORE SOFTBALLS

We're past the softball phase of the interview, and now I'm going to ask a hard question. This isn't a brainteaser or a technical question; this is a question that is designed to give you the chance to tell me a story. I want to see how you explain a complex idea over the phone to someone you don't know and can't see.

Again, who knows what the actual question will be, but you need to be prepared for when I ask the question that is clearly, painfully open ended. I'm not looking for a quick, clean answer; I'm looking for a story that shows me more about how you communicate and how you think. Being an amazing communicator is not a part of most engineering jobs; I know this. I'm not expecting Shakespeare, but I am expecting that you can confidently talk about this question because I found this question in your résumé, and that is the only piece of data we currently have in common. If we can't have an intelligent discussion about that, I'm going to start wondering about the other ways we aren't going to be able to communicate.

YOUR TURN

We're 20 minutes into the phone screen, and now I'm going to turn it over to you when I ask, "Do you have any questions for me?"

When I tell friends that this is my favorite question, the usual response is "So, you're lazy, right? You can't think of anything else to ask, so you go for the path of least resistance." It's true. It's an easy question for me to ask, but it is essential, because I don't hire people who aren't engaged in what they're doing. And if you don't have a list of questions lined up for me, all I hear is: *you don't want this job.*

A well thought-out question shows me that you've been thinking about this job. It shows me you're already working for it by thinking about the job outside of this 30-minute conversation. Yeah, you can probably wing it and ask something interesting based on the last 20 minutes, but the impression you're going to make with me by asking a question based on research outside of this phone screen will make up for a bevy of yellow flags. It shows initiative, and it shows interest.

The Close

And we're done. It went by pretty quickly, but the question is, How'd it go? Here's a mental checklist to see how you did.

LONG, AWKWARD PAUSES

Were we struggling to keep things moving? Were there long silences? Well, we didn't tune appropriately. Again, not a deal killer, but definitely a negative.

ADVERSARIAL INTERACTIONS

What happened when we had different opinions? Did we talk through it, or did we start butting heads? This happens more than I expect on phone screens, and it's not always a bad thing. I'm not interested in you telling me what I want to hear, but if we are on opposite sides of the fence, how do we handle it? If a candidate is willing to pick a fight and dig in their heels in a 30-minute phone screen, I'm wondering how often they're going to fight once they're in the building.

HOW'D IT FEEL?

This is the hardest to quantify, but also the most important. Did we click? Now, I haven't done a technical interview in years. Others with more recent experience are going to drill down on these elements if we bring you into the building. There's a risk that if you get past the phone screen and you don't have the technical ability, we're going to waste a half day of my team's time interviewing someone who can't do the job, but I'm vetting a more important aspect of you.

You are not a cog. The story we tell ourselves when someone we like chooses to leave the group or the company is: everyone is replaceable. This is true, but this is a rationalization designed to lessen the blow that, crap, someone we really like is leaving. We are losing part of the team. Professional damage is done when a team member leaves, and while they are eventually replaceable, productivity and morale take a hit.

All of my softballs and questions are designed to answer the question, Are you a person who we'd miss if you left? As the leader of my group, I am hopefully representative of my team, so if after 30 minutes you and I haven't figured out how to communicate, there's a good chance you won't click with part of the team as well.

SPECIFIC NEXT STEPS

How did I leave it? Did I give you a song and dance about how "We're still interviewing candidates and we'll be in touch within the next week"? Well, that's OK, but what you're really looking for is a specific next step like "I'm going to bring you in" or "Let's have you talk with more of the team." An immediate and actionable next step is the best sign of success with a phone screen. If I don't give you this as part of the close, ask for it. If I stall, there's a problem.

A phone screen is not an interview; it's a sanity check. I already know you meet the requirements for the job by looking at your résumé. The phone screen is going to tell me whether you meet the requirements of the culture of my team.

Unlike your résumé, where you send your hope to an anonymous recruiting address, the phone screen gives you leverage to show who you are. It's the first time you get to represent yourself as a person. It's still a glimpse, but it's the first time you can actively participate in your next job.

5

The Nerves

There's a collection of emotions competing in your head before an interview, and no matter how many interviews you go through, some version of them will always show up. I think they can be collectively viewed as the Nerves.

The Nerves are the jumble of every single emotion and question bouncing around your head trying to get out. Questions like:

- Who am I going to meet?
- Are they going to ask me to code?
- Can I accurately communicate how cool the stuff is that I build?
- Is my love of this potential new job going to come off as desperation?

My opinion is that the biggest source of the Nerves is judgment. In the next six hours, your career is literally on trial. You are about to be cross-examined by a handful of strangers regarding your education and your experience. The result of this cross-examination will be a decision regarding your future livelihood.

An interview is a crucible where everything you've learned and everything you've done is being measured and understood in a day, and it's your responsibility to elegantly and eloquently describe this experience to a bunch of strangers.

I understand why you are nervous.

In this chapter, I'm going to give you a simple strategy for handling the hardest part of the interview: answering questions.

Question Types

First, let's understand the questions that are going to show up. There are three classes of questions you're going to encounter:

Specific

> These questions are focused. *How'd you end up at that company? Why'd you leave?* While the answers to these questions might make them feel open-ended, these are warm-up feeler questions intended to give the interview context. They're exploring you and your résumé, but they haven't really asked a hard question. Answers to the questions are short, specific, and don't require much strategy.

Problem solving

> These questions are intended to qualify and demonstrate ability. *How many times a day do a clock's hands overlap?* These are the dreaded coding or brain-teasing questions that, while hated, give the interviewer an idea of how you think. You go into these questions intentionally not knowing the answer, because they want to see how (and if) you arrive at an answer. These are "show your work" questions intended to shine light on your thought process.

Open ended

> These are like problem-solving questions, except they're for the other side of your brain. *Explain your design philosophy. Tell me about your biggest failure.* Even though we all dread the problem-solving and coding questions, I believe open-ended questions are where we screw up the most, and I blame the Nerves.

While I think the strategy listed next helps with any of these question types, I think it's best suited to tackling ambiguously slippery open-ended questions.

The Answer Process

First, understand the request.

> *Tell me what you learned at your prior gig.*

It's a big, ambiguous, open-ended question, and because you have the Nerves, you're going to want to just start talking, but before you say a thing, before you even think of an answer, you need to make sure you understand the question.

Sure, I learned all about design in my last gig and...

Stop, no. You're answering and you still don't understand the question. It's not what you learned, it's what did you learn that this specific person is going to care about? Who is this person, and why is he asking the question? If it's an engineer, it's the engineering version of the answer. If it's a program manager, go for the program manager version.

You're spinning these folks by altering your answer. They asked a big, huge, vague question and you, hopefully, learned a ton at your prior gig and are using some of that knowledge to give the interviewer an answer that will be relevant to him.

OK, can I start talking now?

No.

Before you do that, you need to have an answer.

You understand who is asking and what he's asking, but do you have an answer? You don't open your mouth until you can feel the answer. My biggest interview pet peeve is when I ask a question and the candidate wastes three minutes of our time talking and never answering the question.

The flawed reasoning here is that you need to say something immediately. But since you don't immediately have an answer, you're going to open your mouth and, hopefully, verbally wander toward one. This strategy can work, but when it fails, when you're two minutes into a rambling answer that has nothing to do with what I asked, we're both going to know it. Two minutes have passed and all I've learned is that you're mentally messy.

Wait until you have an answer. Wait until you can feel it, and don't start talking until you do. If a couple of seconds have passed, and the silence is becoming palpable, it's one of two situations:

1. You really don't understand the question, or

2. You really don't have an answer.

Here are three moves:

- If you don't understand the question, clarify. "Are you asking what I learned that I cared about or what I learned about relative to design?" The clarification demonstrates active participation in the interview, and I love it. I love that someone is past the Nerves and is engaged in the interview and actually listening.

- If you don't have an answer, if you've clarified, maybe twice, and you're still drawing a blank, I have a cheap trick that is going to give you another 10 seconds: repeat the question.

  — Yeah, repeat it. Word for word. It's lame, but you've got a mental logjam in your head. Maybe it's the Nerves. Maybe you really don't have an answer, but the simple act of sounding out the question can sometimes fire the right neurons.

  — Don't look at the interviewer; the Nerves are going to tell you that they're wondering why you're stalling. Look at the ceiling, look at the window, and repeat the question.

- You've clarified twice, repeated, and you're 10 seconds into another round of silence. Still nothing. The Nerves are screaming, but I want you to ignore them. The Nerves see silence as a weakness, but I believe silence demonstrates composure and thoughtfulness, and you're going to need that composure because your next move is to look them straight in the eye and say, "I don't know."

It feels like interview suicide, the admission of ignorance, but look at the alternatives: rambling, praying, and hoping that inspiration strikes.

Both problem-solving and open-ended questions are designed to show me how you think. Even though I'm giving you space for being nervous, when your answers come out as a rambling mess, I'm wondering how much control you have over your faculties. Where's your head going to be when we're three months into a shipping death march? Are you going to be rambling then? How about when you're demoing to the executives?

I understand the courage it takes to acknowledge ignorance during a time when you're pitching yourself as a worthy hire, and it's that courage that will make an impression.

The Confidence of Knowing a Thing

Understand the question and have an answer. As interview advice goes, it's pretty simple, but you've got to keep it simple because of the Nerves. Think of your last interview when you totally blew the question and went so off-topic that neither you nor the interviewer knew where the hell you were going. Tell me about the Nerves after that disaster of an answer.

By keeping your answer strategy simple but making sure you understand what is being asked and being certain you have something to say, you're providing comfortable mental structure around your interview; you're making it a bit more predictable.

The mental state I want you in is the one after you nailed that open-ended question. They vaguely asked you about your design philosophy, you clarified, you considered, and then you spoke for three whole uninterrupted minutes about your philosophy, and as you watched the interviewer, you saw him getting it.

Your job in an interview is to lose the Nerves and show them who you are. With each successful answer to a question, you provide a more complete picture of who you are and gain confidence, and confidence kills the Nerves.

6

The Button

Getting your head on straight and having well-constructed answers to questions is only half of the game. An interview is an exchange of information, and the first and best way to screw that up is to forget that it's as important for you to gather information as it is to give it.

You may really need this job, and this might give you the impression that the steady flow of people who are grilling you are calling the shots. And yes, if you let them, they will be, but while they need to learn about you, you need to learn about them. You need to figure out their Button.

Creatures and Structure

Before you start pushing buttons, you need some context in the form of the interview list. Some employers don't want to share this until you're in the building, but even in that case, you can spend a few minutes figuring out your day.

Who do they have talking with you? Is it just your peer group? OK, then this is round #1, and if things go well, there will be another round. Is it the entire org chart? Well, looks like you're interviewing at a startup and will be exposed to the entire business. Awesome.

The next thing you want to discern is whether the interview schedule is structured or unstructured. This is likely not going to be obvious until the interviews have begun.

In a structured interview, each person interviewing you has a specific topic area: people skills, technical skills, etc. This means that each interview has a specific purpose, and no two interviews that day are going to be alike. Someone has put in the effort to make sure the different interviewers don't step on each other's toes.

The unstructured interview is a free-for-all. There's an interview list, but no one has been given guidance about what to ask, so they wing it. With each person who walks in the door, an unstructured interview is a study in personality identification. More on this in a moment when I explain about interview creatures.

In general, the participants in structured interviews come prepared. There is a process that occurred before you showed up. This might have involved a pre-interview meeting. They've read your résumé, and each person is likely capable of skillfully managing the interview.

Unstructured interviewers waste the first 10 minutes of the interview doing the homework they should've done before you arrived. It's annoying, but, as you'll see, it's a great way to figure out what they are about.

As an aside, my preferred use of interview time is a structured/unstructured hybrid. While I don't give interviewers specific topics to cover, I've chosen specific people because I know they gravitate toward certain professional areas, such as technical aptitude or cultural fit. This structural ambiguity means interviewers can creatively adapt their questions to each person while also assuring that I get a complete professional picture of the candidate.

Understanding who you are talking with and the structure of the interview process gives you some of your first insight into the organization, but the information doesn't start to flow until you stare at and understand your potential future coworkers.

INTERVIEW CREATURES

Structured or unstructured, each person who walks into the interview will bring a different agenda. The sooner you know what their agenda is, the sooner you're prepared to handle your only job during this interview. You need to get them talking.

That's right. Your goal is exactly the same as their goal, which is to learn by getting them to talk. It might strike you as a bad strategy because if they're talking, they're not learning anything about you, but that is not your problem.

Different personalities are going to walk into the interview, and each personality has a Button. When you press this button, they're going to be compelled to talk. This is not interviewing chitchat. This is essential telemetry regarding their thoughts about their job and the company.

Some personalities hide their buttons better than others, but most people have at least one.

Here's a list of some common interview creatures organized by increasing difficulty of button discovery as well as their likely influence on the interview.

Pissed-Off Pete

Pete's agenda is obvious 30 seconds into the interview because he's pissed off. This isn't an interview; this is an opportunity for Pete to rant to a captive audience. He's going to go through the motions by bringing in your résumé and feigning interest, but all he really wants to do is gripe about "the situation."

The Button: Ask anything. Doesn't matter, Pete is going to twist the answer so that he can ramble some more about how screwed up "the situation" is.

Perhaps your best tactic with Pete is to spend as much time as possible understanding "the situation." If it's so bad that he's going to ignore the opportunity of learning about you, a potential coworker, maybe "the situation" is something you should understand before you consider joining the company. Even better, asking about "the situation" is a great button exploration technique in later interviews.

Influence: Low. These interviews are normally a waste of time, and there are two red flags to consider. First, who thought it was a good idea for Pete to interview you? Don't they know he's a one-trick rant pony? Second, why is Pete so pissed off? What kind of organization lets Pete get this tense?

The Talker

Emily loves to talk, and the moment you ask anything, she'll start, and it'll be hard to get her to stop.

The Button: Ask any question.

Influence: Low. Like Pete, I have concerns about an organization that puts Emily on the interview schedule. Similar to Pete, Emily can be a huge source of information, so use the time well. She'll answer any question: Why do you love your job? Who's a jerk? Why's Pete so pissed off?

Given that Emily is going to do most of the talking, her report on you is going to be vanilla and dull. Don't sweat her.

The Poet

This is an advanced, artful combination of Pete and Emily. Like them, the Poet really has something he wants to tell you about, but unlike them, he's not going to give it up unless you specifically ask him about it. He's aware of what his job is, and that's to ask you questions.

The Button: The Poet is sneaky, but he's still going to reveal his button via his questions. What is he asking about? Where is he repeating himself? *He's an engineer, but he keeps asking interaction design questions. I wonder what happens if I ask him a question about interaction design?*

Wham.

Pure poetry. Listen hard because what's coming out of the Poet's mouth is important, and he's not going to talk for long because, unlike Emily's chattiness and Pete's pissed-off-ed-ness, he's not dedicated to his poetry. He's going to turn it around quickly because he really wants to hear about your poetry.

Influence: Medium. The Poet is articulate and artful, and this will not only color his opinion of you. The distinctiveness of his report will travel further in the organization than the useless vanilla crap captured by Emily and Pete.

Gotcha Greg

Halfway through the interview day, Greg is going to walk into the room and say nothing. He's going to size you up for 10 seconds, and then he's going to ask, "How...would you...test a soda machine...in the dark...submerged in strawberry Jell-O?"

What?

Greg is on a power trip. He believes his job is to confuse you with the dazzling brainteaser. He believes that catching you off guard with this left-field question is going to demonstrate whether or not you're mentally nimble, but I believe that Greg mostly just likes to see people squirm.

The Button: You're going to need to first get past Greg's question, and my advice is to relax and have fun with it. These types of brainteasers are usually designed to demonstrate your thinking process, so think out loud, and when you're done, go on a button hunt.

This can be tricky since Greg clearly likes to be on the offensive, but I've found that interviewers who lead with random, huge, bizarre questions are compensating for the fact that they don't really like having a normal conversation. So. Have one.

Influence: Low to medium. Greg believes his value is high, but it's likely the rest of his team knows what you figured out with his first question. He's a mental bully.

Slick Steve

Now we're getting into some tricky personalities. Slick Steve is probably not a part of the engineering organization. He's the product manager or some other marketing denizen. This means that he doesn't natively speak engineering, but as part of the strategic portion of the organization, he routinely talks to a lot of people, so he can wing it. He's read this chapter, and he knows that you're trying to gather information. He's a tough nut to crack.

The Button: Steve is going to completely ignore your attempts to find his button. "So, Steve, what do you think the biggest challenges are for product marketing?" His response, "What do you think they are?"

Dammit.

You've got to fake out Steve a bit to find his button, and that means getting a little tricky. Try this: hit Steve with an esoteric engineering question you're sure he won't know. Remember, Steve is slick, which means he wants to maintain the calm, controlled elegance of his interview, so being unable to answer a question might trip him up. This is why you follow up with a question you're sure he'll be able to answer. Ask him that lame marketing challenges question again. He'll answer it this time because he's presently feeling ignorant and flustered and needs to get back his feeling of control.

Like the Poet, Steve isn't giving up his button easily, but once you've got him talking, you have a chance to listen and see if you can find it.

Influence: Medium? Steve's here, and he's not an engineer, which means the organization values him. He's here to vet something. The question is: What?

Silent Bob

Bob is a button problem. Bob will sit down, ask his first question, his second question, his third, and you will learn nothing about him except that he's silent. He's not going to engage in witty repartee; he's literally going to ignore your button exploration questions, and this is going to annoy you. Yeah, Bob is the guy who is going to have you code at the whiteboard until you break.

The Button: Don't get rattled. In my experience, Bob is the senior technical guy on the team, and his social skills just aren't that good. He's there to vet your technical chops, and that's it. He has no button. He's not qualified to assess team fit or cultural fit, and he knows this, so show him what you've got.

Influence: Very high. If you're interviewing for a technical gig, this is the interview. This is the one you were losing sleep over. This is why you bought *Dive into Python* and read it over the weekend. No one other than the CEO is going to trump Bob. Good luck.

The CEO

Interviewing with the CEO is not necessarily an interview with the actual CEO; it's the interview with the highest-level manager during your interview process. This is likely the hiring manager's manager.

Where's the Button? Simply put, you need to be prepared for some serious Jedi Mind Shit with the CEO. The feint 'n' jab you used on Slick Steve isn't going to work here. In fact, the CEO may start the whole interview with, "What questions do you have for me?"

Oh good. This is going to be easy.

Yeah, it's not.

The Button: As you'll see, the influence of the CEO is extraordinarily high, and like Silent Bob, I want you to ignore your button acquisition activities with this person. I want you to talk. I want you to sell yourself and tell great stories about your successes. Gather your organizational intelligence in other interviews; this is your opportunity to sell yourself to one of the major influencers in the organization.

Influence: Very high. The CEO is going to say that she isn't the decision maker. She'll say that the hiring manager is, but if you do poorly with the CEO, it's unlikely that the hiring manager will contradict the boss.

A Fresh Perspective

Interviews are exhausting. Baring your professional soul for multiple rounds of interviews with a bunch of strangers will wear you out, and when you're done, you'll be wondering, *What did they learn about me? Did I nail it? Am I a fit? Did I get the gig?* All good questions, but you should also be asking, *Do I want this job? Do I like these people? Is it a healthy organization?*

By the end of a few rounds of interviews, you're going to know more about the health of the group you interviewed than a lot of the people who interviewed you do. Freaky, isn't it? Fact: all the different creatures you interview are lost in the day-to-day of their respective jobs. The fresh perspective that you have after many hours of interviewing is unique and informative, and while you still need many days on the job to figure out what is really going on, you still have a lot of data.

...if you pushed a lot of buttons.

7

The Business

You've had a small number of career-defining moments. These are the select few moments in time when the trajectory of your career changed instantly and drastically. I have two buckets of these: ones I expected and ones that completely blindsided me. While the surprise and subsequent scrambling involved in being blindsided are chock-full of delicious adrenaline, I highly recommend the moments you can predict.

One such predictable moment is the first glimpse of the offer letter for your new gig. This is the culmination of hours of résumé tweaking, a series of phone screen gymnastics (see Chapter 4), and two grueling days of in-person interviews (see Chapter 6). This is a rare moment where you can answer the question, How much does the world think I'm worth?

Fact is, you should already know. You're the business.

You Are the Business

Before I break down the offer and offer negotiation process, I want to reset your head. I've no clue how badly you need your next job, and the degree of your need will affect your negotiating position, but here's some reality. You are the business. If you get an offer and take the gig, I think you should pour your heart into it, but I want you to remember that you'll have 5 to 10 other jobs in your life, just like this next one. This means that for each moment you spend being pumped about the new gig, you'll have an equal and opposite moment at the end of the gig where you can't wait to get the next gig started.

Among these 5 to 10 jobs you'll have, there is one constant: you. You're the one who has to pay rent, ride the subway, buy a condo, get married, have some kids, and build your dream house. Your welfare is not your employer's first priority. It takes one layoff to figure that out.

You are the business; the one consistent metric business is measured by is its growth. A new gig represents one of the few moments in your career when you can directly and forever change the trajectory of that growth. It's backward to think of an offer as a true estimate of your worth; it's one piece of data in a larger story that is your responsibility to define. Let's do it.

Actual Earnings

The offer negotiation process has changed significantly in the last decade. In many US states, employers cannot ask about your current salary. If you volunteer this information, employers are not allowed to use this information in setting your offer.

You still have a chunk of work to do; you need to figure out what kind of offer you'd accept, starting with figuring out what you're currently earning. Go ahead and say your current earnings out loud. I won't tell.

What'd you say? $104K? How'd you arrive at that number? Oh, it's your base salary. You actually earn just over $200K.

I'll explain.

WHAT AM I EARNING?

Like frequent résumé updates, this career maintenance exercise is designed as a professional checkpoint that answers the simple question, How am I doing?

Let's start by breaking down how I calculated what you are earning:

- Base salary: $104K
- Benefits: 30% of $104K = +$31K
- Bonus: +$10K
- Stock: +$60K
- Total: $205K

There are likely two surprises in this framework. First, if you haven't worked for yourself, you probably haven't considered benefits as part of your compensation. That 30% is an educated swag that most companies use to account for health and life insurance and 401(k). You spend much time ignoring this 30% because it involves retirement and health benefits, and you're immortal. There will, however, be a time, probably sooner than you'd like, when you fully appreciate this portion of your compensation.

The other area: stock. This $60K represents a total swag. Levels.fyi claims that stock grants range from $20K to $100K per year for your average engineer in the US. I combined the high and low and divided it in half. Do not confuse this sloppy math with the importance of your stock grants; they often have the most direct effect on your compensation. Much more on this later in this chapter.

OK, grab a piece of paper and use this rough framework to figure out what you make. Don't sweat perfection. You just need to be close.

The Swag

Fast forward. You've just finished the interviews. Traditionally in high tech, the recruiter is the last interview of the day, and their job is to get inside your head and take your temperature regarding the gig. The guiding rule here is: the more they know you want the gig, the less they need to offer you.

And they haven't offered you a thing yet.

There's a time and place for negotiation, and it's not at the end of six hours of interviews on a Friday when you don't even know if you're getting an offer.

So, you wait. You send off a set of references, lie in bed replaying the interviews in your head, and send thank-you emails to the interview team. All professional karma-aligning activities, but what you really need to do is build your own offer letter. Like you built your compensation, I want you to build your offer.

BASE SALARY

The business model everyone loves is built on recurring revenue streams. This is why you can get a good smartphone for nothing. You'll pay for that phone many times over with your monthly subscription of $39.95. You're still happy paying that much a month because that feels like a deal, but carriers don't see $39.95; they see the $1,500 you'll spend over that three-year contract.

While it is often not the biggest potential impact on your salary, your base salary is your recurring revenue stream. It's your financial lifeblood, and we want to get it as high as possible because getting them to add a 1% increase doesn't affect this year; it affects every year after.

For the swag, you need to figure out what you want to be paid in the new gig, and my first question is, "For someone doing exactly the same job as you, how much are they being paid?"

When I originally wrote this chapter, I found the internet surprisingly useless in figuring out salary ranges. There are multiple relevant information sources these days, but even better, you can ask your potential future employer. Many states in the US have passed laws that require them to post job descriptions with salary range information.

Don't get too excited. They are required to post ranges, which include what they pay an engineer in this role for 1 year or 10. Other companies have chosen to combine two jobs into a single role. The result is you're going to discover absurdly large salary ranges.

I have three pieces of advice for your swag. First, talk to friends with similar jobs and figure out what they're making. Salaries vary greatly depending on the industry, geographic location, and specific company, but after you've talked with a few folks, you will have a rough feel for the base salary. Second, ask the recruiter and confirm the salary range and see what else they can tell you about this range. Does it encompass multiple jobs? Or just one? What are the expectations regarding years of experience from the low range to the high? What is the company's philosophy on promotion? How long are folks expected to perform well in a role before they are promoted?

Finally, if you don't have a good signal, take your current salary and add 10%—that's your very low signal salary swag.

TITLE

Titles, like salaries, vary from company to company, but what you're looking for in a new job is a sign that you are growing. Associate software engineer now? OK, drop that associate title. Stuck as a software engineer for three years? I'd be looking for that senior prefix when I jumped ship.

Like salaries, the internal value of a title varies wildly by company. A director at a startup is an entirely different role at a public company. The good news is the legal requirement of published salary ranges has forced many companies to normalize jobs and titles, which means there are fewer aberrant jobs and job titles, which means senior engineer at Company X is likely a very similar position to a senior engineer at Company Y.

Your swag goal: What title do you believe needs to be added to your résumé for this new job to demonstrate that you're actively growing in your career? You need to have a defensible opinion regarding why this is an appropriate title.

SIGN-ON BONUS

It's difficult to swag a sign-on bonus because this type of incentive is often used to augment weak parts of an offer, and you don't have an offer yet. If a recruiter knows you're keen on stock and you'll be disappointed with a lowball stock offer, they might dazzle you with a large sign-on bonus.

Pro tip: sign-on bonuses are one-time cash windfalls that may never appear again. For now, all you need to know is that they're often a short-term Band-Aid, and the question will be: What are they hiding?

STOCK

While representing the largest potential for financial gain, stock grants are also the hardest to swag. There are two likely initial scenarios here: public companies and startups. I'll explain likely stock structures for each.

A public company is public, meaning anyone can buy and sell their stock. More importantly, you can do a deep dive into their financials. You can get a sense of how the company is performing, usually, by how their stock is perform-ing. I like to look at the last five years. What's the average stock price over that time? That's a good swag price per share for your model.

As a full-time employee, you will likely receive a restricted stock unit (RSU) that vests over three or four years with a one-year cliff. This means your initial ⅓ or ¼ of your stock vests yearly, but you won't be able to sell any for a year because of the cliff. After that, you are likely to vest quarterly.

RSUs replaced hard-to-understand stock options grants and are—important point here—just straight-up stock, usually with restrictions regarding voting rights and dividends. Unlike salary ranges, companies are under no legal obliga-tion to tell you stock ranges for a role. Sure, ask. Know this: per-job ranges exist and are far more predictable for public companies versus startups.

Your potential stock situation at that startup is more complicated. First, they might use stock options versus RSUs. Smaller startups tend to offer stock options and then transition to RSUs as they prepare to go public or seek addi-tional funding. Second, and more importantly, how do you evaluate the value of a startup? You can't check the stock price. Yes, you can.

A public 409A valuation assesses the fair market value of a privately held company's stock. A third party defines this price, and the asking price; "What's your last 409A?" is a question you must ask because you need to place a value on the stock. Now, unlike publicly traded companies, the 409A is only done once a year or when there are significant changes to the business (funding events, strategy shifts, or other major changes to the business). In my experience inside these companies, the 409A is often a stale number that does not reflect current company reality, but it's better than nothing.

Even with this information in hand, you don't know one of the most important pieces of information. When is this startup going to go public so you can sell your shares? The IPO market is based on market conditions. After the dot-com boom, the IPO market cooled for two decades until 2021, when it exceeded the dot-com bubble. At the time of this writing, in 2023, the IPO market has again cooled significantly. When will it heat up again? If you find out, tell me.

For both public companies and startups, you are speculating about the stock, but I see no scenario where you don't focus most of your attention on the size of your stock grant. Better said, why would you ever go to a company where you didn't believe in the opportunity? In your growth? And the growth of the company?

Yes, any value you place on stock or options is speculation, but it should be informed speculation. Your value on the stock is one measure of your belief in the company.

Negotiating Roles

You're done. Two phone screens, two rounds of interviews, reference checks, and much waiting have paid off. Before considering your offer, let's determine who you will negotiate with.

In any reasonably sized organization, a strange switcheroo occurs when you start talking money. If you've reached the offer phase, it means you've likely professionally connected with your potential future manager. She's sending you follow-up emails and generally paving the way for a clean transition to you joining the team. The moment you start talking compensation, she might vanish.

This far into the process, you're probably pretty close with the recruiter. You've probably had a couple of professional heart-to-heart conversations and might be under the impression they're representing your best interests.

Wrong.

The recruiter's role in negotiation is the bad guy and deliverer of bad news. Recruiters are measured not only by the number of hires they make but how the compensation for those hires measures up to the rest of the company. Yes, recruiters want to make the hire, but they're also driving toward internal corporate hiring standards that may or may not be aligned with your ideal offer letter.

Your future manager's role is to make a great hire; the recruiter's job is to make that hire and negotiate it so it's fiscally responsible.

You need to be prepared to dig in your heels and fight for what you want. This may be uncomfortable and might involve tense moments with the recruiter, but if you've done your work we just discussed, you have the upper hand.

OFFER COMPROMISE

I've never received an initial offer that I loved. There has always been an aspect that has disappointed me. The stock is off, the title is unexpected, or the base salary isn't that close. I've always needed to construct a counteroffer, and I've done it using facts.

As a hiring manager involved in many offer negotiations, the safest way to get me to ignore any counteroffer is to make it without data:

RECRUITER: The candidate wants a higher base.

ME: Really? Why?

RECRUITER: He just does.

ME: Grrrrrrr.

Negotiation is a discussion of facts. Any counteroffer must be constructed with data. "I want a 10% raise because, based on my research, that represents the average salary for this gig elsewhere in the industry."

Sure, it's still a swag, but your swag demonstrates a defensible opinion. In an interruption-driven industry full of bright people racing around yelling about the last interesting thing they heard, I'm a fan of research. It demonstrates that you are curious and care about your career, and that's someone I want to work with.

As I don't know your problem with your particular offer, I can't advise what you need to say specifically, but here are some common frustrations and a plan of attack.

Lower base salary

If you're staying in your industry and at an established company, I can't see how a pay decrease is ever a positive sign. Yes, if you're moving to a startup, you will trade your base salary for stock. You need to figure out if you're cool with that.

You wanted a 10% increase, and they returned with 5%? Why? Sure, perhaps your 10% was a pie-in-the-sky swag, but how is the recruiter justifying this base salary? They're probably saying something about comparable salaries across the company and how you'd make more than 90% of the people in your grade.

That's a warm fuzzy, but I call it shenanigans: you're in the wrong grade. Push for a higher grade with more compensation headroom.

But it's OK; here's a bonus

If the recruiter is pitching this bonus as a fix for your low base, I call shenanigans again. A sign-on bonus, like a bonus plan, is a finicky thing that has a habit of vanishing. You can't count on them. There's nothing like an instant pile of money to distract you from the fact that, over the long term, you're bringing less money home.

There are two questions you have to ask yourself: What are they covering up for with this sweet bonus, and how will you feel when that bonus money is gone?

Even better, here's a pile of stock

How big of a pile? Your public company offer will likely come with justification for the grant amount, and you can plug that number plus your five-year average and get an idea of potential yearly returns. As I wrote in the previous section, you can ask and should receive a 409A number from the startup to place a number on the private shares. You can also ask about the number of shares that are issued to get a sense of how big a slice of the pie they are offering.

Again, this is speculation. The amount of shares and their future value is a guess, but if you aren't happy with the amount and place a high value on the stock, you can ask about trading base salary for stock.

And this is our final offer

If some part of the offer is below expectations and there's absolutely no way to fix it, you have two options: walk away or find another way to ease the blow. We'll talk about walking away in a moment, but have you considered the following to ease the blow?

- Asking for additional vacation hours right out of the gate?
- A start date a month later than they're asking? There's nothing like 30 days of work-free bliss to improve work-life balance.
- What their work-at-home policy is? Suggest an adaptation that better suits your particular work setup.
- My favorite move is to negotiate a six-month performance review. You know you rock, but they don't yet.

Walk Away

The final strategy I suggest is one that you might think is hard, but if you've done your work, if you have a defensible opinion regarding both what you are worth and what you want out of your next role, this move is simple.

Walk away.

Please note: I didn't write *ghost them*; I wrote *walk away*. If it is clear that this job offer does not meet your expectations, you do this: write to whoever your point of contact is an email that says:

- Thank you.

- And clearly explains the aspects of the offer that do not meet your expectations and why. Note: if any of this context surprises the other party, you've missed a couple of key steps we've discussed.

- Thank you. Yes, again.

This email does not say anything suggesting that "If we can address this gap, I'm in." While this may be an outcome of this step, it is not the content nor intent of this email. You must be clear in your own head about why you are walking away and be 100% committed to doing so.

You are not buying a used car. This is your professional life.

I walked away from what became one of my favorite jobs—twice. The first time was early in the interview process when my spidey sense was tingling: "The job responsibilities aren't right." I told the recruiter briefly, said thank you, and said goodbye.

Recruiters as a species won't take no for an answer. This recruiter quickly got on the phone, tap-danced his way into my head with promises of further conversations and other assurance, and did just enough thinking to convince me to continue. When offer time arrived, all of my responsibilities and cultural concerns remained, so I followed the process above. I sweated every single word of the email. There were very specific concerns I documented, and none of them—none of them—had anything to do with compensation. There were clear concerns about their interview process (and why it was a red flag for the culture), and there was a lack of definition of responsibilities. I included in my email why I believed these concerns would set me up for failure.

When I wrote "thank you" again and hit Send, I was content. I believed in my choice and was ready to continue my search. Yes, I was eager to hear a response, but I was fine if the answer was "Thank you."

The specificity and clarity of my concerns gave them a very obvious response framework. The fact that this was not the first time they'd read any of this information gave my response gravity. Yes, they did respond, and they responded thoughtfully, in person, over multiple conversations. We cleared the air long before it had a chance to become hazy.

And remember, my concerns had nothing to do with compensation.

My single worst gig was one where I got everything I wanted out of the offer letter. A raise, a promotion, ample stock, and a sweet sign-on bonus. In my exuberance for this compelling offer, I totally forgot that my gut read on the gig was "Meh."

Ninety days later, I couldn't care less that I got a 15% raise and a sign-on bonus. I couldn't stand the mundanity of the daily work, and I happily resigned a few months later, taking both a pay cut and returning my sign-on bonus for the opportunity to work at Netscape.

All of this important compensation strategy ignores a simple question you need to be able to confidently answer long before you decide on an offer: *What do I love about this gig?*

Better, Faster, and More

I want a better job. I want a role providing me with challenges I have not seen before. I want to work with a diverse and talented team that, by just existing, teaches me new ideas and makes me better. I want a better company that has figured itself out and is heading, no, charging toward building the next thing.

I want to move faster in my career. I have been doing the same thing for the last three years, and my career is decelerating because my daily learning is decreasing over time. I always have the next goal for my career, and I want to have a job accelerating me toward that goal by providing me with new opportunities with new humans on different products. The speed with which I'm heading toward the next goal should be... breathtaking.

I want more. More accountability means more potential for the products I'll be building. More visibility into how the product is built and how the company is shaped to support building the product. More features that help more humans.

You will note that nothing I listed under my better, faster, and more job goals mentions compensation. This is not because compensation isn't essential; it's because the things that will matter most in your next job have little to do with how you are paid. We gravitate toward compensation as the measure for the next gig because it's so wonderfully measurable and comparable. However, who you work with, how you build, and what you build are aspects of the job you should be assessing.

But how? There are no structured rubrics for evaluating and comparing people, processes, and products. This is why the best word in your response is *feel*. I know your feelings about the compensation, but how do you feel about the humans you will be working with? How do you feel about how they work together? How do you feel about what they build and where they are going?

Feelings are observations collected, compiled into opinions, and finally transformed into an emotion. I want you to feel your offer is fair, but I want you to feel this is a fantastic opportunity to grow.

For any new job, you should be able to quickly explain to anyone why the new job is more compelling than the last and why you will love it. Whether they believe you or not is irrelevant. You've got to believe it because you're the business.

PART II

Deconstructing Management

The list of words that define management is revealing: *direct, in charge, handle, control,* and *force.* Looking at this list, it's unsurprising that *management* has a distasteful controlling Orwellian air.

Over the years, I've begun to use the word *leadership* instead of *management.* Why? Whether you have direct reports or not, you are a leader. It might not say this as part of your title, but I guarantee that on a daily basis, you are guiding someone else, accountable for a situation, and leading your day in a certain direction.

This section of *The Software Developer's Career Handbook* uses the word *manager.* Managing your manager, managing your peers, or just managing to get through the day. Whether you're a manager or not, these lessons apply to everyone on the team because leadership comes from everyone.

8

Your Best Work

I've received some of the best advice from folks I'm trying to forget.

It's usually past mediocre managers. Average folks doing the job, but in an uninspired fashion, in over their heads, or just coasting for reasons I never understood.

Every so often, they land an idea. Maybe I don't hear it at the time because I'm actively trying to not interact with them, or perhaps I'm not ready to hear the advice because I foolishly believe that because they don't inspire me, they can't teach me.

Let's call my manager Zack. He's been hands-off for my first six months on the gig. I think it's because I am so obviously crushing it, but I quickly learn that Zack is hands-off on everything. No one is sure what Zack is doing. He's in the office daily and attending exec meetings, but 1:1s are vapid "How are you doing?" affairs and project managers drive the products.

Zack has one move, which is when something goes exceptionally sideways. Zack has a nose for potential publicly visible imminent disaster, so he schedules a meeting with me; we start by comparing notes, and then he says it. The line I can't forget years and years later.

Zack says, "I'm going to give you the gift of focus."

The Happy New Year

After weeks and weeks of holiday, we're tired of family, we've overeaten, and bam, it's a whole new year. Most of the resolutions are gone by late February. The complex machinations of humans doing things en masse pull us back to the familiar medians of getting stuff done. What a great time to reimagine your life, reevaluate your goals, and resolve to improve.

My experience is that a resolution you can use daily will stick with you. My experience is the smaller and simpler the resolution, the more likely I can transform a New Year's aspiration into a lifelong habit. My experience is the more the resolution appeals to you, the more likely you are to even consider it.

This year, I am going to give you the gift of focus. Too many words. How about just:

Focus.

Focus. When Sarah walks into your office for the 1:1, you spin to face her and give her your full attention. Doesn't matter what you were doing; what you are doing is giving this coworker your full attention.

Focus. When Terrance walks through the presentation with a room full of people, you lean forward on the desk on your elbows and listen to every word he says. When you have a question, you write it down immediately. When it's time to ask the question, you ask, but more importantly, you fully hear his answer.

Focus. Even when you don't have to. Video conference call. Twenty people. Ten who don't need to be there. You aren't a part of the conversation; you aren't going to say a word, but your eyes are on the grid of faces, hearing and understanding every word.

The Entirety of Your Attention

This is the 500th word of this chapter. How many times have you been interrupted while reading this piece? How many times have you stopped...just because?

Our devices are full of needy applications and services. Our planet is full of media outlets desperate for our attention. Our politics are orchestrated as entertainment. Combine this with the fact that we've spent two-plus years working in a distributed fashion where every needy application and delectable headline is sitting in a window directly next to your meeting.

Just a glimpse. Don't worry. No one will know.

Maybe this is easy for you, but two-plus years of videoconferencing and my already focus-impaired brain needs a profound cleansing reminder. Focus is the entirety of my attention focused on one thing. This person, this meeting, this design.

But what about this other semirelated thing? Let's wander in that mental direction for a bit...

No, all I am doing is this.

But you're the people person. Read the room, Rands! What is the intriguing political dynamic of this particular group of humans? I wonder...

No, I am here to do one thing. The reason why I was invited was to participate.

But I've heard his story before, and he's going to be talk, talk, talking for the next five minutes, so you know what I'm going to do? Just check Mastodon real quick. No one will know.

They won't, but I will.

Thanks, Zack

There is a time and place where your primary job as a leader is sustained acquisition, synthesis, and redistribution of information. This practice is likely the majority of your career as a leader. More confusing, it's a learned skill diametrically opposed to the skills you were rewarded for as an individual contributor.

But here's why we must thank the hapless Zack for our gift—this ineffective leader who was nesting and vesting rather than building a team.

Focus, the pure focus on the task in front of you, is when you do your best work. The important achievements of information management are essential but immeasurable. When you focus, intensely focus, you can see the one thing that must be said, to discover the critical assumption that transforms good design to great and to most efficiently transform your years of experience into small, understandable, and unintentional lessons for those sitting right there...focusing with you.

9

The Culture Chart

They played bridge every Wednesday at Netscape. In the middle of the cafeteria. Like clockwork.

The players were a collection of ex-SGI guys, and they worked for a variety of different groups at the company, but as I learned a few months later, this core group of men quietly defined the engineering culture of the company...with a bridge game.

Days

In the first 90 days of a new job, you're going to have a solid feel for the construction of your team. Who is who. Who does what. What they know. Who the oddball is. Who the free electron is. In a startup, when there are only 12 of you, you're done. You know the initial people landscape because from where you sit you can see them all and you interact with all of them regularly. In a larger company, however, 90 days is only going to give you a brief glimpse of what you need to know about your coworkers, the company, and its culture.

Fortunately, in a large company, tools and documents have been created to help you traverse the culture and process and figure out where people fit. For example, what do you do when you get a random urgent Slack from a coworker who is a stranger? Even if the stranger takes the time to explain who they are and what they do, you still fire up the corporate directory with the simple question: Who does this stranger work for?

The corporate directory is the digital representation of a formerly very important document: the organization chart.

A quick glance at the org chart answers a lot of ego-based questions like:

- Which org does she work in? A cool one?

- How many direct reports does she have? More power?

- How close is she to the CEO? More influence?

As sources of information go, the org chart is essential, but it is an incomplete picture of your company, which brings us back to bridge at Netscape.

Bridge

If you looked up the four core bridge players on the org chart, you'd learn a bit. One engineering manager, another guy from some oddly named platform team, another guy who had a manager title but no direct reports, and the last guy who looked like a program manager.

My org chart assessment: *Meh.*

What I learned months later was that the folks sitting at that regular bridge game not only defined much of what became the Netscape browser, they also continued to define the engineering culture, or what I think of as a *culture chart*.

Unlike the org chart, you're not going to find the culture chart written down anywhere. It doesn't exist. The culture chart is an unwritten representation of the culture of your company, and understanding it answers big questions that you must know:

- What does this organization value?
- Who created this value system?
- Given this value system, who contributes high value?
- Who is most aware of how value is being created?

This is fuzzy philosophical mumbo jumbo, so let's bring it home. In your current job, right now, tell me what it's going to take to get you a promotion.

"I need to work really hard."

OK, so you knew you would need to work hard to get a promotion before you set foot in your current gig. My question is, What specific thing do you need to do in order to be promoted? I'd argue that for any engineer who is actively managing their career, it's essential to figure out the answer to this question as quickly as possible, and to do so, you need to understand the culture.

Detecting Culture

If you are going to be promoted, you are going to succeed when you provide a certain group of people with things it thinks it needs. Now, your gut instinct is that this group of people is the management team, and that's a good org chart–

centric answer. The guy who signs the checks might be the guy who instigates promotions. The problem is it's your job to stay ahead of your manager. You're not going to get promoted by giving your manager what he wants; a promotion comes when you give him what he wants as well as what he does not expect but desperately needs.

It's unfair. This guy is tasked with your career development, and I am saying it's your job to tell him what he wants. You don't have to do this; you can take the reactive cues from your boss, but I derive intense professional satisfaction when I deliver the unexpectedly needed, and I discover the unexpected by first finding the culture.

To deduce the culture of a company, all you have to do is listen. Culture is an undercurrent of ideas that ties a group of people together. In order for it to exist, it must move from one individual to the next. This is done via the retelling of stories.

"Max was this nobody performance nerd, and three weeks before we were supposed to ship, he walked into the CEO's office with a single piece of paper with a single graph. He dropped the graph on the table, sat down, and said, 'No way we ship in three weeks. Six months. Maybe.' The CEO ignored the paper and told him, 'We lose three million dollars if we don't.' Max stood up, pointed at the chart, and said, 'We lose ten if we do. We must not ship crap.'"

Whether this story is true or not is irrelevant. The story about how Max saved the company $10 million by telling the CEO no is retold daily. In hallways. At the bar over beers. The story continually reinforces an important part of this company's culture.

We must not ship crap.

There isn't a corporate values statement on the planet that so brutally and beautifully defines the culture of a company.

There are other stories that you're going to hear over and over again, and inside these stories are the real corporate values. Each one, while designed to be entertaining, teaches a lesson about what this particular company values, and learning how to deliver that value is how you're going to get promoted.

There's a chance you're not going to find these stories. My hope is that you're in a company where engineering is valued and, as such, has an influence on the culture of your company. If it's been six months, you've been actively looking, and no one has told you a great story about how engineering shaped the fortunes of your company, there's a chance that engineering doesn't have a seat at the culture table in your company. My question is then, How are you going to succeed, how are you going to be promoted, where engineering doesn't have a seat at the company culture table?

Culture Definers

After you have a healthy collection of stories, you're going to have a good idea about some of the culture, but you're still missing essential data for your culture chart. See, the folks who tell the stories about culture usually aren't the folks who created them.

Stories are told, but first they are born.

The people who are responsible for defining the culture are not deliberately doing so. They do not wake up in the morning and decide, *Today is the day I will steer the culture of the company to value quality design.*

They just do it. The individuals who have the biggest impact on the culture and company aren't doing it for any other reason than they believe it is the right thing to do, and if you want to grow in this particular company, it's a good idea to at least know who they are and where they sit. You need to pay attention to this core group of engineers because as they do, so will the company.

Game Over

Your company is networked in more ways than you can possibly imagine. Just because you've reverse engineered the development culture in your team doesn't mean you've got a complete map of the overall culture. There are endless connections tugging any decent-sized group of people in multiple directions at once. There's the been-here-forever network, the I-survived-the-layoff people, and the untouchable did-something-great-once crew.

Culture assessment is an information game, and it's never over. Your career depends on your ability to continually situate yourself in such a way that, as quickly as possible, you can assess subtle changes in the culture of your company.

I wasn't concerned when Netscape started losing market share to Microsoft. I didn't sweat it when the stock price stalled. The reason I started thinking about my next gig was, months before either of these two events occurred, one person from the lunchtime bridge team left.

The game stopped. The small group of four no longer spent a long lunch quietly, unknowingly defining the culture of the company, and everyone who was watching noticed. They noticed when one of those who had humbly done the work that defined the company no longer believed enough to stay.

10

Managing Managers

Everyone knew something was up. The executive team was scarce. Meetings weren't being canceled—they were being ignored. It smelled like a re-org, but the startup was doing okay. We'd closed another round of funding three months ago. The adjectives in the all-hands were positive, so where were the execs?

Finally. A hastily scheduled meeting with executives and senior managers.

"We're letting the VP of engineering go."

My boss? Tony? He's, like, good. I...don't understand.

In hindsight, the disconnect between my VP and the rest of the executives was never clearly explained, but understanding boardroom shenanigans isn't the point of this chapter. The two brief lessons that have nothing to do with this chapter are: first, just because you like your boss doesn't mean he's playing nice with others, and second, expect surprises. Always.

A solid replacement was quickly found. As new bosses go, Gimley was an easy transition. The lights were on. He soon scheduled a meeting with me and made it clear it was my meeting by letting me vent for a solid 20 minutes. "Get it out of your system, Rands, I'm here to listen."

It wasn't a meeting to resolve anything; it was a rough sketch of the playing field in the company. A high-level getting-to-know-you. Gimley didn't say much, he nodded a lot, but at the end, he had his marching orders ready. There was only one, and I was initially disappointed with its simplicity.

"Rands, I want no surprises."

It was a deceptively simple request, but the more I thought about it, it was an empowering one. *Rands, I trust you to know when to keep me in the loop.*

A Management Assessment

The one thing I know about managers is that they are different from you. There's a book to be written about all of these differences. Still, for this chapter, I want to focus on how you communicate with your manager because until you figure that out, you're not even going to know how different you are.

Whether you've just inherited a new manager or are in year three of this professional relationship, the following set of questions will give you insight into how your manager communicates, as well as their appetite for information.

IS THERE A 1:1?

It pains me to write this, but my first question about your boss is this: Is he taking the time to talk with you in a private setting? A 1:1 is a frequent, regularly scheduled meeting between you and your boss, and if it's not happening, I, uh, don't really know where to start.

A 1:1 is a time for the person responsible for your professional well-being to check in and see how it's going. Yes, a 1:1 is a time for team and project status, too, but I'm certain that information is bouncing around elsewhere in the company. A 1:1 should regularly involve a frank discussion of how you are doing professionally.

There are large and successful companies like Google that have stunningly large employee-to-manager ratios, which means there is no practical way for regular 1:1s to occur. My question is, How are these employees growing? Yes, there's a world of experience to be had writing your code, arguing with Felix (the QA guy), and working 27 hours straight to hit a deadline. Still, there's free and hopefully painless valuable experience sitting in your boss's brain right this very second.

One of the hats your boss should wear is that of a mentor. He's likely seen more than you, which means there's a high likelihood that you can bring any random question, idea, or disaster to his desk, and he can comment...hopefully, valuably.

The absence of a 1:1 is the absence of mentorship, which means you need to gather your experience in the trenches. And while there is nothing to replace "real-world experience," I'm wondering what the value add of your boss is. If he's not taking the time to pass on what he's learned, isn't he just a project manager?

If you don't have a 1:1, ask for one. Maybe it's not every week, maybe it's once a month, but it's an essential time to reflect on your job and career and to plan.

IS A STAFF MEETING A CASUAL OR STRUCTURED AFFAIR?

Your boss's appetite for information can be discerned by how she runs her staff meeting. By understanding how she constructs and runs this one meeting, you can get a good idea of how she wants this information presented. I have a spectrum that I use to assess engineers that also applies to managers. They're either *organic* or *mechanic*, and I'll describe each briefly.

An organic manager uses the word *feel*. A lot. He understands the personality makeup of his team because, of course, he has 1:1s. He wants to know how you feel because he understands that the messy parts of being a human very much affect his team and his projects.

The mechanic manager understands the world through structure. Like any typical geek, her interaction with the world follows the mental flowchart of "how things work." The mechanic manager values predictability, consistency, specificity, and facts.

With that brief description, let's see how these personalities define a staff meeting:

- Is there an agenda? *Mechanic.*
- Is it followed? *Mechanic.*
- Is random debate encouraged? *Organic.*
- Can debate occur without involving the manager? *Organic.*
- Is debate limited to a specific time? *Mechanic.*
- Is the time allotted for the meeting always filled? *Mechanic.*
- Can it go over? *Organic.*
- Does it always go over? *Organic.*
- Is it a fun meeting? *Organic.*

Understanding whether your boss is organic or mechanic is directional, not definitive, data. I'm organic with mechanic tendencies. Your boss is also a mix of both; different aspects of her personality will manifest depending on different scenarios. My last boss was intensely organic until senior management started to lean on him, and then he went completely mechanic.

Your job, if you want to communicate with your boss, is to figure out their particular mix and how they use it.

You don't need to worry about adapting to or shaping your communication style for a primarily organic manager because they are willing to adapt to whomever you are and how you communicate. The organic *gets* people and, as such, will deftly manage the conversation toward the information they need.

Mechanics need structure. Mechanics need predictability. I had a manager who was so mechanic that if I changed the order of my 1:1 updates, he became visibly flustered. "We talk about people before products, right?" You don't wing it with mechanics. You tell them what to expect, deliver, and then confirm the delivery.

Contrasting communication styles are a hindrance to the ability to communicate effectively. Mechanics think organics are frenetic babblers. Organics think mechanics are passionless automatons. We're both wrong.

If you are on the other side of the communication chasm with your boss, remember that it's just as much his job to build the bridge as yours.

ARE THERE STATUS REPORTS?

Over my career, I've gone back and forth on the value of status reports. The mechanic manager in me loves the weekly structured rhythm of ascertaining and communicating your week. My organic tendencies remind me that if you're relying on a status report to understand what's going on in your organization, you're probably hiding in your office too much.

The presence of status reports is a sign of a mechanical manager, and it might not be your boss; it might be his boss, but that's not interesting data. Let's assume it is your boss who is asking for status reports. What do you learn?

My impression is that the presence of status reports indicates that your boss doesn't trust the flow of information in your organization. I'm not talking about paranoia; I'm talking about unfulfilled information acquisition needs. Your boss sees the status reports as a means of filling a perceived information vacuum.

The question you need to answer is: Why is he seeing a vacuum? Maybe he is intensely mechanic and doesn't have the social skills to gather the data in the hallway. Maybe status reports are just how he's always done it, or perhaps he'd prefer more data in your 1:1?

If status reports are a corporate mandate from on high or just part of the culture, you're likely stuck with them, and I say embrace it. A good status report doesn't read like a passive-aggressive, boring bulleted list. It's your chance to write what happened this week, why it matters, and what's next.

If your boss is just requesting the status report for no valuable purpose, your job is to kill it, and you do that by determining what communication gap he's trying to fill:

- He's mechanical and doesn't like face-to-face communication. OK, how about 1:1 with a well-structured agenda sent in advance, strictly adhered to, with the meeting completed on time? Yeah, it's not really a 1:1, but it's a start, and over time, maybe he'll loosen up.

- She has too many direct reports and doesn't have time. Great, how about adapting staff meetings to have aspects of a good 1:1?

I'm heavily pushing direct human-to-human communication because while status reports might be structured and reliable, nothing compares to the understanding you gather when you look someone in the eye and hear what they say.

WHAT MEETINGS DOES SHE SCHEDULE?

Another good way to assess your boss's information appetite is to look at the meetings she schedules outside of 1:1s and staff. I'm not talking about the meetings she attends; I'm talking about the ones she takes the time to schedule, either regularly or as one-offs. These are not the meetings she has to attend; these are the ones she *wants* to attend.

There are two classes of meetings you'll find:

Technical

> The technical deep dive. This is a meeting where your boss wants to go deep on the technology. This isn't a review of already-made technical decisions; this is where the decisions are debated and made. Technical meetings scheduled and run by your boss are her way of reminding herself that she, too, was once an engineer.

Alignment

> Project meetings, status meetings, all-hands; the alignment meetings have a million different names, but they all serve the same purpose. They answer the question, Are you and I on the same page? These meetings are usually the domain of project and product managers who have their fingers on the cross-functional pulse of a project, so the question is, Why is your boss scheduling an alignment meeting? Who isn't on the right page?

In your scheduling assessment of your boss, you're less interested in a single meeting than in the meeting aggregate over time. You need to step back and look at two weeks of boss-scheduled meetings. Lots of technical meetings? She still thinks she's an engineer. Alignment meetings everywhere? Your boss is attempting to reconcile differing opinions somewhere in the building.

Conventional wisdom is that when you become a manager, you will forego the technical aspects of your career. Let those closest to the bits make the hard decisions. But I think there's a balance to be struck here. A totally technical manager won't see the larger project landscape and will stumble when tricky people-based issues get in the way, whereas a project-focused manager has likely forgotten the basic rules that motivate engineers.

Like organics and mechanics, you want to know where your boss lands on the technical/alignment spectrum because you want to know what they need to hear. Are you bringing in the technical minutia or the project details?

HOW OFTEN IS HIS HAND IN THE COOKIE JAR?

If everything is working, your boss can get everything he needs to know from you, his boss, or his peers. However, "everything working" is rarely the case in companies. Information moves at different speeds in the company based on a dizzying number of factors that we'll discuss later. And there will be times when your boss will inexplicably put his hand in the cookie jar.

The cookie jar metaphorically represents when your boss crosses an organizational boundary that he shouldn't. The classic cookie jar move is when a senior manager bypasses one of his direct reports to talk to one of their direct reports. There are perfectly acceptable reasons for this manager to make this request, but there are equally many ways this can screw up team communication and morale.

I'll explain. Senior manager Frank has a manager named Bob who has a bevy of employees, one of whom is named Alex. One day Frank is frustrated that a bug hasn't been closed in Bob's group, and Bob is nowhere to be found—virtually or otherwise. In frustration, Frank goes straight to Alex, who owns the bug, and asks what's up. Alex happens to be all over this bug and has proven it's a user error and is happy he's able to instantly defuse Frank's frustration. Everyone's happy, right?

In isolation, this is fine; this is a team of people communicating, but now Frank knows he can get instant bug gratification from Alex, and Alex knows he did a solid for the big boss. My question is: Where the hell is Bob?

Maniacal rules regarding the chain of command are the domain of the military and don't belong in software development. Still, the organizational chart, and the manager and employee relationships, exist for a reason. These relationships define who is accountable for what. The precedent unintentionally set by a cookie jar violation is that it isolates people who should be in the know.

A cookie jar violation can occur in any direction on the organization chart. It is deliberately circumventing individuals from the flow of information and decisions. If your boss is a cookie jar violator, he's either not getting the information he expects or he doesn't understand how teams of people communicate.

The Essential Elements

It's going down. Third floor of headquarters. You're sitting in a cross-functional meeting where a VP stands up and says something innocuous. It's designed to be a throwaway line, but when you hear it, you see the entire game board. You see him making a move to grab one of your boss's teams and the people who work on it. Oh yeah, it's going down.

With this information in hand, my question is, How will you present this essential, time-sensitive, and contentious information to your boss? Yes, I assume you like your boss and want to keep him in the loop. How are you going to shape the information just right for efficient transfer? The organic manager wants the impassioned plea quickly: "He's stealing your team!" The mechanic wants the data delivered deliberately and constructively, at the appropriate time.

The shaping doesn't stop there. What aren't you going to say? Where are you going to add your opinion? It's an honorable instinct to want to share every piece of information with your boss, but if that's your strategy, what exactly are you doing other than moving data from point A to point B? I can do that with Slack, Twitter, or two cans and a string.

The trick is to boil the story down to its essential elements, insert your opinion if appropriate, and deliver the message according to your boss's appetite. You can skip details. Trust me, he's heard this story before. Not exactly the same story, but that's why he will ask lots of questions. He's using his experience to figure out which version of the story you're telling.

The Loop

Gimley was a declared organic with passive-aggressive mechanic tendencies. This meant that he held regular, productive 1:1s, worked the hallway, and played well with a diverse set of personalities. When he was stressed, when he was cornered, or when he was pissed, he turned into a raging mechanic diving deep into every detail, volunteering to help with the code, and generally regressing back into an engineer.

He initially requested "no surprises" because he was aware of his personality quirks. He knew that when the sky fell, he was not on his game, so he instructed his directs, "No surprises," which implied, "You're not going to like what you get if I end up surprised."

Managing Up

We wanted the VP fired.

The architect, the director of product, and I wanted him out. It was a startup, and he was absent when we were grinding away on weekends. When he was in the building, his ideas felt reactionary and knee-jerk—he lacked vision. Most importantly, during a time when we were pouring our souls into the startup, he did not inspire us.

The three of us stood at the whiteboard in the boardroom for three nights, enumerating our reasoning, documenting our experiences, and cross-checking our evidence. After constructing our arguments, we finally scheduled a meeting with the CEO.

"What's up?"

Our pitch was clean. Each of us had a well-defined role in describing, relative to our jobs, how the VP was a zero. Twenty solid minutes of incontrovertible professional negligence. Solid and sold. When we finished, the air was filled with potential.

"So?" said the CEO.

So? we silently thought.

"So, what's your proposal?"

Proposal? Aren't you the boss? Don't you decide what...

"It's clear you're justifiably upset, but what are you going to do about it?"

What are we going to do about it? What are you going to do about it? You're the boss.

On Experience

In order to appreciate this chapter, you need to make a leap—you need to believe that your boss's experience is valuable. You need to believe and accept the fact that since he's been doing this 10 years longer than you means his opinion is more informed. His decisions are based on something more than gut feeling and delusions of grandeur.

We're knowledge workers, which is an awkwardly lame way of stating that we don't actually build physical things with our hands. We build nonphysical things with our minds. We create interesting arrangements of ones and zeros in the confines of our caves, coalescing our ideas into things that are, hopefully, useful enough that someone else is willing to pay for them.

There are no sets of physical tools we need to collect and master to make our jobs easier. Our toolsheds are empty. Our skill is entirely dependent on the kung fu of our minds. Relative to your career, the only thing your boss has to give you is his experience, and sometimes you need to ask for it.

I get issues with authority. I get how power corrupts otherwise bright people and gives managers a suspicious air. I know you want to figure it out on your own, but sometimes it is more efficient to go to your boss, lay out the problem, and let him weigh in. You're not going to get the educational satisfaction of knocking together the solution yourself. Still, you are going to be living the #1 rule of teamwork: together, we can do more than separately. Together we scale.

The word *scale* sounds like management-ese. It's an executive way to say, "I want better, more, and faster." While managerial definitions normally give me the shakes with their punchy venality, this definition of scale works for me.

Whether your gig is as an individual or manager, given any professionally tricky situation, your job is to decide what decisions you can handle and when you're going to need help from someone with more experience.

There are risks and rewards at both ends of the spectrum. If you're asking for help all the time, my question is, What value are you adding? If you're never asking for help, it statistically means you're screwing up unnecessarily by ignoring the experience of those around you who've probably already efficiently solved this particular problem.

When do you choose to manage up? Let's define that.

Up

At each level of the org chart, each manager is responsible for the folks below them. I mean it. The CEO is responsible for the care and feeding of each and every person in the organization. This doesn't mean that she's going to understand the minutiae of you; it means she's responsible for you and your well-being, and she can be fired for your screwup.

How, in an organization of one thousand people, does she accomplish this? Well, she has minions. She has her staff, who have their staff, and so on. This is the organization chart, and while HR will tell you the org is held together with reporting relationships, it's actually the flow of information that holds the org together.

The traditional view of how information moves around an org chart is that information, decisions, and strategy are being designed by those with more experience who are further up the org chart. That information slowly makes its way down the chart. It's called trickle-down. However, an equally large and important amount of information moves up the chart, and that's what happens when you're managing up.

An org chart only scratches the surface in describing how work gets done in a company. I guarantee your org chart is broken in some fascinating way, but figuring that out is another chapter. Your job is to figure out what information your boss needs and when—not only to keep her in the loop, but also to help make your work life easier.

Partial Information

Let's start with the Issue. We're not going to be too specific regarding the Issue. All we're going to say about it is that it's stopping you in your tracks. It's unique, and unfamiliar, and your first thought is, *I...don't quite know what to do with this.*

Good. Figuring out the unknown is the best way to learn. The question is: Are you going to pull in the boss to handle the Issue?

The simplest rule to remember about deciding whether to involve your boss is that if you ask, she will answer. There is no half-engaging your boss when it comes to her opinion. When you say, "We might have an issue here," there's officially an Issue.

I'm not suggesting that your boss isn't informed and well-intentioned, but she is living in a constant state of low-grade fear induced by being partially informed. This state began the moment she decided to be an engineer no longer and jump into management. See, she believes what you believe, that the only truth is the code, but she doesn't code much anymore, so she's developed a semi-irrational fear—*What's going on out there that I don't know, and is it going to screw me?*

The irony is that while your boss expects you to do your job and handle all the issues in your area, she's also unreasonably expecting you to keep her in the loop on everything. You can't. You won't. You're getting paid big bucks to do exactly the opposite. Things are going smoothly when you're efficiently and independently handling the issues in your team—and your boss doesn't hear a damned thing except for the efficient silence of the productive.

Some issues need to be pushed up, though, and here's the checklist I walk through as I size up the Issue and determine whether I will engage the boss:

Is it your Issue?

> Is this Issue your responsibility to handle? Would an external, informed stranger look at this Issue and say it's yours? If it's your Issue, you must handle it. The Issue not being obviously yours isn't necessarily a reason not to handle it. Handling an Issue outside of your area of expertise or responsibility can have a significant political upside but also has equal risk. Successfully resolving an external Issue makes you a hero; failure leaves everyone asking, What the hell was he doing there in the first place?

Can I handle it?

> What's your gut feeling on the Issue? Can you handle it? Have you seen it before? Is it similar to other Issues? Do you feel like you have a chance to handle it *sans* management intervention? OK, keep reading.

What's the magnitude of the Issue?

> How big a deal is this Issue? There's an important threshold that, when crossed, requires immediate boss notification. Some of the obvious ones are any issues involving HR or lawyers, sticky personnel matters, or extremely juicy gossip that might be related to your team. No matter whether or not you think you can handle the Issue, confirmed big deals need to be pushed up to your boss as soon as possible.

Is this Issue at all related to one of your manager's hot buttons?

> What are the three areas your boss is always interested in? Performance, scale, and anything related to that manager she hates in that other group, right? OK, what are her high-octane pet peeves? What are the topics that, when they land on her desk, she loses it? Is the Issue at all associated with areas your boss is always interested in? Unless there is a compelling reason to keep her in the dark, you pull the trigger on engaging her. Failure to at least give the boss a heads-up on issues related to hot-button topics is a sure way to incur her micromanagerial wrath.

What's the upside of solo success here?

What happens if you nail this Issue *sans* management intervention? Experience, trust, and credibility—these are all valuable aspects of what you might get when you solo an Issue without your boss. Confirmed success can even cover the sketchier aspects of handling the Issue. Not your direct responsibility? *Who cares? It's fixed!* Didn't give the boss a heads-up on a hot-button topic? *No problem, I knew you could do it, but maybe next time you'll tell me what's going on?*

What's the downside of the solo screw-up?

Conversely, can you estimate the damage if you screw this up? Is your boss going to trust you less? Is she going to fire you? Are there additional people who get pulled in if you blow it? Is unsuccessfully resolving the Issue just going to create more Issues? If this isn't an Issue you've handled before, know that theorizing about the downside or the upside is tricky business. Can you effectively predict what is going to happen?

Will you learn?

This is one question that I can answer for you right now. If you're sitting there carefully considering the Issue, if you're walking through this list of questions and trying to decide whether to go it alone or not, I guarantee you're going to learn something. Success or failure, choosing to tackle this Issue is going to give you knowledge and experience.

While the goal is a job where you can handle all the issues without help, remember the leap—we're assuming that your boss has something to add. Her experience can help you crack the issues faster because she's seen them before. This alone is a reason to occasionally lean on your boss, but there's one more reason.

Beware the Doof

Right, let's pitch the leap and admit the truth: there are useless managers. They vary by uselessness and ineptitude, but I want to describe one in particular: the Doof.

The Doof used to be healthily paranoid. He used to care about what he did not know, but he gave up. Maybe he had had enough success and began to believe he could do it all in his sleep. Maybe he began to believe that he'd seen it all and lazily thought there were no more surprises. Whatever the reason, he became the Doof.

Because he believes he's figured it all out, the Doof sits back and lets it all happen. The issues show up on his desk, and he quickly maps them into prior experience, throws down brief judgment, and hands them back to you without helping.

The frustrating thing about the Doof is that he sounds like he knows what he's talking about. When you bring him the Issue, he nods knowingly, he asks insightful questions that give you the impression he knows what to do, and you leave the meeting thinking, *Alright, I did my job. I managed up.*

A week passes, you're back in your 1:1, and you bring up the Issue again, and you have precisely the same feel-good conversation you had a week ago.

Whatinthewhatwhat?

You've been doofed.

You manage up for two reasons: to communicate and to ask for help. Managing up to the Doof accomplishes neither, and having worked for many Doofs in my career, I believe it's partially my fault.

Yes, a good manager knows when it's time to swoop in and help. Yes, it's your manager's job to have his finger on the group's pulse and be thinking several steps ahead, but they miss stuff. Important stuff. The upside of getting a team of people to work together is that, collectively, we error-correct for each other. Part of your job is to catch the things your boss and your team miss, and part of your job is to ask for help with the things you miss.

The most important part of managing up isn't that you've chosen to manage up; it's that you insist on help. The Doof is created by extensive experience conjuring the illusion that the game has been won and the puzzle has been solved. When you decide to bring your boss in on the Issue, it is your responsibility to see past their management spin and seek out what I hope is their valuable experience. If you don't, if you let him allow you to believe his clever words are action, you're contributing to the creation of the Doof.

Everything

I love working in an industry where everyone believes they can do everything.

While I understand wanting to be in a world where you have the experience, intelligence, and chutzpah to make all the decisions yourself, you're never, ever going to get there. While experience and choosing to tackle issues are going to help you get better at making decisions, you're also going to get better at knowing when you shouldn't. Yes, the goal over your career is to make the transition from asking for help to giving it, but you're always going to need help.

Yes, the Issue was that the VP we wanted to fire was a Doof. Yes, the CEO's question, "What are you going to do about it?" is the right thing to ask a senior management team: *don't bring me a problem, bring me a plan.* The problem was we needed specific help that only the CEO could provide.

We'd walked through all the risk assessment questions before we talked with the CEO. We knew we had a problem with our manager. We knew it was an Issue of magnitude, and we knew there was a significant upside if we could instigate a change. But we could only describe the problem; we could not execute the change.

I remember this story because I remember the disappointment when we walked out of the CEO's office feeling like we'd failed. We'd failed to define the Issue, but more so, we'd failed to bring a solution into the room. Years of hindsight have altered this disappointment and turned it into frustration because I know our failure to get the CEO to act was our first step into letting him turn into the Doof.

12

The Leaper

On my short list of professional competitive differentiators, I would list my inbox strategy. I have a zero-tolerance policy for unread emails. Zero. Any email, however big or small, that lands in my inbox is instantly read. There is an industrial-strength set of mail filters that move mailing-list noise out of the way, and yes, that means I ignore a good portion of my incoming email, but most email addressed directly to me is consistently and expediently read.

There are other inbox strategies I employ to figure out when and how I respond, too, but I admit the combination of these strategies is not foolproof. I read emails and never respond, despite having good intentions to do so. I passive-aggressively ignore emails I just don't want to answer, and sometimes I just forget to respond. I have a carefully constructed excuse when I'm called on these email transgressions. It's a standard preface in all emails and phone conversations where there needs to be an acknowledgment of neglect and it's...

"Sorry, I've been swamped..."

This isn't a lie; it's an excuse.

Now, there is a bit of pride in that I have a life where I'm scrambling. Yes, I'm proud that I'm busy. I'm a happy member of the Busy Club because I've been to the Boring Club meetings, and they're boring.

But, in this moment when it inevitably happens, the pride vanishes in the guilt that there was neglect. I forgot to respond, I screwed up in some manner, and here I am with my standard disclaimer: "swamped." The guilt is the emotion that lingers. I just checked my sent box of 20,483 messages and found the word *swamped* 712 times...in the last year. How unoriginal and pathetic.

And then I remember the worst part. It's pathetic because when I use the excuse that I'm swamped, I tell you absolutely nothing.

On Excuses

I had a boss—we'll call him the Leaper for reasons you'll understand in a moment. The Leaper was a bright guy, a worthy mentor, politically savvy, and generally, a person who would look out for his team. The Leaper had a lot of responsibility as VP, so his management strategy was to randomly sample his teams, looking for—you guessed it—places to leap.

The Leaper's skill lay in his ability to detect bullshit. Being bright, a former engineer, and familiar with the problem space, he could tell when he was being spun. He knew when he heard less than the truth. Generally, he understood when he sampled ambiguity, but there was one sure way to get him to leap: answer a question with an excuse.

The Leaper attacked excuses as a personal affront. He wouldn't let anyone leave the room until it was painfully clear that the excuse card had been played, that it was unacceptable, and that the proper steps were taken to ensure it would never happen again.

For first-time excusers, it was a painful perspective adjustment. See, when the Leaper asked a question that the answerer wasn't comfortable answering, they did what I did when I ignored an email: they made an excuse. It's a knee-jerk reaction with seemingly little consequence, but that's not what the Leaper saw. He saw the lame diffusion of blame and a weak defense.

An excuse is an abdication of responsibility, and there are no healthy excuses. I'll explain.

On Delivery

"But Rands, it's really Antonio's fault! He owns the deliverable; he missed the date; it's his screw-up." Calm down. You're arguing about the wrong part of the excuse.

An excuse has two parts: the content and the delivery. Your Antonio content may be spot on, but the reason the Leaper is going to leap on you is your delivery. It sounds like you're redirecting; it sounds like you're spinning. You're delivering the facts, but what's being heard is the emotion. Maybe it is Antonio's fault, but why'd he miss the date? Do you know? No, you're stuck on the fact he screwed up and, by association, screwed up you, and that's what you're conveying, and that's what is being heard.

Yes, you can confidently deliver weak content and not trigger a leap, but this only delays the inevitable. Your chutzpah may disguise the content, but since your content is weak and you don't actually know what you're talking about, you're eventually going to take the reputation hit...three times: first, when the crap content is discovered; second, when everyone realizes you were pitching your facts on false confidence; and third, every time in the future when the same people will be listening to you and wondering, *Does he actually know what he's talking about?*

Well done there.

The irony is thick. To avoid looking like you didn't know what you were talking about, you opened your mouth and only added to the confusion. If you told the Leaper, "I don't know, but I will know tomorrow," he'd be cool.

Life in a big or small company is an information game where you are judged by the amount, accuracy, and timeliness of your information. This game becomes more complex as you leave the individual contributor role for management. Still, even as an individual, you are expected to be aware of your surroundings and honestly able to describe them to others.

I know that feeling when someone in authority spends 30 seconds looking at something you've been working on for six months and immediately finds a painfully obvious flaw. The mental conversation starts with, "There's no way he could...," and it finishes with, "Holy crap, how could I miss that?" It's disorientating, and when the question is asked of you, "Why didn't you think of that?" I know where the excuse comes from. It's alarmed spin; it's poor marketing, it's the uncomfortable admission of guilt.

So, what are you going to do? There's a reputation hit here, so what's the right move?

Remember, it is likely that an excuse got you here in the first place. Someone somewhere abdicated responsibility for an important part of your product, and that's why everyone is staring at each other dumbly at this conference table. Take a small amount of time to say something real. Honest, clear, and brief. Sure, these executives might be angry, but the last thing to do in that scenario is to add fuel to the fire by actively demonstrating your discomfort.

Some executives like to see you squirm and revel in discovering flaws. While they might be right, this does not give them the right to be cruel. I'm talking about that deliberate dead silence after the flaw has been exposed, and everyone sees it now, and everyone is wondering, *How could we miss that?* At that moment, someone is expected to say something. This is your opportunity to say something of value.

Say Something Real

Working for the Leaper for years, I can now sense the moment before I'm about to employ an excuse. I can feel the chain of events about to occur as I construct my weak redirection of responsibility. I hear what I'm about to say in my head—*It's not my fault*—and then I stop.

I want you to think of the very last conversation you had, and I want you to think of one thing that you did not say. Maybe you were in a hurry and you blew off someone's question. Maybe you were in a great conversation. Perhaps you were talking to your dad. What is the topic you should have brought up? What is the small thing you could have said to make that conversation more valuable?

This is everything that crosses my mind after I stop with the excuse. I think about all the throwaway phrases I use where I could have actually said something valuable. I once wrote, "Every time you say blah blah blah, a creative writing teacher dies," and I meant it. Each time you open your mouth, you can build something. That's the perspective you want during the uncomfortable dead silence, not the victim-based emotion of excuse.

I'm in a hurry, but being in a hurry isn't an excuse for not taking a small amount of time to say something real.

13

The Enemy

The $150,000 mistake, the discovery of a critical and unfixable architectural flaw three weeks before shipping, and the Really Bad Hire (aka, we're being sued).

These are not screw-ups, these are disasters, and they aren't about to happen—they're here. They're guaranteed. When you discover them, the air leaves your lungs, the back of your head tingles, and there's an odd metallic taste in your mouth. Your mind goes blank except for the crisp mental picture that is a disaster of your own making.

Initial personal discovery is shocking, but what I want to examine is secondary discovery. This is when your boss learns of the disaster, and you shouldn't be worried whether there's an odd metallic taste in her mouth; you should worry about who she's about to turn into.

Management Transformations

Ideally, your boss is the levelheaded type, and she'll manage your disaster cleanly and easily using her years of experience. Still, disasters knock people off their game and out of their comfort zone. Disasters create unusual stress, and stress can mutate normally sane people into unrecognizable caricatures of themselves. Let's talk about the leaders that might show up.

THE INTERROGATOR

The Interrogator's approach is an endless stream of questions: When did the customer first call? Who triaged the bug first? What were the results? How did we proceed from there? It goes on and on.

What's annoying about the Interrogator is that she actually only wants to ask one question—*the* question—but she's putting you through the paces to build a sense of context. This stream of questions will demonstrate the relevance of the one question. The one question is the only question that matters, and when it shows up, it's time to start the meeting.

While you're being grilled, I want you to remember this: the Interrogator is blowing off steam while asking an endless list of questions. This process of question and answer is laborious, but with each piece of data you convey, you can paint a more detailed picture of your disaster and increase the chance she can help.

Some Interrogators don't actually have one question that they're driving toward, and these managers need managing. If you're 27 questions into your 1:1 with no clear direction and a total lack of context, it's time to dig in your heels and ask, "Hey, Boss, what are you really trying to figure out here? Are you just pissed, or are we trying to make progress?"

THE PRIORITIZER

Meetings with the Prioritizer start with a complete inventory of the to-do list for your team. He wants to know everything you plan to do to resolve the disaster, and if this list doesn't exist or isn't complete, you might as well reschedule the meeting because there is no other way to satisfy the Prioritizer.

With that list in hand, the Prioritizer will now put you through the agonizing process of prioritizing every single task on the list. If he's in a really bad mood, he will want to talk through your mental prioritization process for each task. What he's doing is sniffing for a lack of knowledge on any of these tasks, and if he finds it, you're screwed because any lack of knowledge or confidence this close to the fuckup erodes his confidence that you've actually got a plan.

Unlike the Interrogator, there is no obvious point where you'll understand, *Oh, this is what he wants to know. This is the plan.* He wants to know everything. Your disaster has him freaked out, and his reaction to this is to gather as much data as possible. Feels like micromanagement, right? It is. More on this in a moment.

THE RANDOMIZER

The insane version of the Prioritizer. This is the manager who is going to swoop into the situation with good intentions, but he's mostly going to randomize the team with his endless good intentions.

The warning signs of the Randomizer are easy to recognize: his marching orders to address the fuckup change every couple of hours. You might not initially see this because the Randomizer is the boss. His passion and urgency is intoxicating because everyone wants to get to the other side of the fuckup.

They want to succeed. After the third drastic change to the plan of action, the team is going to start scratching their heads and thinking, *How is running around bumping into stuff actually helping us?*

Your job as the minion of the Randomizer is to get back into the 1:1, close the door, and see if you can summon the Prioritizer. Your boss should be your strategic muse, not your tactical nightmare.

THE ILLUMINATOR

The Illuminator is on the same mission as everyone we've already talked about, but she's subtle about it. You may not even know the Illuminator is in the room when you show up for your 1:1. I love the Illuminator. I love being the Illuminator.

See, you screwed up. The Illuminator isn't going to interrogate or prioritize you for an hour; she is elegantly, calmly going to get you to realize the magnitude of the situation and also get you to suggest a reasonable course of action. You'll be proud of yourself halfway through the meeting when you slap your forehead and say, *Wow, this is what happened and this is what we should do!*

The transcendent Illuminator experience is when you don't realize the Illuminator is gently mentally course correcting you and providing silent guidance. The cherry on top is, even if you do see this management manipulation, you realize, *Oh, she's trying to help.*

THE ENEMY

On the opposite side of the spectrum of the Illuminator is the Enemy.

Like the Illuminator, the Enemy isn't going to reveal his colors immediately, but unlike the Illuminator, he will not revel in silently providing guidance; he loves going on the attack. The Enemy is pissed. The Enemy is angry about your disaster, and the Enemy believes that dragging you through that anger is a useful learning experience.

Here's the terrifying reality regarding the Enemy: unlike all the other personalities I've talked about, the Enemy is not on your side. As long as your disaster didn't involve breaking the law, your manager is part of your team, and even if he's furious with you, he should always be trying to lead and help because you are his responsibility.

If the Enemy shows up, your disaster instantly doubles in size. You've got a disaster, and you've got a manager who doesn't believe in you. I hope the Enemy is a mood; it's the peak fury of your manager's reaction to your disaster, and, fingers crossed, it should fade into a calmer personality. Still, even when it does, you need to figure out why your manager doesn't trust you when he's freaking out.

The M Word

Yes, everyone except the Illuminator is a micromanager, and while being micromanaged sucks, see, you have a disaster on your hands. It'd be great if your manager remained even-keeled, but we humans are a squishy, moody bunch, and how we react when a disaster is thrown in our laps varies by the day.

Whether you're being interrogated, randomized, or prioritized, you must remember two things.

First, it's your job to figure out how to bring your calm, levelheaded boss back into the room. Every personality save for the Illuminator is looking for the same thing: *explain to me what we will do to fix this, why this is a fix, and when it will be done.*

Second, as you stare at this strange person who was your boss, you need to remember that people with more experience can teach, you can learn from them, but you might need to wait for it.

While you wait for the storm to pass, might I suggest a healthy dose of proactive disaster triage? Unless you're working for the Enemy, your boss will eventually help. Still, long-term success here will be taking an active role in understanding the full scope of your disaster and determining what needs to change to ensure it never happens again.

14

The Impossible

Right now, there's a CEO standing in front of his 85-person startup at an all-hands meeting and he's saying, "In the next ninety days, we need to do the impossible."

The particular version of impossible doesn't matter. What matters is that everyone in the room is shocked when he says it. You can tell by the intensity of the silence.

"We're going to what in the what?"

What gives this guy the right to ask the impossible? Sure, he's the CEO, but does that mean he gets to stand in front of the room and ask the team to build a levitation machine?

Yeah, it does.

However, this does not mean the CEO isn't screwing up.

Asking for the impossible is an advanced management technique, and it's one that is particularly abhorrent to engineers. Engineers are very clear on what is and isn't possible because they're responsible for building and measuring all the possible. When you ask an engineer to do the impossible, they often laugh in your face, not only because they think it's an absurd, irrational request, but they also have the data to prove it.

Yet, given this irrefutable data, we are still going to consider this request. There is an upside to pulling off the impossible. Not only is it a great morale booster, but it can also be incredibly profitable, because all your competition thinks the impossible is, well, impossible. Better yet, *Who doesn't want a flux capacitor?*

There are three measurements to take with regard to your CEO and his request when the team has been asked to do the impossible. These measurements aren't going to help you pull off the miracle, but they will help you size up the impossibleness of the miracle as well as the character of your CEO.

A Hint of an Insane Plan

First, let's figure out whether your CEO is insane. Listen carefully to the actual request. If your CEO is standing in front of the engineering team asking you to transform lead into gold, you should grin, nod, and start mentally editing your résumé, but don't bolt from the room just yet. Now, if he's asking you to reduce your release cycle from 90 days to 10, you can let yourself be shocked, but be relieved by the fact that you're not being asked to perform matter transmutation.

There's a subtle difference between insane and impossible.

You should respect your gut when that internal "he's insane" flag starts waving, but that doesn't mean you should stop listening. There's more data to gather, and there are times where an insane approach might be the right thing.

Our next assessment has to do with legwork. Has your CEO done any preliminary work to actually figure out whether the impossible idea is achievable? What is his strategic intuition about this crazy idea? Is he able to articulate, however vaguely, why this idea is a good idea for the company and how you might pull this off? You're not looking for a definite plan, more the strategic broad strokes, a point from which the managers can begin sketching in the details.

A word of warning: there are managers and executives out there who can pitch the impossible on confidence alone. They need no intuition or evidence regarding feasibility to get their teams' buy-in, and while these chutzpah-laden individuals sure are inspiring, you should trust that nagging feeling that shows up later when you're driving home, the high fades, and you're left with a strategic emptiness. That emptiness is the practical result of the CEO's request lacking everything but confidence. The absence of some thread of an idea about how you're going to do the impossible means you might be screwed.

The lack of a glimpse of a plan beyond the charisma translates to a lack of hope.

Skin in the Game

Next, you want to figure out how much skin your CEO has in the game. How much of the company is he betting on this request? If this is a bet-the-company decision, I'm comforted by the fact that he's backing this impossible request up with his job. He knows that failure means everyone is looking for a new gig. That's motivation.

If the request is smaller, if this is a bet-the-department request, well, the risk is more localized. The cost of failure will likely be borne by the senior folks running the show. I'm not suggesting the CEO thinks any less of the importance of this impossible request, but trust me, he knows that it's not necessarily his job on the line if the team blows it.

What you're assessing here are two things: size of the request and level of executive commitment. Having a gut feeling for these two things is often a moot point. Depending on your seat on the org chart, you might not even have a chance to choose whether you're saddled with the impossible. However, developing this swag out of the gate means when the impossible hits the fan, you can be one of the first to act.

The Importance of Respect

The glimpse of a plan and confidence. These two fuzzy mental assessments are in play when deciding to ask the impossible, but there is one more that needs to be considered.

Remember, this is an impossible request. This isn't, "Hey, can you fix these ten bugs by Friday?" It's, "Hey, can you rewrite this major component in half the time it took you to write it the first time?" Forget whether it's remotely feasible. Forget whether the confidence is oozing out of every pore of your CEO. You're not going to be convinced, and more importantly, you're not going to engage if you don't respect the person who is asking you to do something.

Financial rewards, promotions, IPOs, promises of future interesting projects. All of these incentives matter and can be used to light a fire under a team, but an individual's decision to engage in the impossible starts with the question, Do I respect this person enough to tackle the impossible?

There's a book to be written about how to build respect in an organization. My brief advice is, when you are asked the impossible, carefully consider every hard request already made of you. Does he ask the impossible every month? Every Monday? Does he follow up on his impossible requests, or does he expect you to run with them? Have we ever successfully completed an impossible request? Is he there at 3:00 a.m. on Sunday morning with everyone else, looking like he hasn't shaved in a week?

I don't know how many impossible requests you get, but I do know that frequent impossible requests result in an erosion of respect and a decaying of credibility. And that means when the CEO is standing up in front of the troops asking them to perform magic, all they're thinking is, *This crap again?*

What He Really Wants

Nothing I've described is concrete. Nothing I've described is going to placate your initial intense, negative engineer reaction when your CEO asks you to do something utterly absurd and irrational.

It gets worse...I mean better.

There are times when your leadership should be unencumbered by your version of reality. There are times when it's important that your CEO isn't intimately familiar with a product space or lifecycle. Day to day, doing business requires reasonable expectations and an adherence to plans, but those things actually prevent the extraordinary from occurring. The extraordinary requires a catalyst like an impossible request.

What's important when the CEO asks for the impossible is that he's pushing the definition of possibility for what the team can accomplish. Maybe your CEO only has an idea and can only feel the possibility in what he's asking, but it's not his job to make it all happen. That's where you come in. You're the person responsible for transforming the feel, the intuition, the glimpse of a plan, and the confidence into knowing and doing.

You're the one who is actually responsible for delivering the impossible, and all I'm asking is that you consider the request because agreeing to engage in the impossible shatters normality and ignores fears.

15

Knee Jerks

There was a fight on the roller hockey rink this morning. Anaheim bumped into Philadelphia at speed, and Philly didn't like that, so he elbowed Anaheim in the chest—hard. Anaheim pushed back, shoving Philly into the goal, where he tripped and fell. Swearing, more shoving, and then we spent the next five minutes keeping them separated.

This hockey rink is a remnant of the first internet bubble. Built by Netscape, the rink has held a game every Saturday since 1998. A majority of the folks who show up know each other, so the game is mellow. Finesse, not fighting. A fight is an unusual once-a-year thing.

When Philly, who I believed was at fault for this whole situation, got the bench, someone asked him what had happened. His answer: "Anaheim ran into me, and I protected myself."

One-Eighth of a Second

I want you to think of the last time you were surprised. Good, bad, I don't care. When was the last time you were really surprised? Got it? OK, now think about the first thing you thought about the surprise. I don't want to know how you eventually handled it; I want you to think about your instantaneous first reaction.

How do you react when you're surprised? Is this how you always react when a surprise lands? My guess is yes.

On the hockey rink, Philadelphia puts up his shields when he's surprised. It's a natural reaction, protecting yourself, but what's interesting isn't Philly's very sensible reaction to the perception of being attacked; it's everyone else's interpretation. We all saw him hold up his arms in defense of Anaheim's unintentional attack, and we all thought, *Man, Philly. What a goon.*

In any group of people larger than one, these instantaneous reactions to unexpected situations happen often. Understanding their range and impact is important to navigating awkward, tension-filled, and professionally tricky situations.

The Jerks

These are knee-jerk reactions, and the first thing you need to know about them is that they should be first viewed without judgment. I'm not a psychologist, and I don't know why some people are aggressive knee-jerkers, and others are passive. I don't know if these reactions are a function of upbringing or genetics, but I do know that we as a species have little control over these initial reactions, and there are many of them.

In my head, the complete set of reactions fits on a spectrum labeled Fight or Flight. The first step in understanding a knee-jerk reaction is first figuring out where on this spectrum the reaction lies. Is this a person who will take on the surprise, or will they let it wash over them? Will they bolt? Will they wilt? If there is one thing you want to know quickly about those around you, it's their penchant to fight the surprise or flee it.

Again, no judgment. A person who automatically has the fight instinct is not necessarily a jerk—it's just the default instinct when the world unexpectedly and rapidly changes. I know who on my team will attack a surprise. They'll leap on it. I also know the ones who will silently digest the surprise. I know who will return three hours or three days later with a totally different attitude because they'll have processed the surprise.

The base assessment of Fight or Flight gives you a starting point regarding what might first happen when a surprise lands; but other instantaneous reactions occur, and understanding them gives you an idea of what you need to do next, if anything.

For the sake of this chapter, I assume that a surprise has landed, and it's bad news. These reactions apply regardless of the type of surprise, but let's assume it's professionally bad news with negative consequences and it's being delivered in a group setting. Here's whom you might see across the table.

DR. NO

Denial. That's the reaction. Doesn't matter if the surprise is reasonable, understandable, or well explained. Dr. No's only reaction is fighting, and she does it by saying, "No."

"No, I'm not going to let her go."

"No, I'm not moving organizations."

"No, we're not shutting down this group."

Remember, knee-jerk reactions are not rational, they are not considered, and while they are tactically interesting, they are not strategically useful. Dr. No's denial is not her thoughts on that topic; it's her reptilian brain's reaction to a surprise.

No.

If this is a group surprise and Dr. No is sitting in a conference room full of people throwing down the "No," there's a chance for everyone to go off the rails. Well, Dr. No said no and I agree, so *No as well.* Immediately after the surprise goes down is not the time to take any action except to allow folks to react. There will be Nos and a bevy of other reactions, and if it's your meeting, it's your job to let folks talk—let them react. The goal with Dr. No and everyone else in the room is to get their reaction out so that we can figure out what to do next.

The follow-up: The good news is that Dr. No has got it out of her system. She's expressed her displeasure, which is half of the game. The next time you chat, there will be residual "No," but Dr. No knows that she's been heard and will be willing to brainstorm what to do next about the surprise.

RAGING BULL

Perhaps the most dangerous of the reactions, Raging Bull wants to fight. They're taking the surprise personally, they're going to say no, and they're going to pick a fight. Raging Bull is Dr. No with attitude.

The move with Raging Bull is to know that it's coming, to know that you've got a Raging Bull on your hands. Suppose you have any control over the surprise. In that case, you want to put the Raging Bull in a safe situation where he can react to his heart's content without afflicting psychological damage on others or sparking a mob mentality where he infects a mindless horde of mini-Raging Bulls. If it's a pure surprise and it's a group setting, my advice is to end the meeting as quickly as possible. Like Dr. No, Raging Bull is expressing his shock. Unlike Dr. No, the Raging Bull isn't going to feel complete until he has the emotional satisfaction of picking a fight with someone else.

The follow-up: Everyone needs time to contemplate a surprise, but no one needs time more than Raging Bull. Each knee-jerk reaction scratches a particular psychological itch. In the case of Raging Bull, he believes that getting someone else to participate in his mental and verbal freak-out will help.

It won't.

Of all the reactions, Raging Bull's behavior is the one that I've found likely to repeat itself after the fact. Raging Bull will often continue to pick fights days after the initial surprise, so it's your move to get him thinking, as quickly as possible, about what's next. What are we going to do about the surprise? What specific thought does Raging Bull have that is crucial to navigate this surprise successfully?

STILL WATER

This reaction reads like flight because she's not fighting. She's just sitting there, but Still Water is taking it all in. She's not missing a thing. In her complete silence, wearing her poker face, she is meticulously processing and evaluating all possible permutations, best- and worst-case scenarios, and potential impact on her day-to-day.

This processing results in one of two very different Still Waters. There's the true Still Water, who is going to maintain a calm demeanor for the entire duration of the surprise. See, this Still Water's processing has resulted in a comfortable plan. She believes she knows what to do about the surprise, and this realization has brought her peace.

The second Still Water is mentally losing her shit. Sure, externally, she looks calm, but internally her processing has resulted in increasingly loony nightmare scenarios regarding the surprise. Without quick action, Insane Still Water will find a reason to become a Raging Bull.

The follow-up: You want to get to Still Water as quickly as possible in a safe location after the surprise because Still Water isn't still. Unlike Dr. No and Raging Bull, who had their opportunities to weigh in, Still Water is still in her head, and the longer she remains in her head, the higher the probability she'll tell herself a tale that will drive her insane.

You need Still Water to say out loud how she feels about the world when it suddenly changes. Like Raging Bull, you need to engage Still Water in the surprise and move the problem out of her head and onto the table where everyone can take action.

DISTILLER

This is my favorite knee-jerk reaction because the Distiller attacks the surprise with questions. Why did this happen? How come we didn't see it coming? OK, what's the impact? Right, what are we going to do?

This is a fight reaction but a constructive one. The Distiller is as uncomfortable as anyone with the surprise, but his coping mechanism is aggressive understanding. He's not going to stop asking questions until he feels he has a complete understanding of what actually happened.

In a group setting, I let the Distiller have free reign during the landing of the surprise because his incessant questions are helping everyone in the room contemplate what actually happened. The Distiller focuses the surprise on facts rather than feelings.

The follow-up: You're going to feel you've got a good idea where the Distiller is at because of his endless questions, but now's a good time to explain that everyone comes down from a surprise in different ways, which is why everyone needs that personal follow-up. A Distiller can turn into Raging Bull after a night's sleep. Still Water might go Distiller. You just don't know who will walk into the building 24 hours after the surprise. This is why most surprises are engineered to occur late in the week; there's a belief that all the knee jerks will calm down over the weekend. Maybe. More on this in a bit.

THE HANDLER

The first flight reaction sure doesn't feel like a flight. The Handler is not surprised. He's fired up to handle whatever the surprise might be. He makes it appear that he knew this surprise was going to occur. How'd he do that?

The Handler is a calm facade. Where the Distiller understands via questions, the Handler's coping mechanism is the illusion he's got it all figured out—that he's 10 steps ahead of everyone else. This is a convenient reaction when you've got the Raging Bull standing on the conference table challenging anyone to hand-to-hand combat, but the Handler needs help.

The follow-up: The Handler crumbles hardest. The Handler is actually Dr. No, except without the denial. There will be a quiet moment in the middle of the night when the Handler realizes absolutely nothing has been handled, and then you'll see his actual reaction.

MY BAD

This flight reaction is one of accountability. My Bad's impression is that he's personally done something to incur this particular surprise. He believes that if only he had done just one thing differently, no one would've had to deal with the surprise.

There's hope inside My Bad's reaction. His empathy regarding the surprise is constructive, as opposed to the destructive social tendencies of Dr. No or Raging Bull. Still, you don't want him wallowing in his overdeveloped sense of accountability.

The follow-up: My Bad is not responsible for the surprise. While his sense of responsibility is admirable, My Bad needs to understand the actual cause behind the surprise. His actions didn't lead to it, so he shouldn't feel like they did. The more he focuses on feeling responsible, the less energy and focus he has for making progress.

WE'RE DOOMED

The most common flight reaction is also the reaction that, I believe, everyone will experience as they digest the surprise. Despair.

In a room full of geeks hearing a surprise for the first time, one of their first thoughts is, *How does this surprise fit into my mental system of how things work?* Failure to map the surprise into the mental model results in an uncomfortable realization: *The world does not work as I expected. Therefore, other surprises are guaranteed to happen randomly. QED. I have no control whatsoever. Shit.*

The follow-up: A perceived lack of control or understanding of our world is a confidence-shattering experience for the geek, and the best way to attack this despair is with a project. Doesn't matter if the project is surprise-related or not; they need something to do. They need the blissful distraction of building something. It's during this constructive distraction that they'll actually figure out how they feel about the surprise.

I QUIT

The last knee jerk is our strongest flight reaction. An extreme version of We're Doomed, I Quit does exactly what you'd expect: he threatens to quit on the spot.

He's not quitting. Well, he might, but not right now. You need to translate "I quit" into what he's actually saying: "I am very surprised, and I don't like being this surprised." Unfortunately, this is his reaction, especially in a group setting, because I Quit's attitude can create mass professional hysteria, which means this needs to be handled immediately. You can't wait until after the weekend to explain to I Quit that his reaction at this moment might be vastly different after a night's sleep. You need to hold up a mirror in front of him and ask, "No matter the surprise, why in the world would you eliminate so many options by quitting on the spot?"

The follow-up: I Quit will calm down and land on another opinion, but his knee-jerk reaction is a sign of a larger problem. I don't know what your surprise is, but I know if someone wants to quit, first, it's a big surprise, and second, he values his job less than his peace of mind.

Stages of Jerk

With people, it's never as easy as just a name. These labels for the knee-jerk reactions are deliberately simple, but people are conspicuously complex.

As I hinted earlier, I've found it commonplace that you will see multiple knee-jerk reactions as a corporate surprise is comprehended. These reactions, like grief, have stages, and your job as a manager or a concerned coworker is actually not comparably complex. Your job is to listen.

The reason there's a knee-jerk reaction is that the unexpected occurred. It kicks off the process of assimilation, and that's what we care about—the understanding of the surprise, not the reaction to it. While everyone has a different reaction, they're all going to end up trying to figure out what just happened, and part of that process is having someone they trust sit there and listen to their assessment. Verbally walking through our thoughts is one of the ways we organize and understand them and begin finding a comfortable, constructive conclusion.

I'm just as uncomfortable with a Raging Bull as anyone, but I know this knee-jerk reaction is not who they are; this is just how they react. Understanding these varied potential reactions is the first part of digesting a surprise. It helps you understand what to expect so you can figure out what to do next.

16

Invest in the Boring

I admit it. I love it when the sky is falling. There is no more delicious state of being than the imminent threat of disaster.

During these times, I've done great work. I've taken teams from "We're doomed" to "We made it." Yeah, we had to cancel Christmas that one time, and there was that other time I didn't leave the building for three days straight, but it was worth it because there's no more exhilarating place to hang than the edge of chaos. We're wired to escape danger.

There's a reputation you get after successfully performing the diving saves. You're "the Fixer." You're the one they call when hope is lost, and while that's a great merit badge to have, it's a cover story. It's spin. See, someone screwed up badly. Maybe it was you. When the sky falls, it means someone somewhere underestimated the project, didn't make a decision, or let a small miss turn into a colossal disaster, and while fixing a disaster feels great, you're not fixing anything.

Management by crisis is exhilarating, but it values velocity over completeness; it sacrifices creativity for the illusion of progress.

Still, right now, the sky is falling, and rather than let it fall, immediate action is necessary, and my first bit of advice is that everyone takes a deep breath.

Sigh

Your body has a distinct natural reaction when you see an impending crisis. When considering the crisis, you take a long, deep breath. You often don't notice this, but if I sat next to you, I would hear you *sighed*.

A sigh is associated with despair. *We're screwed. Sigh.* My interpretation is different; this long, deep breath is one of preparation. Let's break it down: breathe in. Gather your strength. *Oh shit, how am I going to deal with this?* Hold it. Hold it. OK, breathe out. *OK, not sure what the plan is, but let's roll.*

The interesting part of the deep breath is when you hold it. Try it right now: take a deep breath and hold it. What are you doing when you're holding your breath? Well, first off, you're slowly asphyxiating, but in that moment of life-threatening tension, you're doing interesting work. It's a subtle transformation from building tension to calm release. It can also be a deliberate moment of consideration.

You can let that breath out now.

It's a metaphoric stretch, but it's around the deep breath that I build my team's communication structure. I'll explain, but first, a story.

The team at the startup was in a design crisis. The 1.0 version of the product was out and doing well, and everyone wanted to do...well, everything. Every feature was being considered. Unbridled ambition is an excellent problem to have for about a week. After a month, we had three different design directions in play with various levels of support. The creative rush of developing a new release was degrading into useless design meetings where different camps were building strategic fortifications rather than talking. Decisions were being made and not communicated. Confusion was replacing creativity.

In times of crisis, a few human behaviors can make everything worse:

- In the absence of direction, people make stuff up. Nature abhors a vacuum, and in the absence of solid information, people generate their own information to fill that vacuum. They're not lying; they have no ill will; they're just trying to build a semblance of structure among the confusion. This is only exacerbated by the fact that...

- Human beings provide mutual group therapy by endlessly talking about the crisis at hand. This isn't the creation of new content; it's just the regurgitation of the latest news. At the right time, this hallway cross-pollination is a great way to evolve an idea, but if all we're doing is talking about the crisis, we're scratching at the worry rather than dealing with it.

- Finally, everyone wants to know everything. Combine the communication vacuums and the group therapy creating a fire hose of additional questionable content, and it's not surprising that everyone on the team wants to know everything. *Before I proceed, I want total disclosure. I have something unique to add and I better get a chance to do so.*

It was an information communication disaster. There were brilliant ideas wandering the hallways, and there were stickies with great ideas hanging from monitors, but in the confusion that was our communication structure, everyone was running around panicking, and no one was taking a deep breath.

THREE MEETINGS

Starting on a Monday, I imposed a new meeting structure. Let me first describe the meetings, then discuss the purpose. There were three types of meetings:

1:1s with my staff

Monday morning. First meeting of the week. Thirty minutes for the folks who are cruising. One hour for those in crisis. The agenda is a simple deep breath:

> What are you worried about?
>
> Here's what I'm worried about.
>
> And discuss...

Staff

With air from our 1:1s still in our lungs, I have my staff meeting. Two hours, right after the 1:1s are complete. It sounds like a long meeting, but when this meeting is run well and full of the right people, it's almost always over before you know it.

Staff is where we can continue to worry publicly, but Staff is where I want to turn the corner, where we turn from inhale to exhale. *OK, we're worried a lot, but what will we do about it?*

The tone and content for this meeting vary wildly by where we're at in the development cycle. If we're early in the cycle, we're talking about the design state. If it's late in the development cycle, we're looking at confidence in the quality.

There are three buckets of topics that I work through at my Staff, and they're increasingly slippery. We start with Operations (Where are we?), move on to Tactics (What are we going to do about that?), and finally, Strategy (No, really, what are we going to do about it?). I'll explain each:

Operations: Where are we?
> Operations topics are hard, nondebatable measures. How many bugs do we have? Where are we at with hiring? When are we moving to a new building? Charts. Graphs. Yay. Any hard piece of data that we collectively need to know. No debate, no discussion, just alignment. What gets measured gets fixed.

Tactics: What are we going to do about that?

Now we're working. Tactics are changes, tasks, events, and things we're going to do as a team over the next week to address the worry we found in our 1:1s. Like operational topics, tactics are measurable, consumable things, but these are not topics we're reporting on; this is where we're taking action. *We will scrub every bug in the next product milestone to ensure it belongs. Jason is going to provide the new design by Thursday.* By defining these tactics, you're defining the agenda for the last meeting on my list, but we first need to talk strategy.

Strategy: No, really, what will we do about it?

All of these well-defined tactics are great. They are real work that, hopefully, by the end of the week, will define measurable progress. Go you. There are some organization, product, and people problems that you won't be able to tackle in a week...or a month. Strategy involves deep changes to policy and culture. *Our quality isn't great, so we're going to institute a code review culture. Our design is all over the place, so we'll define a style guide.* Strategic topics during Staff are my absolute favorite because they represent the most significant opportunity for substantive change in the group. They're also the hardest to define as well as the hardest to measure.

Worse, strategic changes are also tricky to implement during sky-is-falling situations because everyone is working to prevent the sky from falling—they're intensely and correctly tactical. This doesn't mean strategic discussions aren't important during Staff. You might not discover a strategic change, but just having the debate around the idea of change will give a glimmer of future hope to those who are hyperventilating.

When my Staff meeting is done, I've not only taken a deep breath, but I've also begun the process of calmly exhaling...*I now know what we need to do this week.* This is generally where people screw up. They confuse the relief associated with the exhale with having a plan, with actual progress. You haven't done anything yet, except sit through three hours of meetings, and we need one more.

"Look What We Built" meeting

Four o'clock on Friday. This meeting exists for one reason: to measure the tactics we defined at Staff. *Did we do what we said we were going to do?* From an agenda perspective, this meeting is a no-brainer. The list of topics and measurements were hopefully well defined on Monday. Again, the content varies as a function of where we're at in the development cycle, but some version of this meeting always occurs on Friday. *Let's review the design. Let's look at the bug charts. Let's confirm that we've made that big decision.*

The "Look What We Built" meeting is the time to demonstrate progress, to show that even when the sky is falling, we know how to make progress. It's also an excellent time to celebrate—briefly.

MAKE ROOM FOR SOMETHING ELSE

It's not just during a crisis that this calm, repetitive meeting pattern pays off—it's always. I know you've been working with your favorite designer for three years. I know you believe you're totally in each other's heads, but this psychic confidence doesn't mean you should skip your 1:1 with her, even when the sky isn't falling.

Communication in a group of people is an endless exercise in alignment. No matter how well you know your team, you can never predict where the internal dialogue of your team's internal dialogue will wander. What this meeting structure does is set organization expectations:

- Everyone knows when they will get their moment to speak in private.

- Everyone, whether in the meetings or not, knows the system by which a lot of information moves around the building.

- Everyone knows how we measure success weekly, and whether the sky is falling.

Equally important to these meetings' existence is that they occur with obsessive, robotic regularity. Years from now, when your team has been disbanded, I want you to look at your clock at 10:15 a.m. on Monday and think, *I've got my 1:1 with my boss in 15 minutes.* This regularity is not a threat; it's not a stick; it's the basis for building trust in a team. *I know I have a say.*

And I haven't even told you the best part yet.

This structure, all of this boring meeting repetition, exists to make room for something else. Whether you're designing as an individual or as a team, when you're being creative, you need two things: an environment that encourages the random and time to live there. An obsessive meeting schedule is an investment in the boring, but by defining a specific place for the boring to exist, you're allowing every other moment to have creative potential. You're encouraging the random, and random is how you're going to win. Random is how you discover a path through a problem that no one else has found, and that starts with breathing deeply.

17

Gaming the System

On my list of creative management solutions to dire situations, I offer the rolling whiteboard.

The rolling whiteboard was a curiosity at the startup. Not a full-size white-board, but a door-sized whiteboard on wheels, suitable for rolling into conference rooms and cubicles alike. I never knew who owned it; I just grabbed it in a moment of desperation.

It was the end game. The time in the project where you pay for every single shortcut you've taken, for every specification you didn't write, and for all the warnings from engineers that you've ignored. All the data is grim. Bug arrival rates are skyrocketing while bug resolution rates are pathetic because, uh, we are still finishing features.

Like I said, grim.

The endless stream of bad news was grating on everyone. We were already three weeks into working weekends with no end in sight. A normally pleasantly pessimistic engineering staff had gone uncomfortably quiet. Everyone was star-ing at "the date we can't miss" and thinking, *I guarantee we're missing it.*

I needed a game.

An Entertaining System

Engineers are system thinkers. We see the world as a very complex but knowable flowchart where there are a finite number of inputs that cause a similarly finite set of outputs. This impossible flowchart gives us a comfortable illusion of con-trol and an understanding of a chaotic world, but its existence is a handy side effect of a life staring at, deducing, and building systems. It's also why we love games—they're just entertaining systems—and the more you understand this fascination with games, the better you'll be at managing us.

As with all mental excursions with engineers, there's a well-defined process by which we consume a game, and it goes like this:

- Discovery
- Optimization, Repetition, and Win
- Achievement

DISCOVERY: FROM CONFUSION TO CONTROL

The initial joy of a game is discovery. This is a delicate balance of confusion and progressive disclosure. A game is initially attractive because it starts out chaotic and unknowable, but even in the chaos, there's always a hint of the rules...of structure. *What are the specific rules that govern this game? And how might I learn them?*

We are searching for a single source of joy in this initial state. It's the sense of discovery and progress toward a currently unknown goal. *I want to see the engine that defines this particular universe...I want to know how it works.* We're looking for those edges because as soon as we find this wall, we know this is a containable and knowable place, and that is comforting because the game becomes a controllable thing.

There's creative flexibility in rule discovery and pacing, and it tends to be a function of the size and the intent of the game. The beauty of *Tetris* is that the initial rules are immediately obvious. But the wonderful curse of a massive online game like *World of Warcraft* is that while there are rules, they are vast and, as we'll see in a moment, they are changeable.

This discovery is the hook where we're going to know in just a few minutes whether this particular game suits our particular appetite. But getting past the initial phases of discovery doesn't mean you've successfully engaged us. The real test is...

OPTIMIZATION, REPETITION, AND WIN: A PARADOX AND A WARNING

With the basic rule set discovered and defined, the process of optimization begins. *OK, I get how it's played, but how do I win?* This is the phase where, now equipped with the rules, we attempt to use them to our advantage.

There's a discoverable structure to the rules. There's a correct order that, when followed, offers a type of reward. It's the advantage of thinking three blocks ahead in *Tetris* or holding onto those beguiling hypercubes in *Bejeweled*. This is the advanced discovery of the system around the rules that leads to exponential weird joy.

There's a paradox and a warning inside of optimization and repetition.

The paradox involves the implications of winning. We will furiously work to uncover the rules of a game and then use those rules to determine how we might win. But the actual discovery of how to win is a buzzkill. The thrill, the adrenaline, comes from the discovery, hunt, and eventual mastery of the unknown, which, confusingly, means if you want to keep us engaged in a game, you can't let us win, even though that's exactly what we think we want.

Think of it like this: Does it bug you that there's an absolute high score to *Pac-Man*? It bugs me.

To get around this entertainment-killing paradox in subscription-based games like *World of Warcraft*, game designers freely change rule sets as part of regular updates. The spin is, "We're improving playability," which translates into, "The community is close to figuring it out, and we can't have that, because they'll stop paying."

This paradox does not apply to all games. It's hard to argue that there is much more to learn about *Tetris*, but folks continue to play it incessantly, which leads to the warning.

There's a socially frightening act inside of optimization that normal humans don't get, and it's the calming inanity of intense repetition. In a game like *World of Warcraft*, many of the tasks involve an exceptional amount of repetition. Repetition like, "Hey, go kill one thousand of these guys and come back, and I'll give you something cool." Yeah, one thousand. If each kill takes a minute, you're talking about 16 hours of mindless hacking and slashing. This is not a task that requires skill or thought...and that's the point.

If you walked in and looked over my shoulder at troll kill #653, you'd think I'd dropped into a twitchy, fugue-like mental state, and I have. *I am...a machine.* Machines don't have a care in the world, and that's a fine place to be. This is the act of mentally removing ourselves from a troubled planet full of messy people, combined with our ability to find pleasure in the act of completing a small, well-defined task. This is our ability to lose ourselves in repetition, and it is a task at which we are highly effective.

In the defense of game designers, there are no quests that read, "Go waste 16 hours of your life doing nothing." They are more elegant with their descriptions; they splice all sorts of different tasks together to distract you from the dull inanity of large, laborious tasks. But they know that part of what makes us tick is the micropleasure we get from obsessively scratching the task itch in pursuit of the achievement.

As I've never designed and shipped a game, I can confidently and ignorantly say the compelling magic in games comes from the design in optimization and repetition. This is the portion of the game where we spend the most time and effort and derive the most pleasure. It is this abstract mental state we long for when we're not playing.

But there is one last phase to consider: achievement.

ACHIEVEMENT: WHO CARES IF YOU WIN BY YOURSELF?

Once we've learned the game by discovering how to win, we become interested in advanced winning. We're interested in how our win fits into the rest of the world. We want to compare and measure and answer the social question, "Is my pile of win bigger than yours?" We believe we've mastered the game, but reputation—achievement—is nothing unless someone else can see and acknowledge it.

Before the internet, winning was a private thing. You entered your three-letter name into the local *Pac-Man* machine and then anonymously stumbled off in search of *Donkey Kong*. In an interconnected world, games became social, and once we discovered each other in these virtual worlds, we looked for a means to compare our feats. We began to understand that achievement was not just becoming great at a game, but also being recognized for being great.

Achievement can be as simple as a score, a numeric means of comparison, but the more sophisticated the game, the more complex the achievements. In *World of Warcraft*, you'll be busily into your seventh hour of mind-numbing troll extinction when you see that night elf run by with...what's that? A staff...where the hell did she get that staff? It's sweet. *My world will not be complete until I own that staff.* Now, what was four more hours of troll killing becomes the quest for the staff.

There's no well-defined rule that says, "To win, you need this staff." Sure, it might make those next two hundred kills easier, but that is not your entire motivation. For you, the staff is your own personal badge of mastery, and you don't wear a badge for yourself; you wear it for others to see.

Most achievements do have an empirical value, but that's not what makes them important. The point of an achievement is to have someone you know or don't know look at your Violet Proto-Drake and say, "Holy crap, do you know what he had to do to pull that off?" It's wondering exactly how far you'll go to get the Legendary badge on Stack Overflow.

In a world where we spend a ton of time with people we'll never meet, achievements are the currency of respect and identity.

THE RULES OF THE GAME

Now that we understand how games float the engineer's boat, we can tease out rules you can use to build your own business-centric games. This will take a creative leap on your part because I don't know in what way your particular situation is grim. Perhaps your bug count is crap like mine? Maybe you can't hire fast enough? Maybe you can't measure how screwed you are? I don't know what game you need, but I know you need to follow the universal rules of games.

The rules need to be clear

Whatever game you design must stand up to scrutiny. Test the rules with selected team members before you roll it out. Find the holes in your game before you're standing in front of the team describing a game that makes no sense. Ambiguity, contradiction, and omission are the death of any good game.

The rules must be inviolable

Enforce rules with an iron fist. A rule not followed is twice as bad as a poorly defined one. A violation of the rules is an affront to an engineer. They react violently to violations of the rules because it's an indication that the system is not working. Rules make a game fair, and when they stop being followed, the engineers stop playing.

The playing of the game must be inclusive, visible, and broadcasted

Include everyone on the team. Those not on the team should be aware of the progress and implications.

Use money as a reward only as a last resort

It's a knee-jerk management move to use money as an incentive. Problem is, money creates drama. Money makes everyone serious, and while you may be in dire straits as you design your game, do you/don't you want the team stressing about who is getting paid; you want them to stress about the work.

This is not to say that rewards in a motivational game are verboten, but step away from the money and think about achievements. One of the best trophies I've awarded was a horrifically ugly ceramic blue rhino the size of a pit bull. The winner proudly displayed the rhino achievement in his office for years.

It's not a game

Just because I'm using the word *game* all over this chapter doesn't mean it's trivial, simple, or something not to be taken seriously. Your team will treat the game as a motivational tool as seriously as you choose to treat it in building and rolling it out—because they want to win.

The Whiteboard Game

Everyone was working on a Sunday night as I stared at the blank portable whiteboard in my office. A weekend of hallway conversations, bug scrubbing, and informal testing confirmed what I already knew: the product was shaky, the bugs we were discovering were alarmingly bad, and there were too many of them.

OK, a game. The game will be called *Focus*, and it will concentrate and structure our attention on the worst parts of the product. I thought of the 10 worst bugs I'd found during the weekend and listed them on the board. Next to each bug, I drew four boxes:

- Root cause
- Fix identified
- Fixed
- Tested

I grabbed a handful of dry erase pens, rolled the board into the architect's office and said, "This is all we're working on."

He stared at the board for 10 minutes and finally nodded. "Good, but each person needs their own color, and you should assign points for each of the boxes. 10 points for root cause and fix identification, 5 for fixes and tests."

"Points for what?"

"Points for points. We're engineers."

"And everyone has their own color?"

"Yeah, so we know who has the most points. Give me a blue pen. I've already got root cause on bug number three."

"Blue?"

"Yeah, I'm always blue."

18

Managing Werewolves

If I move a muscle, I'm dead. Jane, who I'm pretty sure is a Werewolf, is jumping from one player to the next, testing individuals' will and looking for weakness. She's looking for a sign of guilt or discomfort, and it's not just her. The room is full of people looking for someone to be their next victim.

The game is *Werewolf*, and I'm both exhilarated and terrified, which is odd because I'm paid to play this horrific game every day.

A Dangerous Scenario

Werewolf is a party game described by its creator as "a game of accusations, lying, bluffing, second-guessing, assassination, and mob hysteria." Understanding the basics of how it's played is important to understanding why this game will help your critical thinking skills at work.

A moderator begins by handing players cards that indicate their role: Villager, Seer, or Werewolf. With all the cards distributed, each player announces their role in the village, and everyone says the same thing: "Hi, I'm *My Name*, and I'm a Villager."

Now, some people are lying. There's a bunch of Werewolves, and they're not going to admit that, because the Villagers want to kill the Werewolves before they kill us.

The moderator then announces that it's nighttime, and all the players close their eyes. The two things that Werewolves are afraid of are, obviously, cows and zombies, so all the players make one of the following sounds: "BraAaaaaaaaAaaaains" or "MooOoooooooOooooo."

These sounds are an auditory cover for what really goes on at night when the moderator asks the Werewolves to awaken and pick a Villager to kill. Once the Werewolves have silently selected their victim, they go back to sleep. The moderator then wakes the Seer, who points at one player. Via a thumbs-up or thumbs-down, the moderator confirms for the Seer whether that player is a Werewolf or not. With everyone back to sleep, the moderator then awakens the village and announces who has died.

Then the game begins. The village must collectively choose someone to sacrifice, whomever they decide is a Werewolf based on whatever meager information they've gathered from either the Villager introductions or the previous night's killing. It's not much information, but they must kill someone because, each night, each turn, that's exactly what the Werewolves do, too. And when there are more Werewolves than Villagers, the Werewolves win.

We can't let the Werewolves win.

I've explained the mechanical basics of the game, but I have not explained its beauty. I love *Werewolf* because it's a game where you can safely learn how to deal with the worst people you're going to meet in the most dangerous scenarios possible.

People Lie, Some Are Evil, Others Just Want to Screw You Over

I have a long-standing policy of optimism. It's my leadoff mindset. I assume that we're a team working collectively to do the right thing. As a strategy, optimism has served me well, but here's the bad news:

- People can vary from being poor communicators to being outright liars.
- Politics and process often screw up people's value systems beyond recognition.
- Evil things happen. Sometimes randomly.

In your career as either an individual contributor or a manager, you are going to be faced with these unexpectedly shitty situations involving other people with devious agendas. While the HR department is furiously working on cleverly named workshops about conflict management and situational leadership, there's really no replacement for having someone lie straight to your face and having to figure out what to do next.

This takes us back to a critical part of *Werewolf*: the accusation phase. In the morning, the Villagers wake up and must select someone to sacrifice. What's the process for this? Who leads this process? How is this potential Werewolf selected? While the moderator keeps track of time, it's the Villagers who organically guide this process.

Invariably someone in the village jumps into the leadership position. They start questioning people and guiding the accusation process. Why are they leading? What's the motivation? Every word and every movement in this situation has differently perceived meaning. This is, effectively, your boss's staff meeting, except in this meeting, people die.

When the group has selected a potential victim, the moderator asks the initial accuser why they think this Villager is a Werewolf. The reasoning can vary from "He's twitchy" to "Well, we have to kill someone." The victim is given a chance to defend himself against this accusation, which, in the case that he actually is a Werewolf, means he sits there and comfortably lies to the entire room.

This is why I love *Werewolf*. Where else can you hone some of the sketchiest but most important skills you need in groups of people? Some of these skills are:

Rapidly size up a person based on how they deliver a single sentence.
> "I...am a Villager." Where was he looking when he was speaking? Did he make eye contact? Was he fidgeting? Is he usually fidgeting? Why'd he stutter? *That strikes me as...wolfy...*

Observe the rapid evolution of roles in high-pressure scenarios.
> Who comes forward to lead? Are they challenged? Do they last? Why is she leading now? *She was quiet last time.* Who does she question? What kinds of questions is she asking? What kind of nonverbal language is she using? And why does she appear to be aligning with him?

Figure out how to fluidly integrate yourself into a group of strangers.
> How do they develop alliances based on little information? Who already knows each other? How are they communicating? Who is really playing, and who is just trying to figure it out? Who am I instantly connecting with? Why am I being let into this particular clique? *I don't trust her, but for some reason she's got my back.*

Learn how to lie without the guilt or getting caught.
> What's the difference between sinning by omission, twisting the facts, and outright, blatant lying? When is lying just temporarily convenient versus long-term trouble? How many lies can you tell and still keep your story straight? What are the keys to a convincing lie? What does this particular group of people want to hear? *You can't kill me. I'm the Seer and I know where the Werewolves are...really.*

Aggressively turn the spotlight off you and onto someone else using nothing but chutzpah.

Who is the weakest in the room, and how did they make themselves weak? What's the balance between sounding credible and desperate? When is answering a question with a question the right move? Can they sense you're aggressively trying to hide? How do you defuse the leader's authority and credibility? *No, I'm not a Werewolf, but I'M CERTAIN SHE IS!*

Perfect the poker face.

Can you hide your emotions and reactions? What is the right type and amount of eye contact, body language, and tone of voice? When is calm believable? When is it not? Who can you look in the eye while maintaining your cool? Who is a liability? When is it time to completely shift your personality to make a point? *I...am a Villager.*

This Isn't Role-Playing; This Is Life or Death

Werewolf is a game, and games are fictionalized simplifications of life designed with a mythology and a rule set that allow you to explore in ways you normally cannot.

In real life, there's a subtle, detectable flow to how a group of people interact. There are standard roles that people will adopt. There are discernible rules to how people will act. Unfortunately, it's an impossibly long set of rules because the rules vary as much as each person is different.

In *Werewolf,* there's a very small set of rules:

- Villagers kill Werewolves as best they can.
- Werewolves kill Villagers as best they can.
- Sleep when you're told to.
- Make cow or zombie noises when asked.
- Survive.

Interwoven within these rules is the actual game, and therein lies the brilliance of a solid game of *Werewolf.* It's a crucible of people dynamics, improvisation, and intellectual combat. In just a few short hours of gameplay, you realistically experience some of the worst possible meeting scenarios you can imagine paired with the agility and amazing motivation to handle these situations because, well, you don't want to die.

Now, I'm optimistic and, sometimes, realistic. I don't actually believe some-one will deliberately lie under normal circumstances or that they are purely evil. I think there are those who have an agenda that doesn't align with mine, which gives them incentive to work against my interests. But they're not just out to screw me; they're out to succeed...just like me.

In reality, I know most meetings aren't these high-pressure, survival-of-the-fittest slugfests. Many meetings are well-structured affairs with hardly a drop of blood spilled. I also know that each time you speak in a meeting is a moment in the spotlight to explain that, yes, you understand what's going on, you are clear about the fuzzy rules of this particular game, and you're in it to win.

We Can't Let the Werewolves Win

I suspect Jane is a Werewolf because she's running the show this round. She's keeping the spotlight on herself, and that means she's excited, she's got a lot of energy, and I suspect, a thirst for blood. I'm waiting for her to make her way to me, to accuse me, and I know she will.

I'm being quiet. Intentionally. I'm setting a trap because I've played with her before, and I know that she believes what I believe:

"We kill the quiet ones because they aren't helping."

19

BAB

My management team was bickering. Two managers in particular: Leo and Vincent. Both of their projects were fine. Both of their teams were producing, but in any meeting where they were both representing their teams, they just started pushing each other's buttons. At every meeting on some trivial topic, a variation of the following would occur:

LEO: *Vincent, are you on track to ship the tool on Wednesday?*

VINCENT: *We're on schedule.*

LEO: *For Wednesday?*

VINCENT: *We'll hit our schedule.*

LEO: *Wednesday?*

Endless passive-aggressive verbal warfare. Two type A personalities who absolutely hate to be told what to do. My 1:1s with each of them were productive meetings, and when I brought up the last Leo 'n' Vincent battle of the wills, they immediately started pointing at their counterpart: "I really don't know what his problem is."

I do. They didn't trust each other.

On the Topic of Trust

There's a question out there regarding how close you want to get with your coworkers in your job. There's a camp out there that employs a policy of "professional distance." This camp believes it is appropriate to keep those they work with at arm's length.

The managerial reason here is more concrete than the individual reasoning. Managers are representatives or officers of the company and, as such, may be asked to randomly enforce the will of the business. Who gets laid off? Why doesn't this person get a raise? How much more does this person get? Professional distance or not, these responsibilities will always give managers an air of otherness.

Here's my question: Do you or do you not want to be the person someone trusts when they need help? Manager or not, do you see the act of someone trusting you as fitting with who you are?

Yes, there's a line that needs to be drawn between you and your coworkers, but distancing yourself from the people you spend all day, every day with seems like a good way to put artificial barriers between yourself and the people you need to get your job done.

Is that who you are or who you want to work for?

The topic of trust is where I draw a line in both my personal and management philosophy. My belief is that a team built on trust and respect is vastly more productive and efficient than the one in which managers are distant supervisors and coworkers are 9-to-5 people you occasionally see in meetings. You're not striving to be everyone's pal; that's not the goal. The goal is a set of relationships where there is a mutual belief in each other's reliability, truth, ability, and strengths.

It's awesome.

And it's something you can build with a card game.

BAB

It's pronounced how you think. Rhymes with *crab*. It's an acronym for a game that, with practice, will knit your team together in unexpected ways. It's Back Alley Bridge. The rules are included in the Appendix at the end of this book,[1] but before I explain why this game is a great team-building exercise, you need to understand a few of the rules:

BAB isn't bridge

The game does have a few important similarities with bridge. First, it's a game for four players, involving two teams. The folks facing each other are on the same team and share their score. Second, it's a trick-based game where the goal is for each team to get as many tricks as possible. A trick is won when each player turns up a card and the highest wins, unless someone plays a trump suit, which, in the case of BAB, is always spades.

---

1 Also available as a PDF: *http://randsinrepose.com/assets/BAB.pdf.*

Bidding

Also, like bridge, BAB has bidding, meaning each team bids how many tricks they think they're going to get after the cards have been dealt. Scoring is optimized to reward teams who get the number of tricks they bid and heavily punishes those who don't get their bid. Bidding is a blind team effort—you have no idea what your teammate has in his hand other than what you can infer from his bid.

Decreasing hand count

Unlike bridge, the number of cards each player gets decreases with each hand. Each player gets 13 cards in the first hand, 12 in the second, and so on. Play continues down to a single card and then heads back up to 13. A work-friendly modification I've made is to only play every other hand (13-11-9, etc.). This number of hands fits nicely into a lunch hour.

Hail Mary

There are two special bids: Board and Boston. A bid of Board indicates the team is going to take every single trick. A bid of Boston indicates the team intends to take the first six. Achieving a Board or Boston can be an impressive feat and is rewarded handsomely from a scoring perspective. Failure results in a scoring beatdown. Both of these special bids allow for wild variances in the score, which can be handy for teams who are falling behind.

Scoring, game play, and other information are in the complete rules. Now, let me explain why I picked this game as a recurring weekly lunch meeting.

In BAB, you talk shit

I've landed BAB in three different teams now, and in each case, the amount of trash talking that showed up once players became comfortable with the game was impressive. This is a function of my personality, but it's also a byproduct of any healthy competition among bright people. It's also a sign of a healthy team. I'll explain.

Trash talking is improvisational critical thinking—the art of building comedy in the moment with only the immediate materials provided. As I'm looking for candidates for my next BAB game, I'm looking for two things: Who will be able to talk trash and who needs to receive it?

The art in talking trash is the careful exploration of the edges of truth. When someone effectively lays it down, they say something honest and slightly uncomfortable. The ever-present risk with trash talking is when *that* line is crossed. It's that one thing that is said that goes too far and offends, but it's the presence of that line that makes talking trash so much fun.

It's these honest and dangerous observations that form the basis of trust. When a coworker makes a big observation about you and shares it with the other players, you take note—someone is watching. It sounds problematic, but remember, we're just sitting here playing cards. It's safe.

In a new BAB game, it takes players time to get used to the trash talking, especially in a situation like Leo and Vincent's. Adversarial coworkers playing on the same team need to learn to ditch the business for the game. They need to understand there is a relationship outside of the daily work, and there's nothing like a comedic verbal beatdown to remind them to lighten up.

In BAB, you learn things unintentionally

Once you've got an established game with regular players who all know the rules, you'll learn two things: people get better at trash talking with practice, and information travels in unpredictable ways in groups of people.

It goes like this:

PLAYER #1: I bid 3.

PLAYER #2: I bid 1.

PLAYER #3: Pass.

PLAYER #4: Kevin's quitting. I'm sure of it.

PLAYER #1: Yeah, I know.

PLAYER #2: Sucks to be you.

Out of nowhere, in the middle of the game, you're suddenly assessing the departure of a coworker. I see this as a sign of a thriving, healthy BAB game because the team has begun to trust each other more. In the safety of the game, they're letting the worries of the moment spill onto the table for all to see, which is impressive, since everyone knows that anything on the table at BAB is fair game for talking shit.

In BAB, you're having work experiences without the work

Relationships need time to bake. Trust doesn't magically appear; it's cautiously built over time via shared experience. The majority of these experiences are created during the regular workday, and I'm certain there are a great many healthy professional relationships that are defined and maintained in this manner, but I want my teams closer. I'm not suggesting group hugs and voices united singing "Kumbaya." I'm looking for each team member to have the opportunity to understand each other slightly more than through what they see when they're at work.

The more you understand how your coworkers tick, the better you're able to work with them. You'll stop seeing them as the role, the title, or the keeper of a particular political agenda. They are just...Phillip. And you know what I know about Phillip? He's the manager who used to wait too long to speak in a meeting. He had plenty to say that mattered, but he used to be too shy to say it.

Two months of trash talking over BAB showed me his reservations, so I learned to pull Phillip into the meeting conversations as quickly as possible. After a few pulls, he started to do it himself. After a few weeks, you couldn't get him to shut up.

The Second Staff Meeting

The inspiration for the game came from a regularly scheduled bridge game at Netscape, and there's nothing special about BAB that makes it the perfect lunchtime game. I chose BAB because it's a team-based game that fits nicely in a lunch hour.

You bet I maneuvered Leo and Vincent onto the same team for weeks on end. There was no magical moment during one game when they suddenly understood each other. Leo and Vincent continued to bicker in meetings, but over time the tone changed from the passive-aggressive to the playful talking of trash. They turned competition into something healthy and fun.

In the safe competition that is BAB, you learn how to work together better by understanding that winning doesn't always mean hitting your dates, getting paid, or receiving a promotion. Winning can be a simple, playful thing: "We were awesome as we kicked your ass."

More importantly, BAB is a regular forum for experiencing that relationships are not defined just by the work we do together, but who we become with each other when we aren't looking.

20

Your People

In your career, there's a list of essential career intangibles. These are the things you need to do in order to be successful, which are also maddeningly difficult to measure. There is no direct correlation between completing these activities and a raise. It's unlikely that accomplishing these indefinite tasks will end up in your review, but via organizational and social osmosis, you've learned these intangibles are essential in order to grow.

I want to talk about one: networking.

There are two types of networking. Basic networking is what you do at work. It's a target-rich environment with coworkers, your manager, and those of interest in close proximity. It's work, but it's easy work because your day is full of those you depend on, and you've learned that professionally befriending these people keeps you comfortably in the know.

I'm going to call the other type "people networking," and it's harder work. This is when you put yourself out there. It's attending a conference where you know no one. It's driving to the city to sit in a coffee shop with 10 strangers bonded by a programming language. It's a leap for the socially awkward, but the infrequent reward is that you discover Your People.

I don't have a good definition for these people, so I made a list. My hope is that as you read this list you'll think of at least one person you know who is already Your People:

- Your connection with Your People is instant and obvious; it transcends age and experience.

- The best way to discover whether someone is Your People is absence. If, when they return, it's as if they never left, they are Your People.

- There are more of them than you expect, but their number is disguised by the ebb and flow of their presence in your life.

- An investment of time with them will be repaid, but not in a way you can predict or expect. That is the point.

- Your People will piss you off because the relationship is genuine. They do not coddle and they do not spin. Consequently, Your People error-correct you in ways that others cannot.

- You may call on each other without reason, randomly. During these random visits, hours of time will vanish, and neither you nor Your People will notice.

- Conversely, long silences are also acceptable and comfortable.

- Your People have a knack for showing up when you need them, even if you didn't know you needed them prior to their arrival. I don't know how they do this, but the more People you have, the more likely it is that this will happen.

- Your People rarely demand anything. But when either you or they make a request, neither the request nor the agreement to do it is ever in question.

- Your People keep you in balance. Their presence reminds you first that you're never flying solo yolo and, second, that there are two sides to every story.

- Your People instinctively know who you are and are able to say accurate and valuable things to you and about you with stunningly little data.

- You get email and messages all day from everyone, but you stop whatever you are doing and respond whenever Your People reach out.

- Your People reach out randomly...delightfully.

- Your People will always be Your People—even if they leave and never return.

When I'm talking about Your People, I am not thinking of your best friend. Sure, your best friend might be Your People, but I'm talking about a larger population who aren't necessarily your friends and who aren't your family. These are a strange lot of people you've discovered in a motley array of places because you were searching for them.

Furthermore, I am not suggesting that those who are not Your People are somehow less valuable. In fact, the majority of the folks in your life are going to be extraordinarily more work than those who are instantly familiar. The work in bridging the gap between you and those who are harder to know is also an essential intangible skill.

Lastly, while Your People may be less work, they are harder people to have in your life. These are not people that let you sit in place; these are people who hold a mirror up to your disasters, and who explain, in excruciating detail, exactly what you don't want to hear. If they did not do these things, they would not be Your People.

Share What You Build

It's going to take quite a shove to get you out of your cave and into a situation where you're likely to stumble upon Your People. A list twice the size as the one here isn't convincing you to move an inch, because strangers are, well, strange. They're unpredictable nobodies who have no idea they're supposed to be your new genuine friends.

My end run around my social insecurity has always been my hobby: writing. It's late on Monday night and I'm blaring "T'Pau" because one-hit wonders are my thing while I'm transforming this article from a blog entry into a chapter for the book. The lights are all off, and I'm wearing a hoodie because this month I'm a better writer when my head's covered. Go figure.

This writing hobby, this wonderful, dark, antisocial place, has the fortunate upside of appealing to people I do not know, and when I'm not looking, I find ways to use my writing to find more people. I publish a blog entry and carefully read every comment for a sign of a person who I need to follow up with. I turn a chapter into a presentation. A presentation that I give to a room full of strangers who, when I'm done, occasionally approach me to talk about these things I write when I'm alone. These presentations are often at conferences that I've discovered are target-rich environments for people I need to know.

Engineers build stuff. I'm not sure what you build, but when no one is looking, you build something. I'm not talking about what you're paid to build; I'm talking about what you build for yourself. You have a different relationship with this work than the work you've been asked to do. You have more confidence about work that is entirely yours. I see no reason why you can't parlay that confidence into conversation with others who share your interest in the intimacy of that which you build for yourself.

More good news. Likely candidates are nearby. You probably already know who they are, and you likely already talk with them daily, but you've also likely never seen them.

Just because you have hundreds of Twitter followers or a Discord list chock-full of names doesn't mean you've found Your People. The final addition to my list is, "They're Your People because you know them." I'm not suggesting your Facebook pals aren't an important part of your life, but until you've sat in a bar arguing about the relative benefits of your favorite programming languages until 2:00 a.m., you don't know how someone is built.

The internet connects us, but the medium also filters out the aspects of humanity that make us interesting and knowable. You're not going to know me until you see that I talk with my hands. I'm not going to know you until I realize that when you're really thinking about a thing, you can't look anyone in the eyes, because it distracts you.

You Tell Stories

All day. It's a constant story being composed in your head. You're doing it right now. You think you're reading this paragraph that I've written, but what you're actually doing is telling yourself the story of reading this paragraph. It's your inner dialog, and it's often a convenient lie biased in your favor.

I'm not saying you deliberately lie to yourself. OK, maybe I am, but we're all doing it. We're all gathering data through the course of the day and creating a story based on that data, our experience, and our moods. It's a perfectly natural phenomenon to guide the narrative in our favor. We see the world how we want. As we edit our days into these stories, there is always a risk of fiction. This is why you need to identify and nurture Your People.

You tell these stories to Your People without reservation. Your People love your stories—fiction and all. They love how you tell them; they laugh about the lies you tell yourself, and then they stop and they tell you the truth.

Networking is the art of finding those who are willing to listen to and critique your stories, so go look at your inbox. Better yet, go look at your sent box. Check your phone and see who you call the most and who calls you. I'm certain that, right now, one of Your People wants to hear a story and they have one for you, too.

21

Wanted

Jesse walked.

Monday is the day we set aside for new hires. All the new hires spend the morning learning about the company, figuring out how to create accounts, and becoming indoctrinated in company culture. When lunchtime arrives, managers pick up their new employees and take them to lunch.

Their morning starts at 9:00 a.m., and at 9:15, I got a call from HR: "Jesse's not here."

Bad traffic, miscommunication, there were a dozen good reasons he wasn't there, but I instantly felt a rock in my stomach: "Jesse walked."

A quick call to my recruiter, and the mystery began to unfold. "Oh, yeah, he called just before five on Friday and said he wanted to chat. I was off Friday; should I call him now?"

Yeah, call him. Tell me what I already know.

The recruiter discovered that Jesse was firmly ensconced in a code of silence because his Friday call was his cold-feet call. After three months of phone screens, interviews, offer negotiations, and acceptance of said offer, Jesse called to tell us that while he had resigned two weeks ago, a last-minute counteroffer had shown up. He'd decided to stay...at 4:45 p.m. on his last day.

Jesse walked.

As I sat at my desk, lightly tapping my Zebra Sarasa .5 gel pen against my forehead, I thought how simple it would be to be pissed. In terms of respect, trust, and professionalism, Jesse had screwed me in just about every manner possible, but in this case, the fault would be mine.

I had not explained to Jesse that he was wanted.

The Requisition Situation

Whether you're a manager or not, I will make sure you know two things: first, that you understand how urgent it is to hire, and second, how to ensure those hired actually show up. There's a huge pile of work in the middle of this process involving phone screens, interviews, and offers, but for this chapter, we'll just focus on the beginning and the end.

Let's start by understanding where this whole hiring process starts. We need to talk about requisitions.

In many companies, jobs are ruled by requisitions ("reqs"). These imaginary pieces of paper give you, the hiring manager, permission to hire, but they serve two other purposes. First, they document and formalize the process of hiring a new full-time person, and more importantly, they give executives visibility into the state of the company's growth.

It varies by company, but reqs—specifically open, approved reqs—are one of the more popular organizational levers the execs have to measure and control the company's growth. In software development, one of your larger corporate expenses is base salary, which means the moment uncertainty appears on your company's horizon, reqs (read: the largest obvious expenses) are one of the first things to vanish.

This leads to painful lesson #1 regarding requisitions.

Note

Reqs vanish randomly, often without notice, without reason, and at the least convenient time.

In larger companies, the bureaucracy involved in getting an approved req is impressive. When the req is finally approved by the 17th person you don't know, you have a false sense of accomplishment. You believe this req is yours, but there is really only one way to make it yours—make the hire.

It's not just corporate nervousness that causes reqs to vanish. Your boss is a likely req-stealing culprit. *Anton's got a guy right now who is perfect for his team, and we've only got one req. He can hire him right now, and I swear we'll get you a req when you find someone.*

You believe your boss. You trust your boss, so you give him your req, and Anton's a happy guy, and you feel like you've done the team a solid. Except that when you actually find someone, guess what? You don't have a req. Neither does your boss because sometime between when you gave your req and actually found someone for your position, the first rule was invoked: every single req in the company was frozen.

I'm guessing 50% of the reqs I've managed to get approved in my career have resulted in a hire. Meaning a flip of a coin would as accurately predict whether or not I could hire someone.

From the moment there's a hint of an idea of a req in your future, you need to work on improving your chances that you'll be able to hire. And that means, as quickly as possible, you need to: find the person, phone screen them, interview them, interview them again, negotiate an offer, get that offer accepted, and get them in the building. Think of that as you're staring at your shiny new req. Think that the industry average for hiring against an approved req is 90 days—three months—and each of those days represents a day that someone, somewhere, can steal your req. This is why you need to...

SPEND AN HOUR A DAY ON EACH REQ YOU HAVE

We'll discuss how to ensure they'll show up in a bit, but to start, you need to get the pump primed. A former boss helpfully suggested, "Spend an hour a day on each req on your plate."

An hour?

If you've got an approved req, you have approval to grow your team. To add new skill sets. To build more stuff. In your role as a manager, I ask, What's more important than growing your team? No, this isn't a draconian hour; this is a daily reminder that you must grind away at this req until you've hired someone.

Rands, I have no candidates yet. The req was just approved. I...

Again, reqs vanish. Randomly. At the end of each workday, you must think, *Phew, no one stole my req.*

Here's how to start:

- Search the internet for candidates. *Show me a stranger who will be perfect.*

- Mail friends who might know the perfect person. *Know anyone? How about you?*

- Annoy your recruiter. *Where are my résumés?*

- Ping folks who have turned you down in the past. *Are you ready now?*

- Scan your inbox and sent folders for folks you need but may have forgotten. *Really, are you ready now?*

- Read your job description for additional inspiration. *Do I actually know who I'm looking for?*

But isn't this why I have a recruiter?

It's terrific that you have a recruiter. They will streamline your entire hiring process, but you still need to spend an hour a day for each req. A quality recruiter will find candidates and do time-saving phone screens, and they can keep in-flight candidates warm. When it comes to offer negotiation, they're great at providing you with essential compensation telemetry, and they're good at playing bad cop. Still, as we'll see, it's your job to demonstrate that the candidate is wanted.

I FOUND THEM! I'M DONE!

No, you didn't, and no, you aren't.

No, really! He verbally accepted, and he starts in two weeks. It's a done deal.

No, it's not. If randomly vanishing reqs are painful lesson #1 of hiring, there is also a painful lesson #2.

Note

People lose their minds during job transitions.

Think back to your last job transition. Think about the mental turmoil. When did you actually fully believe that you were going to accept the new gig? For me, this happens about two months after I start.

You keep recruiting and searching for the perfect employee until your new hire is sitting in their office. It's not common for an accepted offer to be declined, but it must happen once for you to learn the lesson and suddenly realize, *Oh, I need to start over. Crap.*

Until he's sitting in the seat, in the building, badge hanging from his belt, you haven't hired anyone.

Deliberate Want

Michele's team was embarking on a new technology direction, and while she had the basic talent in place, she needed two more hires, and we had the reqs. In a recruiting brainstorm, I sketched out the type of person we needed. "OK, we need Alex. He's the senior architect at this other company, but he's the right combination of technical brilliance and architectural jerk. We need someone with that technical ability and the will to enforce it because we're starting from the ground up."

HER: *Why not hire Alex?*

ME: *He'll never leave his startup.*

HER: *Have you asked?*

ME: *No.*

HER: *I'll ask.*

She did, and although it took six months, Alex, the perfect fit for the team and the project, joined the team. Halfway through the recruiting stint with Alex, when it looked like he might not budge, I threw another perfect candidate on her plate and said, "Maybe ask him, too?" Sean was on the team a month after Alex.

Two hires we had absolutely no chance of hiring. Both were on the team in a matter of months. Your question is, What's her secret? And the answer is dangerously simple—deliberate, consistently expressed, and reinforced want.

Both of the positions we had were attractive. Senior engineering gigs working on a 1.0 product in a name-brand company. But these guys were at the top of the field. Recognized names. There are a number of opportunities across the Valley that would be attractive. How'd we win?

We continually and consistently explained that they were wanted.

The idea of a new gig, a fresh start, is appealing because of its simplicity. You know nothing about your future team; you have no idea about potential death marches or that guy down the hall who just bugs you for no particular reason. It's simple to think about the future optimistically because the future hasn't screwed you...yet.

This optimism fades in the middle of the night when you open your eyes, startled, and think, *Why in the world would I leave a solid gig with people I know and a bright future?* The reasons are myriad, but that's not the point. The point is for any big decision, you will question it from every angle. You're going to have endless inner dialogs with yourself. You're going to talk yourself into the gig, and then you'll talk yourself out of it.

It's exhausting.

Michele's message during the entire hiring process was, "You are the best person for this gig. We want you." Remember that we're not talking about random, anonymous candidates; we're talking about handpicked candidates.

Before any interview, she'd drive to them, explain the gig, and begin, "You are the best person for this gig. We want you." After the first round of interviews, her message was the same: "See, this gig is perfect for you. We want you."

When we started the offer negotiations, she worked with the recruiter and knew exactly what we'd need to do to lure the candidates. She knew that base salary was a big deal for Alex. She knew Sean was going to be a stickler about stock. There was no offer negotiation because Michele constructed offers that would be accepted. She presented them: "This is the offer you wanted. This gig is perfect for you. We want you."

Once the offers were accepted, Michele didn't change her tone or message a bit. She'd had rock stars walk before, and she knew the slippery inner dialogs that were going on. She knew that change begets more change and that the easiest time to lose someone was during that postcourtship purgatory between gigs. She had her team take them for drinks. She planted seeds of future work that would need to be done. She reminded them, "We want you."

This strategy reads like a massive ego stroke for an attention-starved engineering rock star, but it's not. Whether you have preidentified a candidate for your gig or you're lucky enough to randomly find a great fit in a pile of anonymous résumés, the strategy is the same: you consistently remind the candidate that they are wanted. In the mental chaos of a career change, you and your gig are unchanging in your message. You're not coddling them; you're a constant among chaos.

Hire for Your Career

The strategy I'm proposing steps on a lot of recruiter's toes. Recruiters are professional relationship people, and their instinctive reads on candidates can be eerily accurate, but their job is the hire, and once the hire shows up, the recruiter vanishes. The relationship has ended because the job is done.

Your professional relationship with those you hire and work with is never over. If you're hiring well, you're hiring people not just for this job but for your career. These are the people who, for better or worse, will explain to others what it is like to work with you. They'll explain your quirks, your weaknesses, and your strengths. When they eventually leave the group, they're taking your reputation with them. You may never talk to them again, but they'll continue to talk about you, and my question is: What stories will they tell?

Your daily, hands-on management of your hiring isn't just going to improve your hiring process; it's going to improve your career because, from the first moment you interact with your future employee, you demonstrate that you care.

Jesse didn't decide to turn us down at 4:45 p.m. on his last day. The decision began long before that, and I wasn't listening. I didn't hear the parts of his current job he loved because I didn't do the phone screen. I didn't understand his concerns about leaving his first job since college, which he loved, because I didn't build enough trust in the interview. I didn't hear him drifting away during the offer negotiation. The last thing I heard about Jesse was that he walked.

22

The Toxic Paradox

Everyone is an adjustment. When you're interacting with anyone, you leave the core *you* and become slightly *them*. This is not a betrayal of who you are; this is the middle ground we define between any two people. It's a place of compromise so we can communicate.

There are those people with whom this is an easy, natural place to reach. It's that friend you haven't seen or heard from in six months, and how you know it will take 12 seconds for both of you to get back into a familiar place where those six months vanish.

Then there are those people who are more work. They require a protocol of context setting, translation, and cautious check-ins. *Hi, I said this, is this what you heard? OK, good.* This set of abilities, of communication skills, is more work and is a skill you refine over the years. It is a requirement of seasoned managers who are constantly thrown into meetings with strangers where they need to move quickly and efficiently past the "getting to know you" phase and into the "we've got work to do" portion of the meeting.

My guess is the majority of our relationships fall into either the natural or slightly-more-work buckets. The majority of the folks you surround yourself with, both inside and outside of work, are manageable. Not all are natural, so they are work, but you can live with them and are willing to do the work to maintain the relationships.

Then, there are those you can't handle. These are the folks who, for reasons you may never understand, behave in a way that you'll never grasp, can't define, nor will ever like.

These people are toxic.

Big Fat Toxic Assumptions

This chapter starts with two large, uncomfortable assumptions.

First, as I explain the serious issues with toxic coworkers, I must remind you that when it comes to disconnects between two people, there are always two vastly different stories regarding perceived toxicity. If I were to say that Felix had a toxic personality, you would do well to spend some time with Felix and learn about his perception of me. While I might have done as much due diligence as possible to examine every possible personality angle regarding Felix, there would still be essential data to be gathered directly from him.

A declaration of toxicity is a judgment. Sometimes defined by a group, sometimes spearheaded by an influential individual who simply cannot find a healthy way to relate to this person, but regardless, never trust a toxicity label without doing your own research.

Second, this chapter isn't about fixing this toxic person, but rather your perspective of them. I assume you're done trying to bridge the gap between you and this person. If you're a manager, this is hopefully the end result of months of careful negotiating, delicate compromise, and hardcore communication.

There are entire parts of your organization dedicated to providing ideas and skills about how to interact better with anyone on your team, and this chapter assumes you've employed all of them.

I won't walk you through strategies for dealing with toxic people because you're past that. This person is infecting the team with their toxicity, and you're vastly underestimating the daily damage this person is doing to the group.

This chapter is here to convince you it's time to make a change.

GO TEAM!

A toxic person kills, and by kills, I mean totally destroys teamwork.

Teamwork is one of those painful management-ese buzzwords that is clumsily used at inopportune times as a means of motivation. "We need better teamwork to improve efficiency and productivity." I know what you mean, but there are better ways to say it. Fact is, teamwork—teams of people actually working together—is magical.

It's not actually *magic*. It's years of practice, starting in elementary school, where you learned the basics: raise your hand when you want to speak, say "please" and "thank you," and don't eat the glue. In school, you learn just as much about how to deal with different types of personalities as you do about the world, so when it comes time to jump into the workforce, you already have years of experience in social interactions with a variety of personalities.

However, all of these hand-raising, glue-free pleasantries barely prepare you for a toxic personality.

Let's go back to the personality buckets I described at the start of this chapter: natural, work, and toxic. Let's say the cost of natural relationships is 1x. It's the base unit. It's no work; it's simple. Let's say that the work relationships are 2x. It requires twice as much effort on your part to bridge the communication and social gap. It's not difficult; it just works. You reduce this cost as you gather more experience and as you get to know people a bit, but these relationships will never be totally natural. Fact of life.

A toxic relationship cannot be measured in terms of these work units because, at its core, it does not work. You never get to a state of comfortable communication in these relationships. They are never predictable nor very productive because you are in a constant state of social corrosion. There are brief moments of clarity where you have a lightning strike of insight: *She's this way because I said that, and this is how she always reacts to that...so I won't do that. Brilliant!*

These moments of respite are short-lived. For reasons you may never understand, you are incapable of reverse engineering this personality, or your patterns of reaction to it, and it's only a matter of time before you rediscover this basic disconnect and move back to thrashing around, trying to figure out the unknowable.

Yes, this is a worst-case scenario.

Groups of people get along because they all subscribe to a similar culture. Yes, these people are all unique, but they get along because they have a similar belief system and buy into the same goals. This similarity of beliefs has a lot of benefits, but the biggest win is that it reduces organizational friction. There are heated arguments, but they are arguments based on similar beliefs, and the presence of these beliefs means these arguments have a chance of resolution.

Now, think about your base interaction with this toxic person. You sit down in the conference room across from them, and the topic at hand is easy. *We're discussing a small change to the architecture, and since you own a big part of it, I wanted to get your opinion.*

Reasonable. Professional. Respectful.

This isn't a small change. You haven't thought this through. Why wasn't I consulted earlier? How could we consider this given what I said 14 months ago on this very topic when I was ignored...?

It's a flood of incomprehensible toxicity. Now, inside the flood is a bunch of historic mistakes on everyone's part, but go back and read that previous paragraph. Are you seeing any of the content, or are you seeing the toxicity?

Do the math. This is one meeting, and while you might pull off a meeting win when everyone's calmed down, you're spending the first 30 minutes of the meeting being blasted. And here's the bad news: a majority of the team is having similar experiences. Most of the folks interacting with this person are spending their time trying to figure out how to keep this person from going ballistic rather than actually getting work done.

After a time, this results in even more damage. People stop scheduling meetings with this person. They stop traveling to this person's part of the building. And again, I'm not talking about one or two people here; I'm talking about the majority of the team.

My definition of *toxicity* isn't based on the idea that you are incapable of getting to a professional place with this person; it's based on the idea that the culture of your group, your company, is literally rejecting this person. Everyone is avoiding this corrosive person, and this avoidance is affecting productivity and morale across the board. It's a daily emotional tax of frustration and demoralization.

A culture rarely changes for one person, and in the case of a toxic person, a culture will protect itself through rejection.

A TOXIC PARADOX

Rands, he's just not getting along with the right people.

No.

This is not high school. I'm not talking about cliques here; I'm talking about culture. Cliques are inevitable microcollections of people who like the look and sound of each other. Culture is the foundational broad strokes of beliefs, values, and goals in a group of people; and a healthy culture is inclusive. It seeks out new members who evolve the culture into something new and better. It's constantly growing in interesting ways because of the people it's built on.

A rejection by the culture, while not pleasant for anyone involved, is not a rejection based on individual taste, and it's not because someone doesn't like someone else. It's a rejection because of a lack of shared core beliefs. Vastly different personalities get along famously when they share a common goal.

Yes. People get petty, and people dislike each other for seemingly inane reasons, and yes, it's a manager's job, along with HR, to figure out how to build a constructive working relationship among these people, but this is not the situation I'm describing. I'm talking about trying to shove a toxic square peg in a cultural round hole. It doesn't work. Keep pushing all you want, but...it's not happening.

It's hard to remember this when a toxic person is yelling at you, but they're not actually yelling at *you*. They're yelling at the culture. They're angry because their belief structure isn't a fit with just about everyone else's, and they know it. They know that they're not winning this argument...ever. They know that in order to win this argument, they'd need to restart the culture of the company, and such an endeavor makes a re-org look like a walk in the park.

And here's the worst part: they might be right.

The history of Silicon Valley is full of stories of toxic people who were, well...right. These people were physically removed from their respective companies, but their agenda, and their ideas, however unpalatable to the existing cultural regime, were actually the right thing to do for that particular company.

The paradox is that we need these toxic people. We need these self-centered assholes to ignore cultural conventions totally and to mix things up beyond recognition. They don't need social grace, and they don't need charisma. Both help, but their value lies in their intense belief in their own culture.

We need these folks, but it can't be at the cost of team morale and productivity. Yes, this toxic person might have a core cultural contradictory belief that is key to the future of the business, but assess the risk. What if the cost of integrating that idea is half the team quitting because they can't work with the idea's toxic architect? Is that a viable solution?

No? Maybe?

The deportation of a toxic asset is a judgment call, and it's based on the fundamental idea that fitting in is easy, but real change is hard.

Everyone Is an Adjustment

Your career is defined by two tasks: What hard problems have you solved? and Whom have you joined in solving these problems? For me, the harder the problems, the trickier the people, the better. In an impossible challenge, I believe there are invaluable lessons.

A truly toxic person is not a disruption; that person is a disaster. When you're measuring the damage and the emotional anguish caused by a single person, the question isn't, What am I going to do?; the question is, How quickly can I do it?

23

By Design

I'm at my first startup. We're between layoff #2 and layoff #3. There's a new VP of engineering running the show and while he's been hired with the request to "turn the ship around," the tech economy is a wreck and his first official act is throwing passengers overboard so we don't sink.

Now this will be the third (and last) layoff. The existing team of three directors completed the first layoff under the first VP and then the second under the interim VP (the head of business development...another story for another time). In each case, it started with an unexpected meeting late in the day after the executive team had reviewed the latest numbers.

Then the request came: "I'm sure we won't need to do this, but can you take this here spreadsheet of your team and document how much each of them is devoted to this set of in-flight projects? Take your time."

Sure.

24 hours passed and they walked into my cube, "Are you done, yet?"

You said take your time...?

"Yeah, I need the information in an hour. It's critical."

OK, sure.

Fast forward four weeks, and there are three spreadsheets of our three teams chock-full with information regarding each employee. We are able to use this spreadsheet to understand who is on the team, their capabilities, what products they build, and what those products will contribute to the bottom line.

However, the three spreadsheets are biased. Each of the three directors has carefully built their spreadsheets to demonstrate why the humans on their team must remain. This does not meet the intent of the exercise, which is to recommend a strategy that allows the company to survive. Both the first VP and the acting VP know we've done this and understand part of the job is a reconciliation of these disparate data sets.

The exercise is about as fun as it sounds, but they each completed this complicated process by defining a set of principles, explaining them, and then applying them to our spreadsheets.

Yes, you're drawing a line on this spreadsheet. The humans above stay, the humans below are let go. Yes, the application of these principles meant the lines shifted, often drastically, and that meant one director eventually was letting go of far more of their team than the other two. It's an awful process I wish on none of you.

And now it's time for the third.

My codirectors already have the spreadsheet ready, we've done the drill, and we do exactly the same thing with our biased spreadsheets. Protecting the team, of course, but not helping the overall business.

When we handed our biased spreadsheets to the VP, he glanced at them, quickly discerned we hadn't done our jobs, and said, "You need to cut more. This much more."

Confused. "Aren't you going to help us do that?"

"No, you're a director. This is your job. By design."

Interlude

I've had this schtick on Twitter for years. Goes like this. I hear something someone randomly says, and in my head I translate it to what I believe they are actually saying. What they say is, "I think it's pretty simple" and what I think is, "Based on your understanding of the parts you can see...which is incomplete."

Tweeted another way, "When you say, 'I think it's pretty simple,' I hear 'I think I understand the parts I can see,'" It's snark. It's usually not what they're actually saying, but comedy is where we park the things we are uncomfortable saying.

This inner translation dialog is a habit I've had long before Twitter existed, and to this day I think of those two words hanging at the end of the new VP's guidance on how to figure out who to lay off from the company. A reminder, he said, "No, you're a director. This is your job. By design."

When you say, "By design," I hear, "I can't be bothered to explain this nuanced thing to you."

Back to layoff #3. We, the three directors, did our best to come to an agreement, but we didn't, so we ended up with different principles for different teams. When it came to layoff conversations, different teams were hearing different narratives and, of course, they were sharing this information both with employees who were leaving and those who were staying. Those who were let go were unclear why they were being let go, and those staying were unclear why they were allowed to stay because different stories were being told.

It was a disaster, it was inhumane, and I can't think of a more defining lesson in my leadership career.

Your Job as a Leader

Your job as a leader is not to make the hard calls. That's ego talking. Your job as a leader is to clearly explain how you made the hard call so that your team understands how you think, what strategy you are employing, and what principles you are following.

If you have no strategy, you take the time to define it. If you don't have principles by which to make this decision, you work quickly with as many humans as possible to clearly define them. A principle is a fundamental truth. It's a foundation for a system of belief or behavior or for a chain of reasoning, and you bet they're hard to define, but that's your job.

By design.

24

The Core of Kindness

For this chapter, I plan to simplify management. Let us assume there are three different hats you wear as a manager. They are the Leader, the Fixer, and the Coach. I will briefly explain each role and how I've screwed up each. I'm going in reverse order because I'm building tension.

The Coach

Your standard persona. You are the more experienced human in this team, and your job is to pass your hard-earned wisdom on to others. Most of these lessons are not planned because we move intently and quickly in business. After all, that's how you win.

Problems arise. Conflict ensues. Some you see with your eyeballs, others you hear about after the fact. In both cases, your job is usually not to escalate but to educate.

You say things like:

- "Did you think about this perspective?"
- "When I've seen this in the past, this is why it happened."
- "Allow me to explain how I've failed amply doing this in the past."

Delivery of this wisdom is key to both building up the team and establishing yourself as an approachable Coach.

And this is how I screwed it up.

Months after I left a prior gig, I received an email from the person who took over my role. A friendly note. They wanted to understand what I could teach them about the team. I responded with an immediate, "Of course."

The conversation was rich. They had a good read on the team after just four months. I dropped some knowledge on several of my coworkers' professional hopes and dreams and asked how else I could help.

This person said something off the cuff that I think about every single day. They were talking about their perceptions of what had changed since I left. I don't remember the entire story, but I remember this phrase. "They liked you. *Perhaps too much.*" A throwaway comment that they forgot immediately, but that I'd never forget.

See, the Coach is nice. They want to be liked, they want to be always approachable, they like positive vibes, and they are conflict-averse. They liked me? Perhaps too much? What I heard between the words was the team appreciated me as a Coach and as a helper, but they did not trust me to make the hard calls because I was afraid of hurting my relationship with the team.

And they were right.

The Fixer

A specialized persona. As it's prone to do as we move intently and quickly, the sky falls now and then. There is no more obvious call to action than the sky falling, and when it does, you leap up and run to the front of the room, waving your hands, declaring, "I got this."

The circumstances that require the Fixer are not fun, but the role of the Fixer is a blast. Why? First, you get to blow through the bureaucracy. Second, everyone wants to help. Third, you get to move exceptionally quickly. It's a delightful change of pace.

I've written extensively[1] about Fixer-esque situations over the years, and that's because I love being the Fixer.

And this is how I screwed it up.

The VP needed us to move to a new platform for reasons. Other directors had made two attempts, and both had failed, leaving us on a janky old platform costing us millions of dollars. The previous efforts were happening outside of my engineering world, but the VP had seen me fix it before, so he tasked me with fixing it again.

Off I go with my fix mandate! I spent the weekend researching how attempts #1 and #2 had failed. I educated myself on the future platforms, building a

---

1 See, for instance, Michael Lopp, "Kobayashi Maru Management" (*https://randsinrepose.com/archives/kobayashi-maru-management*), *Rands in Repose* (blog), August 8, 2018.

lovely pro/con list, a cost analysis to scare the hell out of everyone, and an initial two-week action plan. I finished by scheduling a Monday morning all-hands.

Look at me! At the front of the room! Fixing the thing! Enthusiastically!

The VP dropped by my office on Wednesday at the close of business and said, "Let's take a walk."

Outside, he began, "Thank you, you are starting to fix it. You are moving quickly and purposefully, but there is a problem. Your bedside manner signals to the patient that they will die."

What? Bedside manner? Death? Too many metaphors:

HIM: Do you think the folks who have already worked hard to fix this screwed up?

ME: I do. They did. Twice.

HIM: Yes, they can tell how you feel about them by how you treat them.

ME: But they screwed up.

HIM: Do you think they don't already know that?

The Leader

I've screwed up. More times than I can count. There was a time when I leaned too much into being the Coach, so they didn't believe I could make the hard calls and lead. There was another time when all I wanted to do was Fix, but I killed the team's morale because my well-intentioned actions predominantly conveyed how much I believed they screwed up.

Management isn't a promotion; it's a new job. Leadership isn't management; it's a set of principles you continuously and consistently demonstrate to your team to show what you believe is important. Leadership is how they learn what to expect from you. Managers tell you where you are. Leaders tell you where you are going.

Sometimes you'll need Coach and Fix, but aren't they the same thing? The Coach fixes stuff. The Fixer coaches to resolution. Aren't they vastly different hats?

I finish one of my talks with a synopsis of an article I wrote regarding being unfailingly kind.[2] Go read it. Classic Rands. Invariably after the talk and

---

2 Michael Lopp, "Be Unfailingly Kind" (*https://randsinrepose.com/archives/be-unfailingly-kind*), *Rands in Repose* (blog), August 3, 2015.

during the Q&A, someone asks me a question about kindness in the business place. They have a benign scenario designed to test whether kindness works as a practice, so I make it serious:

"Is it kind to fire someone?"

The room is silent.

"Your gut reaction is no, but you're thinking of the scenario where someone is randomly fired without prior knowledge. They are shocked, and that's not kind at all.

"When you first identify a challenge someone is having, you talk about it with them clearly and constructively. You listen to their reaction and then start to coach them. For weeks. You talk about the challenge with them. For months. And sometimes the challenge can't be fixed.

"You explain this to them, listen to their reactions, adapt your coaching, and talk some more. If letting them go comes up, there's no surprise. There is a probable disappointment, but no one involved is uninvolved.

"And in that scenario, after all that discussion and coaching, the fix is for that person to find a different role. Perhaps at the current company. Or another. And you never call it firing because that's not kind."

The Coach listened. The Fixer acted. They did it with kindness because that's how good leaders behave. Being nice is a part of kindness, but the core of kindness—and leadership—is respect.

PART III

Your Daily Toolkit

The list of essential daily skills you need as a software developer that high school and college did not prepare you for is impressive.

It's great that you can explain Big O notation, but what class taught you about presenting to the CEO? I'm happy you're an Emacs zealot, but do you know who in your 2:00 p.m. meeting needs to learn the most from you?

The stereotype regarding engineers is we want to code—we want to hide in our caves, far from people, and code. And we do. Coding is awesome, but that's not all you want to do. You're halfway through *The Software Developer's Career Handbook*, which means you now understand a larger set of skills necessary to be a successful developer.

Manage your time—an invaluable commodity—obsess about the tools you use, and take the time to understand the people around you. Figure out how to speak their language to learn how to convey your bright ideas to anyone.

25

The Nerd Handbook

OK, we're halfway through the book, so it's time for a break. Much of this book is focused on you. Your current job and your plan for your career. However, this wonderfully narcissistic journey is not one you will complete alone; you have an extensive supporting cast.

It's not just your boss and your coworkers, but also your friends. Renee, whom you've known for years, must meet for a drink and a professional vent every three months. There's Ryan, the annoying guy on the train who randomly lands that quip that changes your day. And Lorraine. She runs the coffee shop, and her mood and coffee can set the tone for the start of your day. You are surrounded by folks who support you, whether you realize it or not, and I haven't even mentioned the most important person—your significant other.

The chapter that follows is not for you; it's for them. I hope you can look up from this book and see them sitting there on the couch. They have questions about you. They don't know how to sit at the computer for five hours straight. They find you funny, but they don't know where that funny comes from.

Stand up and hand them this chapter right now. If they're not in the visual range, turn the corner of the page as a reminder that part of your success will be the understanding of those who support you.

Understanding Your Nerd

Hi. You've just been handed this book by someone important to you who also happens to be a nerd. This nerd would like you to read this chapter so that you can better understand those strange quirks you've already recognized but may not understand.

See, a nerd needs a project because a nerd builds stuff. All the time. Those lulls in the conversation over dinner? That's the nerd working on his project in his head.

It's unlikely that this project is a nerd's day job because his opinion regarding his job is, "Been there, done that." We'll explore the consequences of this seemingly short attention span in a bit, but for now, this project is the other big thing your nerd is building, and I've no idea what it is, but you should.

At some point, you, the nerd's companion, were the project. You were showered with the fire hose of attention because you were the bright and shiny new development in your nerd's life. There is also a chance that you're lucky and you are currently your nerd's project. Congrats. Don't get too comfortable, though, because he'll move on, and when that happens, you'll be wondering what happened to all the attention. This handbook might help.

UNDERSTAND YOUR NERD'S RELATION TO THE COMPUTER

It's clichéd, but a nerd is defined by his computer, and you need to understand why.

First, most of the folks on the planet either have no idea how the mechanics inside of a computer works, or they look at it and think it's "magic." Nerds know how a computer works. They intimately know how a computer works. When you ask a nerd, "When I click this, it takes a while for the thing to show up. Do you know what's wrong?," they know what's wrong. A nerd has a mental model of the hardware and the software in her head. While the rest of the world sees magic, your nerd knows how the magic works, she knows the magic is a long series of ones and zeros moving across your screen with impressive speed, and she knows how to make those bits move faster.

The nerd has based her career, maybe her life, on the computer, and as we'll see, this intimate relationship has altered her view of the world. She sees the world as a system that, given enough time and effort, is completely knowable. This is a fragile illusion that your nerd has adopted, but it's a pleasant one that gets your nerd through the day. When the illusion is broken, you are going to discover that...

YOUR NERD HAS CONTROL ISSUES

Your nerd lives in a monospaced typeface world. Whereas everyone else is traipsing around picking dazzling fonts to describe their world, your nerd has carefully selected a monospace typeface that he avidly uses to manipulate the world deftly via a command-line interface while the rest fumble around with a mouse.

The reason for this typeface selection is, of course, practicality. Monospace typefaces have a knowable width. Ten letters on one line are the same width as any other ten letters, which puts the world into a pleasant grid construction where X and Y mean something.

These control issues mean your nerd is sensitive to drastic environmental changes. Think travel. Think job changes. These types of system-redefining events force your nerd to recognize that the world is not always nor entirely a knowable place. Until he reconstructs this illusion, he's going to be frustrated, and he's going to act erratically. I develop an incredibly short fuse during system-redefining events, and I'm much more likely to lose it over something trivial and stupid. This is one of the reasons that...

YOUR NERD HAS BUILT HERSELF A CAVE

I've written about the cave throughout the book, but here are the basics. The cave is designed to allow your nerd to do her favorite thing, which is working on the project. If you want to understand your nerd, stare long and hard at her cave. How does she have it arranged? When does she tend to go there? How long does she stay?

Each object in the cave has a particular place and purpose. Even the clutter is well designed. Don't believe me? Grab that seemingly discarded Mac Mini that has been sitting on the floor for two months and hide it. You'll have 10 minutes before she'll come stomping out of the cave— "Where's the Mac?"

The cave is also frustrating you because your impression is that it's your nerd's way of checking out, and you are, unfortunately, completely correct. A correctly designed cave removes your nerd from the physical world and plants her firmly in a virtual one, complete with all the toys she needs. Because...

YOUR NERD LOVES TOYS AND PUZZLES

The joy your nerd finds in his project is one of problem solving and discovery. As each part of the project is completed, your nerd receives an adrenaline rush that we will call the High. Every profession has this—the moment when you've moved significantly closer to being done. In many jobs, it's easy to discern when progress is being made: "Look, now we have a door." But in nerds' bit-based work, progress is measured mentally and invisibly in code, algorithms, efficiency, and small mental victories that don't exist in a world of atoms.

There are other ways your nerd can create the High, and he does it all the time. It's another juicy cliché to say that nerds love video games, but that's not what they love. A video game is just one more system where your nerd's job is to figure out the rules that define it. This will enable him to beat it. Yeah, we love to stare at games with a bazillion polygons, but we get the same high from playing

Bejeweled, getting our Night Elf to Max level, or endlessly tinkering with a Rubik's Cube. This fits nicely with the fact that...

NERDS ARE FUCKING FUNNY

Your nerd spent much of his younger life being an outcast because of his strange affinity with the computer. This created a basic bitterness in his psyche that is the foundation for his humor. Now, combine this basic distrust of everything with your nerd's other natural talents, and you'll realize that he sees humor as another game.

Humor is an intellectual puzzle: How can this particular set of esoteric trivia be constructed to maximize hilarity as quickly as possible? Your nerd listens hard to recognize humor potential, and when he hears it, he furiously scours his mind to find relevant content from his experience to get the funny out as quickly as possible.

This quick wit is only augmented by the fact that...

YOUR NERD HAS AN AMAZING APPETITE FOR INFORMATION

Many years ago, I dubbed this behavior NADD, or nerd attention deficiency disorder.

How does a nerd watch TV? Probably one of two ways. First, there's watching TV with you, where the two of you sit and watch one show. Then there's how she watches by herself when she watches three shows at once. It looks insane. You walk into the room, and you're watching your nerd jump between channels every five minutes.

"How can you keep track of anything?"

She keeps track of everything. See, she's already seen all three of these movies...multiple times. She knows the compelling parts of the arcs and is mentally editing her own versions while watching all three. The basic mental move here is the context switch, and your nerd is the king of the context switch.

The ability to instantly context switch also comes from a life on the computer. Your nerd's mental information model for the world is one contained within well-bounded, tidy windows where the most important tool is one that allows your nerd to move swiftly from one window to the next. It's irrelevant that there may be no relationship between these windows. Your nerd is used to making huge contextual leaps where she's talking to a friend in one window, worrying about her 401(k) in another, and reading about World War II in yet another.

You might suspect that given a world where context is constantly shifting, your nerd can't focus, and you'd be partially correct. All that multitasking isn't efficient. Your nerd knows very little about a lot. For many topics, her knowledge is an inch deep and four miles wide. She's comfortable with this fact because she knows that deep knowledge about any topic is a clever keystroke away. See...

YOUR NERD HAS BUILT AN ANNOYINGLY EFFICIENT RELEVANCY ENGINE IN HIS HEAD

It's the end of the day, and you and your nerd are hanging out on the couch. The TV is off. There isn't a computer anywhere nearby, and you're giving your nerd the daily debrief. "Spent an hour at the post office trying to ship that package to your mom, and then I went down to that bistro—you know, the one next to the flower shop—and it's closed. Can you believe that?"

And your nerd says, "Cool."

Cool? What's cool? The business closing? The package? How is any of it cool? None of it's cool. Actually, all of it might be cool, but your nerd doesn't believe any of what you're saying is relevant. This is what he heard: "Spent an hour at the post office blah blah blah..."

You can be rightfully pissed off by this behavior—it's simply rude—but seriously, I'm trying to help here. Your nerd's insatiable quest for information and the High has tweaked his brain in an interesting way. For any given piece of incoming information, your nerd is making a lightning-fast assessment: relevant or irrelevant? Relevance means that the incoming information fits into the system of things your nerd currently cares about. Expect active involvement from your nerd when you trip the relevance flag. If you trip the irrelevance flag, look for verbal punctuation announcing his judgment of irrelevance. It's the word your nerd says when he's not listening, and it's always the same. My word is "Cool," and when you hear "Cool," I'm not listening.

Information that your nerd is exposed to when the irrelevance flag is waving is forgotten almost immediately. I mean it. Next time you hear "Cool," I want you to ask, "What'd I just say?" That awkward grin on your nerd's face is the first step in getting him to acknowledge that he's the problem in this particular conversation. This behavior is one of the reasons that...

YOUR NERD MIGHT COME OFF AS NOT LIKING PEOPLE

Small talk. Those first awkward five minutes when two people are forced to interact. Small talk is the bane of the nerd's existence because small talk is a combination of aspects of the world that your nerd hates. When your nerd is staring at a stranger, all he's thinking is, *I have no system for understanding this messy person in front of me.* This is where the shyness comes from. This is why nerds hate presenting to crowds.

The skills to interact with other people are there. They just lack a well-defined system.

Advanced Nerd Tweakage

If you're still reading, I think your nerd is worth keeping. Even though he's apt to vanish for hours, has a strange sense of humor, doesn't like you touching his stuff, and often doesn't listen when you're talking directly to him, he's a keeper. Go figure.

My advice is...

MAP THE THINGS HE'S BAD AT TO THE THINGS HE LOVES

You love to travel, but your nerd would prefer to hide in his cave for hours on end chasing the High. You need to convince him of two things. First, you need to convince him that you're going to do your best to re-create his cave in his new surroundings. You will create a quiet, dark place where he can orient himself and figure out how the water flushes down the toilet. Traveling internationally? Carve out three days somewhere quiet at the beginning of the trip. Traveling across the US? How about letting him chill on the bed for half of a day before you drag him out to see the Golden Gate Bridge?

Second, and more importantly, you must remind him about his insatiable appetite for information. You need to appeal to his deep love of discovering new content and help him understand that there may be no greater content fire hose than waking up in a hotel overlooking the Grand Canal in Venice where you don't speak a word of Italian.

MAKE IT A PROJECT

You might've noticed your nerd's strange relation to food. Does he eat fast? Like really fast? You should know what's going on here. Food is thrown into the irrelevant bucket because it's getting in the way of the content. Exercise, too. The thing is, you want your nerd to eat healthily so that he's here in another 30 years, so how do you change this behavior? You make diet and exercise the project.

For me, exercise became the project 10 years ago after a horrible breakup. When the project was no longer the ex, I dove into exercise every single day of the week. There were charts tracking my workouts, there were graphs tracking my weight, and there was exercise. Every single day for two years until the day I passed out in a McDonald's post-workout after not eating for a day. OK, so time for a new project. Yeah, nerds also have moderation issues. That's a chapter for another book.

Significant nerd behavioral change will only happen if your nerd engages in the project heart and soul; otherwise, it's just another thought for the irrelevant bucket.

PEOPLE ARE THE MOST INTERESTING CONTENT OUT THERE

If you've got a seriously shy nerd on your hands, try this: ask her how many folks are in her buddy list. How many friends does she have on Facebook? How many folks are following her on Twitter? Mastodon? My guess is that, collectively, your nerd interacts with 10 times more people than you think she does. She can do this because the interaction is via a system she understands—the computer.

Your nerd knows that people are interesting. Just because she can't look your best friend straight in the eye doesn't mean she doesn't want to know what makes her tick, but you need to be the social buffer—the translation layer. You need to find one common thread of interest between your nerd and your friend, and then she'll engage because she will have found relevance.

The Next High

As you discovered when you were the project, your nerd's focus can be deliciously overwhelming, but it also comes to a screeching halt. Once a nerd believes he fully knows how a system works, the challenge to understand ceases to exist, and he moves on in search of the Next High.

While I don't know who you are or why in the world you chose a nerd for your companion, I do know that you are not a knowable system. I know that you are messy, just like your nerd. Being your own quirky self will be more than enough to present new and interesting challenges to your nerd.

Besides, it's just as much a nerd's job to figure you out, and maybe someone somewhere is writing an article about your particular quirks. Good news; he's probably reading it right now.

26

The Taste of the Day

Think of this. You have a job where, whenever you need to, you can find the absolute truth. When someone asks you, "Phil, why is this happening?" you are 100% confident that you can figure out the precise answer.

This is the idyllic situation many engineers on the planet Earth live in, and, well, it's just a great gig.

I exaggerate. Engineers do have blind spots, but for their work, for their specific pile of bits, they are omniscient. They're their bits, and they constructed them into their specific system where they are intimately familiar with the rules because they defined them.

Outside of my career as an engineer, I've been a store clerk, a butcher, a video rental clerk, a lawyer's assistant, and a bookseller—and although it's been over 15 years since I've done any of these jobs, I remember the sense of naive pointlessness: What do I build? Well, I sell stuff, cut stuff, or type stuff. I don't really build anything, I...do stuff.

This made the first engineering gig a revelation. "You. We are building a database application and you own this specific part. It is entirely yours. Don't fuck it up."

Delicious, delicious structure. Sweet, sweet definition.

These basic and essential elements of job satisfaction are at the root of why many engineers make horrible managers. They are trained as and love to be control freaks.

The New Gig

Now you have a new job. As a manager, you have an office and you have a door. On your desk, there's a timer that tracks the number of seconds that it's just you alone in your office. Whenever someone else walks into your office, the timer magically resets to zero.

Today's record for consecutive uninterrupted seconds is 47.

This is not a world an engineer is used to, this interruption-driven day full of people and political calculus. This is where the reputation that your manager does nothing begins. It's your manager who thinks it. It's the close of the day and your manager wonders, *Did I actually do anything today except contend with a constant stream of people coming into my office?*

Try as you might, the structure and definition of your quiet engineering gig is gone. Your days of digital omniscience are over.

This is the big switch between the engineer and the manager. You are leaving the comfortable world of bits for the one of bafflingly configured atoms, where you must figure out how to trust those you work with. Where you need to train folks to make decisions for themselves but also help them understand it's OK to escalate for help. It's a gig where you must keep track of everything and constantly reprioritize but remain strategically limber.

And to do all of this, you need a task-tracking system that allows you to strategically forget.

The Taste of the Day

This is my system. Yes, I'm a manager, but there's no reason this system wouldn't work for anyone who feels buried. This system combines my ability to be a systematic thinker with the reality that there is more to do than I can ever complete. I've been using some variation of it for 10 years now, and it's how I run my day and my week.

It all orbits around a task system. Your first question will be: "What task-tracking system do you use, Rands?" The answer is simple: "Whatever works for you." I've used a homegrown Excel system, Tasks, and I'm currently using Things, but as you'll see, the strategic key here is not the identification of the task-tracking system; it's using it—all the time.

This system is designed to create a living, breathing, manageable list of things you might actually do, and it starts with...

THE MORNING SCRUB

The first task of the day is to set my head. What kind of day am I getting myself into? A quick glance at the calendar gives me the first hint of what to expect. Is this a quiet get-things-done day? A meeting hell day? Or a sky-is-falling day? Each day tastes different, and the Morning Scrub forces me to set my head appropriately. It gives me a rough sense of my capacity, the people I'll meet, and what they might need. More importantly, it reminds me that *priority is relative.*

Humans suffer from a bright 'n' shiny complex, where we're titillated by the new. Think of it like this: Have you actually done anything with that last domain you bought? No. You had the idea for it on Tuesday morning, and you got all fired up, so you bought the domain the moment you got into work. At lunch, you furiously doodled your design in your notebook, fully intending to get home and start on the HTML/CSS, and then you got home...and watched *Lost*.

Take the bright 'n' shiny complex and apply it to your entire group, where everyone is prioritizing their day by their particular inspiration, and it's shocking that we collectively get anything done.

By taking a deep breath and considering the entire day, I'm attempting to ditch all the bright 'n' shininess and gather perspective: What is going to matter today? With this rough priority scale in mind, I do a complete scrub of the to-do list. Yeah, the whole thing. If you can't get through this list in five uninterrupted minutes, your list is either too long or you're bad at scrubbing. Don't worry about that yet.

The purpose of the Morning Scrub is to land each task into one of three buckets:

Today
> This task must be completed today.

Later
> Not today. Later.

Never
> Yeah, I'm never going to do this task. It's gone. This is an important, essential decision that we'll talk about in a moment.

Initially, getting through this list is tricky because, invariably, a task will be so delectable that you'll want to jump into immediate action. Don't. The point of this scrub is not forward momentum; it's complete prioritization. Any deviation from the scrub decreases the chance you'll get through the whole list.

How many Today tasks are left when you're done with the scrub? I don't know because I don't know who you are or how granular your tasks are, but I usually end up with between 10 and 20.

With the Morning Scrub complete, I create the Parking Lot. This is a blank legal-size piece of paper that sits directly to the keyboard's left. New sheet. Always legal-size. Every morning.

Anyone who has sat through an offsite knows exactly what this paper is for. It's the landing spot for any idea/task/thing that is worth remembering but, if acted upon at the moment, will derail the productivity train. Like the Morning Scrub, the art of capturing a bright 'n' shiny idea and landing it in the Parking Lot is an acquired skill. You'll want to move on to the new, and sometimes that's the right move, but you need to answer the question honestly and quickly. Is moving on to this new thing more important than finishing what I'm doing right now?

PRACTICE PRODUCTIVITY MINIMALISM

This is not a chapter where I'll debate the pros and cons of various productivity tools. You get to find a tool that fits your personal quirks, but whatever that tool is, I have some brief advice on how to use it relative to assessing your personal Taste of the Day:

- My task list has no hierarchical organization. I've used systems before that allow me to lump tasks by projects or by theme, and, inevitably, I end up maintaining the structure rather than getting shit done. This pisses me off.

- I do use tags within the Things applications, but only to track who the most important person is, if anyone, for a given task. This is a handy way to run 1:1s. "Show me all Bob-related things."

- No priorities. Really. Again, priority is relative, and while slapping a priority on a task when you create it feels right, it's wrong because two days from now, the priority will be different. Priority is a big deal—as a manager, you want to get the right stuff done at the right time, but the priority that matters is the one sitting in your head right now rather than the one you dreamed up a week ago.

- No dates. I'm pissing off productivity nerds now. I don't track due dates, either. I fully scrub my to-do list every day, which means I'm constantly making real-time decisions regarding scheduling tasks.

As an engineer, your natural inclination is to build an increasingly complex system for tracking your tasks. The risk is that the more structure you put into your list, the more you need to maintain it, and the more you maintain it, the less time you'll have to actually get work done.

THE EVENING

After work, after dinner, or just before I go to sleep, I complete another scrub. The process for the Evening Scrub is slightly different.

First, I scrub the Parking Lot into the Later bucket. This is the first taste I get of how the day actually went. Lots of new tasks? OK, what kind? With the Parking Lot scrubbed, I take a moment to size up the day. How'd I do on taste? My original read was "meeting-infested nightmare"—was I right? This is another priority-leveling exercise. It doesn't matter if I made the right call on the day; the point is to set your head again appropriately.

Finally, I scrub unfinished items in the Today bucket. For each item remaining, I ask, "OK, why didn't I get this done?" Very often, the answer is, "Not enough time," so the item gets thrown back into the Later bucket, but sometimes it just gets deleted. Your question is, "How did a task that was scrubbed into the Today bucket this morning suddenly become irrelevant?"

The efficient, version-control-loving information packrat in you will have a problem punting a task into oblivion. Your thought is, *Sure, it might not feel important right now,* but what if!?

Stop. Delete it. We've already wasted 37 seconds noodling on this semi-essential but tasteless task. Nuke it. By getting this task off your list and out of your head, we're making space. Don't worry, if the task is actually important, it's going to find its way back to your Parking Lot.

This deletion is advanced task management kung fu, and it's based on the insight I don't like to give to new managers because it's a total productivity buzzkill. The insight is: you will never complete everything you should.

I can do anything!

Of course, you can.

Don't tell me what I can't do!

I'm not. What I'm telling you is that management is the art of choosing what *not* to do, which means you need to be ready and willing to look at the task at the end of the day and ask, "OK, I made this urgent this morning. A day has passed, and I had time, but never got to it. Does it matter?"

Priority is relative. What felt so important last Wednesday loses importance five days later when the larger context of your week, your month, and your career shows up. You need to develop a practice of strategic information shedding where you are constantly and intelligently jettisoning ideas and work.

A well-maintained to-do list gives you a daily sense of professional well-being. It constructs the pleasant illusion that you have a degree of control in a world where you have no idea how tomorrow will taste. The system I've constructed to maintain this list is lightweight, built from the practical use of constraints, and designed to sift through an endless crapload of information that passes me during the day, but it's a system that is incomplete.

A glance at my current Parking Lot demonstrates this incompleteness. It's a list of things I need to do. It's a list of tactics that I need to use to keep the management engine running, but dutifully following these to-dos isn't management; it's task execution. You need another list, one that represents the strategy for your team, your career, and your values.

And as we'll learn in the next chapter, that one is called the Trickle List.

27

The Trickle List

There's a gaping hole in the prior chapter, "The Taste of the Day." Yes, it's a handy task management system, but it's incomplete. It describes a process for constant scrubbing of a task list, as well as a handy place to keep distractions out of your way via the Parking Lot, but at the end of the day, what exactly is it helping you do?

Here are three tasks from my current list:

- Headcount Asks

- Lunch with David

- Move Europe Trip

These are tasks for today. They are well defined, measurable, tactical, and must be done today. While it's professionally terrific that I'm actively making sure nothing is falling through the cracks, these are still just tasks. What am I accomplishing when I complete them? I'm getting things done.

Is that what you want to do all day? Things? Stuff?

No.

You're a senior development engineer or an engineering manager or a project manager, and while things and stuff are part of the gig, if it's all you're doing, you're productive, but you're vigorously running in place. You're tactical but not strategic. Tasks are an incomplete picture of what you do and what you need to do.

The curse of any effective task management system is that you get really good at capturing, prioritizing, and executing tasks to the point that you believe merely completing a task is helping your career. After a solid decade of rampant task management, I realized I needed to augment tasks with a system that would strategically guide and remind me that my job was not to do things but to remember the interesting words in my title: *manager*, *engineering*, and *products*. That's what I do.

I needed a guiding force behind these tasks, a way to remind me that I was pushing toward a goal and defining and refining a strategy.

I call it a Trickle List, and it looks like Figure 27-1.

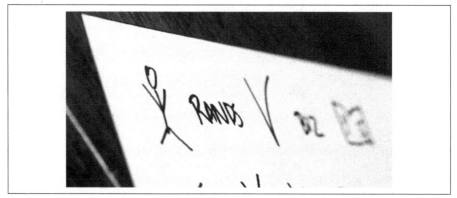

Figure 27-1. Rands' Trickle List

Trickle Creation

My first excursion into understanding the word *trickle* was an idea called Trickle Theory. The argument was simple: you can do more than you think with small, consistent investments of your time.

To understand the Trickle List, you need to first look at the headers at the top of the list. These are the heart of the list, and how you define them is how you define what you want to do.

A good place to start is to figure out what your current job is. If you need a reminder, go scrub that task list again. The question I want to start the Trickle List with is: What should your job be?

OK, got it? You want to be a manager. Good, we can work with that. What simple, regular tasks will point you in a managerial direction? Do you need to network? Do you need to file more bugs? Write more specs? Strategically, I don't know who you work for, or where you're headed, or what your company values are, but here's the good news with the Trickle List: you don't have to be perfect. In fact, imperfection is a great place to start.

Here's my current list:

- People—Have a random chat with someone in the hallway.
- Write—Write something, anything.
- V—Take a vitamin.
- Biz—Learn a part of the business.
- Book—Read something in a book.

Rands, these are simply recurring tasks.

No. They're not. You're doing more than stuff and things with your trickles; you're designing moments of high potential. I'll explain.

Having a random hallway chat usually isn't going to be a career-changer. Nine out of ten of those conversations are lightweight, but those are nine conversations I wouldn't have had otherwise. Plus, it's hallway visibility, and in a gig where 90% of the days are spent holed up in meetings, that's time well spent. And there's the 10th conversation where I learn something huge:

Wait, the project is **how far** *behind?*

Hold it, you're thinking about **quitting?**

By choosing to create a moment where I leave my structured day to have a random conversation, I'm creating an informational opportunity. While these moments may appear to have a low initial return on time investment, you're playing a numbers game. You're counting on the fact that, over time, over many moments, you're creating unexpected potential.

The items on your Trickle List don't need to be huge. In fact, as we'll learn in a moment, the bigger they are, the less likely you'll do them. What they need to be is aligned with where you're headed. However small, they must remind you that you're headed somewhere. The size and the impact of the trickles will come from repetition. A three-month view of the list is shown in Figure 27-2.

Figure 27-2. Completed Trickle Lists

That's not just 90 vitamins I remember to take; it's 47 random hallway conversations that not only increased my hallway visibility, but also resulted in the discovery of some sweet gossip, gave me a chance to deliver some quiet career advice, allowed me to unearth an impending, avoidable disaster, and, oddly, taught me a lot about high-definition TVs.

The Trickle Process

With a couple of defined trickles, let's talk about how to work them into the day. Remember the process in Chapter 26, "The Taste of the Day": the Morning Scrub, the creation of the Parking Lot, and finishing the day with an Evening Scrub. The Trickle List integrates with all of it.

After I've done the Morning Scrub and after I create my fresh, new legal-sized Parking Lot, I pull out the Trickle List for a look at the previous day. Anything that didn't get checked off yesterday gets brief consideration. Any clue why it didn't get checked? Off-site all day? That makes sense.

This is not a guilt-inducing list. I'm not beating myself up when I'm looking at unchecked items. I'm looking for data. *Didn't I check anything? So, I was buried, right? I haven't checked off one item for a week? Is this a trickle I should be trying to do? Yes? OK, why isn't it happening? What larger thing do I need to change?*

If your Trickle List becomes a Must Do List, you'll stop looking at it. The weight of Must Do will slowly transform into, *I didn't do it, so I suck, and I don't want to suck, so I'm going to move my Trickle List out of my line of sight, like, say, to the trash.*

The last step of the morning is adding a fresh new line to the list, starting with today's date, and then I put the list somewhere where I'm going to stumble on it during the course of the day visually. We're off.

Hopefully, during brief moments of calm, I glance at the list, and it gives me a motivational shove. *Now is the time to learn something about the business, and I've got the bookmark right here.*

The Evening Scrub shenanigans, like the morning's, involve assessment. It's the end of the day, and what'd I get done? *Hey, I haven't done this trickle in a week? Why?* Again, the point is not guilt; it's assessment. I want you to add and delete from your Trickle List with glee. In fact, if you're not regularly adding new trickles to the list and removing others, I'd argue that you aren't really using the list. What you need to do as part of your evolving career is, well, evolve. Perhaps you no longer need to focus on the hallway chats, so you haven't checked it off in a week. Fine. Remove it. Move on.

Maybe your trickles are too meaty. I keep trickles deliberately simple and vague because tasks that take more than a few minutes to think about don't get checked. You need trickles that you can easily do. I design trickles for the likelihood of completion rather than perceived impact. Again, the impact is going to come from repetition.

Finally, as you can see from my Trickle List, I often use letters and glyphs as my column headers. My thought is that by giving them fewer definitions, I make more room for me to be creative about how I complete them.

Structured Improvisation

My constant struggle with productivity and task-tracking systems is a struggle with structure. My natural tendency is to build systems that track everything, and that's a silly goal. There's no way I will keep track of and complete everything. I can look at my calendar and tell you what I think I'm going to be doing tomorrow, but the fact is, I won't actually know what I'm going to be doing until I'm doing it.

This is why I'm particularly choosy about the structure I use in task tracking. I need just enough structure not to lose important tasks, but never structure that collapses when the sky randomly falls.

Because the sky always falls. There's always a crisis. If two days pass and I don't feel blindsided, I start to worry that I'm not paying enough attention.

This is my other requirement for my productivity system: it needs to encourage improvisation.

There's a reason I'm scrubbing my task list twice a day. There's a reason I've got the Trickle List taped to my whiteboard. I want both lists to be front of mind all the time, not only because I want to constantly seek opportunities to complete a task or tackle a trickle but also because I want to be aware of the larger themes present in both my lists. This 360-degree awareness will improve my ability to improvise, and that's where I'm really going to kick ass.

Your job is not to check off one thing on your list. It's to cross three things off—at once. It's to have an epiphany so big that you add a column to your Trickle List in the middle of the day—*I must do that. A lot.* The only way you'll come to massive strategic realizations is to have a sense of your entire task list and Trickle List in your head. I'm not talking about memorization; I'm talking about a complete feel of things you need to do and the ability to improvise odd strategic conclusions.

It's the moment in a meeting where I see a hint of opportunity in that thing Phil said. I see the opportunity because I know I've got 12 Phil-related tasks and 2 trickles that, in a way I can never describe but only feel, intersect with what Phil just said.

Strategic insight only comes from well-informed chaos, and you can take a stab at building a productively ephemeral perspective with the tactical information you gain from a structured task list combined with a hopeful strategy provided by a slippery, healthy Trickle List.

The point of your productivity system is not to keep absolute track of your tasks. The point is to keep the important information in the front of your brain, where it will improve your improvisation and inform your whims. A task-tracking system gives you just enough information to calculate your chaos while reminding you to create and act on random moments of high potential.

28

What We Lost

At the end of *Rogue One*, the big reveal is that we see Princess Leia. She's just received the plans to the Death Star and is about to kick off the franchise, except you don't see Princess Leia, you see a CGI rendering of her.

That's not Princess Leia.

Now, fire up your favorite browser, search for Carrie Fisher in her Princess Leia outfit. Chances are that your brain can tell the difference between the CGI and the real person.

How does our brain know it's CGI? It doesn't. Your brain knows that something is strangely off about this image. The eyes are a little too big. They lack life. The smile isn't a Carrie Fisher smile. My brain is fully aware this image is intended to look like Carrie Fisher. Still, my brain also instinctively raises a red flag alerting me "something is wrong" because my brain is shockingly good at receiving and parsing visual information when it comes to the human face. It is essential that I can gather and process signals from the humans around me. Quickly and efficiently.

The dissonance you sense staring at this image is a part of a rich, more significant problem we humans were collectively experiencing during the COVID-19 pandemic.

This Is Not a Meeting

Let's start with disclaimers:

- I'm pro humans working together. Always have been.

- Distributed work has been and will continue to be required.

- There is no doubt in my mind that distributed work works. I believed this before the recent pandemic, and I believe it more now.

With that said, I can confirm that what is depicted in Figure 28-1 is not a meeting.

Figure 28-1. A fake meeting

I suspect this is a staged Zoom call for marketing purposes. How do I know this? Everyone is smiling.

Here's another one (see Figure 28-2). Again, randomly pulled off the internet, but slightly more realistic.

Figure 28-2. A real meeting

That's more familiar. Humans stare in random directions. Many are clearly not listening. Camera is off for one participant. Here's the question: How many humans are on this call?

Zero.

Yeah, I won't let this point go. There are no humans on this call. Yes, there are 14 participants with their video on, one with their video off, and someone dialing in. Yes, you can gather some interesting signals from a single frame of this meeting, but this is a crappy 2-D representation of the team; both essential signal and purpose are missing from this situation.

Five or Seven Senses

You have five base senses: sight, hearing, smell, taste, and touch. Bonus fact: you actually have seven. The mysterious additional two are:

Vestibular system
> The movement and balanced sense, which gives us information about where our head and body are in space. This helps us stay upright when we sit, stand, and walk.

Proprioception
> The body awareness sense, which tells us where our body parts are relative to each other. It also gives us information about how much force to use, allowing us to crack an egg while not crushing the egg in our hands.

Every single one of these senses, yeah, even vestibular and proprioception, are limited in a video conference call. You do not see the entire person; you see them from the chest up. Your hearing is limited and frustratingly altered by the milliseconds of lag and subsequent awkward interruptions to the conversation when someone attempts to insert a vital fact only to be stomped by the current speaker, who hasn't heard the interruption yet. You probably don't think smell, like taste, is essential, but that is because you've been sitting all by your lonesome in your home office for two-plus years (like me) and have forgotten that smell, while not critical, contributes to the information tapestry of an in-person. And touch, the feel of the table in front of you, and the slight echo you experience in the wood when someone sets their coffee cup on the table.

It's an endless list of little things that you think you've forgotten, but you haven't. You are quite literally built to sense an infinite amount of subtle bits of signal from your fellow humans. We were not built to live alone in caves; we were built to live together in them.

Endless Bits of Friction

Relative to the COVID-19 pandemic, the single biggest work question I've been asking myself for two years is, What did we lose? What is the measurable and objective loss for teams not working in close proximity? I've been looking for cracks. I've been looking for leading indicators of future doom. The Great Resignation[1] seems like a proper crack, right? But are people quitting their jobs because they can't work together or because their current job sucks and all this terror in the air has given them a new appreciation of what really matters?

What I see are endless bits of friction:

No, I can't hear you. You're muted.

No, I can't see what you're sharing.

No, I have no idea that you're in a bad mood. You're just the same old postage stamp two-dimensional muted headshot that you were in the last three meetings.

No, I have no idea that everyone hates the idea you just proposed because my ability to read the room has been mostly erased. I can't tell the difference between *we hate this idea* silence and *we're mostly just quiet because it's a chore to speak during a video conference* silence.

Yes, I'm inserting your name into the conversation because I see you aren't paying attention, and I know the conversation is heading in your direction.

Yes, I appreciate that folks are using visual cues like nods and thumbs-up to indicate their agreement, but does everyone remember that we were capable of such understanding with none of the awkwardness?

Yes, I spend an excessive amount of time looking at myself. It's ridiculous.

A video conference is a sterile, dehumanizing experience. A good in-person meeting is pure jazz. It's elegant sparring between those who care deeply about the things they are building, and watching and participating in this banter is one of the joys of my professional career.

---

1 Emma Goldberg, "You Quit. I Quit. We All Quit. And It's Not a Coincidence" (*https://www.nytimes.com/2022/01/21/business/quitting-contagious.html*), *New York Times*, January 23, 2022.

And That Was Not Princess Leia

If I were to ask right after you viewed *Rogue One* whether that was Princess Leia or not, you'd say, "CGI, right?" I'd respond, "Yes, but what was wrong with the image? How could you tell it wasn't Princess Leia?"

To which you'd shrug. "I don't know. Her eyes were a little creepy?"

Suppose you're not a professional computer graphics artist. In that case, you don't know what's precisely wrong with this image, but understanding the specifics is not a requirement for your brain to alert you that something funky is going on. Your brain has been trained and rewarded for successfully deriving information from the simplest facial expressions. You have learned much from listening, from understanding each word they speak, and from listening to the pause between the words because there is information there as well. And you were in that meeting. We all were, and we'll never forget it because, at one point, she stood, slammed her fist on the desk, and yelled, "I can't believe we've let this happen!" I couldn't believe it, either.

Do you want to know why you're fatigued at the end of a long day of video conferences? It's because your brain has been straining to collect essential information that is no longer there.

Together we are more.

29

The Foamy Rules for Rabid Tools

The brother-in-law lives in the burbs and needed five trees removed. Not big trees—10 to 15 feet tall, 6-inch trunks. Not a problem.

I live on the edge of a redwood forest in Northern California. There are sturdy oaks, playful maples, lovely madrones, weed-like bay laurels, and of course, giant redwoods. But the pleasure of living in a forest has a tax. Trees fall and trees die, and in a forest of any significant size, this is always happening.

You need a chainsaw. In my case, I need three. There's Junior (see Figure 29-1), who is great at handling the small jobs. He's light and ladder friendly.

Figure 29-1. Junior

Then there's Marty (see Figure 29-2). He's the everyday, midsized saw that is enough to handle almost any job. Marty would be perfect for a job in the burbs.

Figure 29-2. Marty

Last, there's Rocket (see Figure 29-3). Any tree is Rocket's nemesis.

Figure 29-3. Rocket

Even if you've never handled a chainsaw, you've probably used a handsaw. It's a physical, grinding affair. It's fun for about three minutes, and then you start wondering: *Am I making progress?* The brother-in-law had taken it on himself to use a handsaw on one of the trees. In his three minutes he'd sawed off...a branch.

When Marty and I showed up, we dropped all five trees, cut up the trunks and branches, and stacked them into disposable piles in an hour.

The lesson: the correct tool is exponentially more productive.

That's a long introduction to say an obvious thing, but I'm going to make it even longer. Take a moment and step inside the mind of the brother-in-law. *I've got several trees I want to get rid of...and what do I have in the garage? Two hammers, a paint can full of nails, some leftover wood and...a saw. Perfect. A saw.*

Context shapes perspective, so thanks to the contents of his garage, he knows of no universe where there are chainsaws. He's heard of them and suspects they're much faster than the laborious, sweaty grind of this sawing, but there's no chainsaw here, so he's semi-happily hacking away. To me, standing there with my arsenal of chainsaws, it's absurd. It's a criminal waste of his time.

The lesson again: the correct tool is going to make you exponentially more productive.

The Foamy Rules

As an engineer, you must be rabid about a short list of tools. Rabid. Foaming at the mouth with exuberance.

This is an obvious list of tools, and there's nothing here that you haven't heard before. The news is that you need to care. You need to be able to explain in great detail why using green-colored text on a black background is *the only way to code*. You need to be a zealot about your tools, and zealotry starts with fit.

I was a database guy, then I was a browser guy, and then I became a web applications guy. Each of those professions came with their own set of bright and shiny tools, but the tools were not important. Even a specific feature inside of a tool is not that interesting. I believe you can be just as productive sitting inside of a rich development environment such as Xcode as you can inside of Visual Studio and a slew of terminal windows. The point is not which tool; the point is that the way that tool—your tool—looks, feels, and functions fits how you see, move, and work.

These are my foamy rules, and they may differ wildly from your list. That's cool. My development experience is different from yours. I started working with computers before the mouse, which means I trust my keyboard more. Integrated debuggers had just landed when I began developing, which means, yeah, I like debugging at the command line. Again, the point is to get foamy because what makes you foamy makes you your best.

My foamy rules follow.

MY TOOLS APPEAR DECEPTIVELY SIMPLE

Visual Studio (*https://visualstudio.microsoft.com*). MacOS Terminal. Transmit (*http://www.panic.com/transmit*), LaunchBar (*https://oreil.ly/Ivq36*), and Dropbox (*https://www.dropbox.com*). The mean time to get one of those tools set up is just a few minutes. I can build out my development environment on a new machine in a half hour. This has a couple of handy implications. My tools are readily available and lightweight. I can download and install everything except for an operating system in a short amount of time. Similarly, setup and configuration of these tools is close to zero.

You might think this setup means I'm expecting my computer to randomly explode. No. These tools are not simple; they are well tuned. A Visual Studio user knows it's an onion application. You can keep pulling back the layers and finding new functionality, which is going to make your development experience faster. The same goes for Terminal and LaunchBar. The base functionality just works, and if you have a particular development itch you want to scratch, the tool can scratch it.

MY TOOLS DO NOT CARE WHERE MY WORK IS

How many times have you experienced this? You write a quick script on your local machine to do something clever. You fine-tune it and then plop it on your server and rediscover the rule—there's nothing quite like production.

Any tool that does not allow me to develop live-in production is slowing me down. When someone showed me how to set up Transmit to do editing on remote files, I saw hours of heretofore unknown production debugging issues vanish.

Yes, editing locally is fast, especially when you live on the edge of a redwood forest where latency is an issue, but a tool that doesn't allow me to develop over the wire isn't a tool; it's a debilitating hindrance.

Rands, edit? In production? Are you insane?

No. The tangential background rule is: *if you don't know what you're doing in production, you don't belong there.*

There's a corollary, which is: *I don't care where my work is.* For nonproduction work like, say, writing a book, I don't want to think about where the most recent version of the work is sitting. Yes, I'm talking about version control. But shh, don't call it version control—just call it Dropbox. Provided I have a network connection, this tool magically refreshes a shared directory sitting on each of my machines. I can't think of the last time I worried about which version of a document I was on, and that means I'm spending more time working than worrying.

MY TOOLS ARE DESIGNED TO REMOVE REPETITIVE MOTION

One of my first algorithmic "holy shits" was during my second computer science class as we were learning sorting algorithms. The professor elegantly walked us through the construction of different algorithms, explaining the pros and the cons, and then he landed Quicksort.[1] Holy shit.

It wasn't just the elegance. It wasn't the recursive simplicity; it was the discovery that with imagination there were approaches that were wildly more efficient—and simpler. Whether you're formally trained as a computer science nerd or not, you've learned the value of efficiency—to make each action that you take mean something. You know that when you're efficient, you have more time to do what you love.

This is why I have a simple requirement that any tool I rely on has complete keyboard support. I will fall back on using the mouse for one-off activities, but for any action I take that I know I'm going to do again, my question is, How do I make this action cost less?

Think of it like this. What if I told you that each time you wanted to save a file, you had to stand up, climb up on your chair, and jump up and down, yelling, "I would like to save my stuff now!" The first time you had to do it, it'd be kinda fun, but after that it'd drive you batshit crazy. It's a similar feeling each time I reach for my mouse. I feel I'm engaging in an unnecessary task, which is always going to waste my time because with a mouse sometimes you miss, and missing is a tremendous waste of time.

Finding *any* file or application is, ideally, four keystrokes. Command-Space (LaunchBar), Letter #1, Letter #2, Return. Sometimes I get lucky; sometimes it's three, and you know that puts a smile on my face *every single time it happens*.

MY TOOLS DO ONLY WHAT I'VE TOLD THEM TO DO

Back when Adobe Dreamweaver (*https://oreil.ly/88vBX*) first landed, I wanted to love it. I was so tired of the repetitive motion of developing HTML pages, and the idea of a tool that was going to visually handle that laborious process was appealing. Problem was, Dreamweaver changed my code...without asking.

It what?

Dreamweaver was attempting to be helpful, but the moment it reformatted my code, I threw a fit. *You touched my code!* Dreamweaver never recovered from that horrendous first impression. I'm still mad.

My impression and my opinion of robust integrated development environments is that they can do a lot of good in terms of helping you visualize what the hell is going on. Borland developed some of the best environments for building

---

1 For more information, see the Wikipedia entry on this algorithm: *http://en.wikipedia.org/wiki/Quicksort*.

code back in the day, but I still find myself with extremely primitive development environments where I'm tweaking code in Visual Studio and debugging inside of a couple of Terminal windows.

Yeah, I know all about the glory of integrated debugging, but what I found in many years of development is that embracing the fancy tools means spending time tinkering with your tools to get them to behave how you want.

The corollary to this rule is: my tools don't have a lot of moving parts. Dreamweaver-grade code offenses are few and far between with solid development tools, but the fancy still comes with a cost. You may be fully willing and foamy to embrace that cost, but I'm not.

Am I more efficient than you? Maybe. Do I know where I stand relative to my tools? Yes. Do I have to relearn my development process when the people behind an elegant tool shoot for more elegance? Nope.

MY TOOLS ARE MY TOOLS

Choosing a thing makes it yours. The choice is the result of that unique mix of logic, superstition, stubbornness, and experience that fits you.

You read that right. Green text. Black background. I'll tell you why right now. I'm an old-school DOS guy. My first word processor was WordStar, and that's the word processing program I came to associate with the fugue-like state of maximum productivity: the zone. This is why I continue to favor colored text on a black background in my current favorite editor, Visual Studio. The coloring reminds me of a primal, safe place where the tool is serving its purpose—to get the hell out of the way so I can be exponentially more productive.

This is why, as engineers, we stick with something that works for us. This is why the ancient likes of vi and eMacs continue to flourish. Once we find a tool that works for us, once we've chosen that tool, it becomes ours and remains ours. It allows us to get foamy.

An Evolving Foaminess

My brother-in-law doesn't need a chainsaw. When I took out his five trees, I eliminated half of the population of trees on his property. While a chainsaw is a delicious combination of sound, power, and sawdust, my brother-in-law didn't choose a home where the trees are on the offensive, so he doesn't need defensive weaponry.

He does need to know about a universe where chainsaws exist because every moment of his time is valuable. What differentiates us from the monkeys is not our ability to pick the right tool for the right job, but to pick the best tool.

And you never stop looking. This is why the last foamy rule is the most important: *my tools are always fighting for their lives.*

My current tool set is influenced by all of my experience. Yeah, the elegant simplicity of vi is attractive to me—it reminds me of the uncomplicated early days of development—but vi can't compete with the "holy shit" moment I experienced when I first ran into Visual Studio. *This tool is always five steps ahead of me. I love that.*

But Visual Studio, like all of my tools, must evolve.

Try this right now. Stand up and walk into the office of the best developer in the building. I promise two things: she will be happy to, at length, show you her development setup, and you are guaranteed to learn at least one thing about moving faster. Perhaps it's a tool you've never heard of, or maybe it's the way she deftly manages a tool you've taken for granted.

I don't know what you're going to learn, but I do know you'll see one thing that will instantly and obviously make your universe a smaller, more productive place (Figure 29-4).

Figure 29-4. Now we're electric

30

Up to Nothing

In Silicon Valley, you burn a lot of calories.

It's not just the daily burn of your gig; it's everything else involved in staying afloat in a valley constantly reinventing itself. You sign up for every new service and spend the prerequisite 3.7 minutes determining, *Does this matter?* You surf the web; you tweet, you Slack...all of which brings a constant flood of new data that needs to be sifted, sorted, and assessed.

You have compatriots in this caloric consumption. They randomly walk into your office or your life, bringing additional reasons to burn more calories with them. "Have you seen this? You have to try it. In fact, I'm not leaving until you're jumping up and down excited about this crucial thing."

We are part of an industry that is addicted to enthusiasm, getting things done, and discovering the new; but sometimes the right move is stopping and putting this world on hold. You need to learn how to build quiet moments of nothing as a measure of balance.

Which is why I go to a bookstore.

An Essential Exercise in Inactivity

The moment I walk into a bookstore, I remember what I love about them. They are an oasis of intellectual calm. Perhaps it's the potential of all the ideas hidden behind those delicious covers. Or perhaps it's the social reverence for the library-like quiet. Don't yell in a bookstore; you'll piss off the books.

A bookstore is where I rediscover that while I might be addicted to the nonstop calorie-burning Silicon Valley lifestyle, I also need the serenity only found in the deep quiet of the consideration of nothing. Considering nothing takes work and practice, and the act contains a contradiction: the more I think about what I need to do, the less I'll discover the thing I don't know I'm looking for.

It's confusing, but you need these skills because you have days full of some-things. Your day is probably spent on one of two sides of a spectrum. You're either reacting to whatever is showing up on your doorstep or proactively looking for new things to place on your doorstep so you can figure out what to do with them. Reactive. Proactive. It's how you spend your entire day.

Excursions to the bookstore are essential exercises in inactivity where the whole world stops being a thing to do. My most recent trip to my local Barnes & Noble was in the middle of a two-week period where I'd spent time in both Tokyo and London. Forty hours of flying resulted in five days of meetings that required constant thought, creativity, and focus. During a brief stint back in normality in the States, I had instructions to acquire a children's book for a nephew.

The children's book section at my local Barnes & Noble has been voted "Most Likely to Be a Total Disaster" for three years running. Combining this unique cluttered chaos with a head full of jet lag means my head is overflowing with disorganized somethings, and I'm predisposed to be annoyed. Even worse, I'm not looking for a specific book. I'm running on "get something he'd like" orders, which means I need a modicum of inspiration to be successful.

I must discard everything in my head that's preventing me from looking and being inspired.

This is a surprisingly hard mental maneuver because you and I are both used to days that are not only full but full of well-defined things to do. A lack of structure, direction, and measures throws your brain into fits, and usually, this is when I throw my hands up in frustration and walk out of the bookstore. My brain is rejecting the unstructured ambiguity involved in the search for the unknown.

Look in my head when I start: *Where am I? This looks like the children's section, but this part is full of toys, and I need books. I haven't read a good book in forever. OK, keep moving until something looks right. Since when did they sell candy at a bookstore? Edward Cullen Sweethearts? Please. You know, I don't even know what day it is. OK, dinosaurs, he likes dinosaurs. Wait, can he read?*

My analysis is, *this place is confusing*; I think I'm talking about the bookstore, but I'm actually talking about my brain.

Up to Nothing

Go back to work and think about your average day. How often are you not clear about what you're doing? How often is the goal of the next 30 minutes completely undefined? Yes, you've suffered through meetings with no clear agenda,

and you felt like you were wasting your time, but that's still a known quantity—
I'm currently in the poorly run meeting scenario. Been there, done that.

What happens when there is no meeting, no burning task, and no one in
your office? You wander, surf the web, stare at that calendar on the wall, and
think, *Why do we have leap years again? I forget.* And then you feel bad. *I should be
working. I should be doing something. They're not paying me to reverse engineer leap
years. I have things to do.*

You've built this guilt into your office. It's why your screen does not face
folks walking through your door. You're worried: *They might see me doing nothing.*

You're not up to nothing. You're aimlessly mentally wandering—an act
made famous by every bright idea ever had in the shower. Think of that moment.
Your body is busily on task with the cleaning, and what does your brain do? Sure,
if you're stressed about layoffs, you're going to worry about layoffs, but what
happens on those mornings when nothing is pressing?

Your brain builds something from whatever mental flotsam and jetsam are
in your head. Perhaps it's a useful answer to a question you didn't know you
needed. Perhaps it's just an interesting combination of thoughts put into a story.
It's dreaming, but you're awake.

Back to the bookstore. Remember my orders: a good book for the nephew…

If I survive the mental rejection of ambiguity, the next moment I need is one
of discovery. To ground myself in the silence, I need to discover a single bright
and shiny thing, and there's absolutely no telling what that thing is until it shows
up. It might be based on my mood, the last ten things I cared about, a random
word someone said to me, or my favorite color…the list is endless, indefinable,
and entirely locked in my head.

But there is nothing ambiguous or unclear about the discovery. It's obvious.
It fills an immediate gap I did not know I had.

In this bookstore excursion, it's a black book. It's odd to see a black book
in the endless rainbow of the children's section, but there it is. Black cover
with masking tape surrounding what looks like a handwritten title: *Wreck This
Journal.*[1] OK, interesting. I flip the book open to the handwritten instructions:

Carry this with you everywhere you go.

Follow the instructions on every page.

Order is not important.

---

1 Keri Smith, *Wreck This Journal*, Expanded Edition (Penguin Books, 2012).

Instructions are open to interpretation.

Experiment. (Work against your better judgment.)

And there it was. Exactly what I needed. A reminder of why I go to the bookstore in the first place—to mentally stumble around, defying my better judgment, in a nourishing environment of nothing.

Wreck This Journal was created by Keri Smith (*http://kerismith.com*), who calls herself a guerilla artist, and I've no idea what her book is doing in the clutter of the children's section. It's a journal dedicated to its destruction. One page instructs you to "Rub here with dirt." Another asks you to "Scribble wildly using only borrowed pens (and document where they were borrowed from)." The journal is full of ideas to create unstructured moments of seemingly meaningless activity designed to get you to stop and let something else in.

Don't Look for It

It's a confusing skill, which starts with a question: How will you find what you don't know you need by not looking for it?

A day in high tech rarely encourages the activity of doing nothing. Nothing is not cost-effective. Nothing is not something you'll put in your review. Nothing gets a bad rap, and the more I attempt to define it, the less useful it will be to you because what I need out of nothing is different from what you need.

Moments of nothing are not moments of creativity or consideration. (They might be.) These moments don't last long because your brain can't sit still; it's been trained to burn calories all the time. (The longer it sits still, the better.)

Your brain instinctively and naturally attempts to build something, given whatever world it's currently in. In a bookstore, with effort, I can shed the somethings of my everyday life and find the nothing that I don't know I'm looking for. (And that rules.)

31

How to Not Throw Up

As soon as you decide to become an engineer, either via a university degree or simply because you sit up all night writing Python to scratch your particular technical itch, you think you absolve yourself of having to stand up in front of a group of people and make a presentation.

And you might be right.

Then there's a chance you're going to build or think something brilliant, and no mailing list, weblog, Zoom call, or Slack channel will be able to contain this brilliance. Those who want to hear about your brilliance will insist that you stand in front of them and explain this bright thing that you did or thought.

Conflict. Yes, you want to explain your brightness, but, um, the last time you stood in front of people and told a story was in Ms. Randall's 11th grade English class, and you stumbled through an incoherent ramble about Henry David Thoreau and some pond.

Unlike that pond, you are immensely qualified to talk about your topic, but you're unqualified to present in front of a group of people. It's not just that you haven't had the practice, but that lack of practice has given you the erroneous impression that there's a good chance you might throw up if you have to stand up and tell a story in front of five hundred people.

Not Throwing Up Is a Two-Phase Process

This chapter is about presentations, not content. Both are equally important, but I'm not here to help you write your content; I'm here to transform that content into a presentation that doesn't suck.

Let's say you've written your 30 slides. A rookie presentation move is to: 1) have too many slides and 2) stuff your slides with clutter, like wordy bullet points. Filling each slide with as much content as possible. This is your feeble attempt to get out of actually presenting. Your thought is, *Fill the slides with information and read the slides.* This makes sense to you since I know you're nervous, but my question is, *Why are you nervous?*

I've never presented in front of five hundred people.

So, you're not confident you can do it?

Right.

OK, so let's focus on the confidence rather than creating more horrible slides.

PHASE 1: PRACTICE ENDLESSLY

Confidence will come not when you memorize your slides, but when you move the content from one side of your brain to the other. Right now, your slides are sitting in the linear, left side of your brain, the practical side. This is a fine place for the slides to be while you're creating them, but before you get up on stage, you need to move them to the right side of your brain, the creative side. You need to be able to feel your slides.

Your presentation is storytelling. It's a performance. It's you onstage telling 499 of my friends and me a story about why you're brilliant. That's not a comforting thought since I know you're already nervous about standing in front of 500 people and bumbling through your slides. *And now you're saying it's a performance? My presentation regarding huge performance wins in garbage collection is NOT a performance.*

Of course, it is. Why else would five hundred people be sitting here wanting to hear about it? I promise there's some art, some performance, in your presentation, and the best way to find it is to practice endlessly. The best way to do that is to stand up, walk around your office, and give your presentation to no one. Over and over again.

It takes some getting used to—pacing around your office or hotel room listening to your voice—but that's exactly what your audience will hear. You must figure out how to listen to yourself tell a story while also critically listening to the story. You're the presenter and the audience. Yeah, it takes practice.

Start with those three slides there about that one specific topic. Talk through it and listen to how it sounds. Does it make sense? Does it flow? Are you reading the slide, or are you telling a story? How does it transition into the next point? After you've heard yourself verbally walk through a topic a few times, you start to hear what you're trying to say, and you make discoveries like, *Uh, I'm making no sense. This is supposed to be funny, but it's lame.* Or *This topic doesn't have any relation to anything near it.*

We're talking hours of practice here, but you'll slowly start to notice that you're not just memorizing the content; you're also memorizing the flow. You'll start to notice where you're repeating yourself, you'll find critical points in the strangest places, and you'll stop to reorder and rewrite slides...a lot. Good. Keep practicing.

When you can sit at your desk with your eyes closed and talk through any of your slides, you're going to stop worrying about what you need to say and focus more on how you'll say it. This intimate knowledge of your content is going to give you confidence.

But you still might throw up.

PHASE 2: THROW-UP AVOIDANCE

A few years back, I gave a recruiting presentation at two universities on the same day. Same presentation, same general age group of students, morning versus evening.

The morning presentation was in front of a packed room. Just after 10:00 a.m. I was three cups of coffee into the day, and so was everyone else. Three slides in, I knew this would be a straightforward presentation. Heads were nodding, laughs were coming from the least expected slides, and folks were taking me up on my offer: "Stop me if you have a question." Captivated. Forty minutes of slides. Twenty minutes of intense, engaging questions and answers. Mission accomplished.

Five hours later. I'm in another conference room 50 miles away at another university, and everyone's coffee has worn off. The room is half full, and I'm a little tired, but I've done this presentation 30 times in my head, so when I start on slide #1, it's on. I know this presentation, so why is everyone falling asleep on slide #3? There's no laughing, and by slide #10, someone gets up and walks out. Ouch.

Hopefully, this is normally when you consider throwing up. I say hopefully because there are a great many presenters who don't have a clue when the presentation is going badly. This is undoubtedly a rookie mistake, but I've sat through a fair share of presentations by seasoned managers where they just flopped and didn't have a clue.

You need to stop and listen to what your audience needs. Stop five minutes in if your presentation isn't going swimmingly, stop five minutes in and look around the room. Is the audience looking at you? Or are they staring at their laptops? Has there been nodding? I know it's been 10 seconds, and you're still looking at the audience, saying nothing. It's OK; they're just sitting there wondering if you're about to throw up. You're building tension.

More importantly, you're figuring out the most important part of your presentation: Which audience showed up? Here's the rub: you can write brilliant, compelling slides, and you can practice your slides 40 times, but you can never predict who is going to show up, and you must tailor your presentation for those who show up.

And the wrong audience showed up. OK, now you can throw up.

Improvise

Changing your deck on the fly is hard, and this is where our senior managers, with hundreds of presentations under their belts, screw up. First, they've stopped fretting, which means their presentations lack any sort of energy. Consequently, they don't listen to the audience, so when the audience indicates via their bored silence that they want more, the presenter is deaf. They do not adjust to engage the audience, which is why they sound like a bad used car salesperson; they're just reciting the sales pitch and don't care what you think.

How do you need to improve? What is your audience going to ask for? They want one thing: they want to participate. No, they don't want to get onstage and present your slides; they want to be included in this presentation—in this performance. I'm not talking about waves of applause; I'm talking about looking at a sea of people and *knowing* these people are listening to your every word. It's a constructive silence directed squarely at you, and it's a high when you learn how to read it.

So, what are you going to do? How are you going to adapt? Maybe this crowd wants you to wake them up? How about accentuating your points loudly? How about a bit more walking around the stage, waving your hands furiously? Perhaps you're too amped, and they want you to slow and pause between your words. Give them time for your words to sink in.

When someone walked out of my university presentation, I immediately stopped. They woke up, and I dove back into my slides with my new college buds, who were now clear that I cared about what they thought. I began reminiscing about my college years and the complex protocol I'd worked out for when it was OK to walk out of a lecture. This five-minute irrelevant segue did two things: first, it reminded my semi-lucid audience that I was one of them, and second, since my segue was timely (person walking out) and humorous (maybe), we reconnected.

Fret

No lying. The ability to improvise takes experience, and you'll have to live through and recover from a couple of horrific presentations in order to build up your improv repertoire. For these early disasters, I have three pieces of advice:

- When presenting, talk like you're talking to one person who has a thousand eyeballs. Don't get lost in the sea of faces; pick a person and tell the story. Not for the entire hour, just a few seconds. Then move on.

- Use silence as punctuation. This is my favorite trick in the book, especially since I'm a fast talker. When you hear yourself gaining verbal momentum, stop. Count backward from 5. Walk across the stage. Resume. These breaks will give you and your audience a chance to regroup mentally.

- They want you to succeed. This advice is in every presentation guide because it's true. Your audience is expecting you to rock their socks. They're expecting an A+. That's where you're starting in their heads and walking onstage knowing this helps.

I don't want you to throw up.

I want you to fret about this presentation, and if you're not losing a little sleep, you don't care. You're not going to be motivated. You will perpetuate the idea that engineers can't tell a story. If you've been handed the responsibility of a presentation and aren't the least concerned, give it to someone who will sweat this thing, and then be prepared for that person to end up as your boss.

32

Out Loud

If you're looking for advice on giving a presentation, the internet is chock-full of advice. If you're looking for tips on writing a presentation, the internet goes dark for a reasonably simple reason. To think about how to write a presentation, you need to think about how you speak. I'll demonstrate. Say the following:

I am reading this out loud to no one in particular.

Were you surprised to hear your voice? I was. Did you read it out loud? No? Why not? Sitting in a coffee shop? Worried that the guy next to you will think you're a freak? This basic discomfort is the reason it's tricky to explain how to present in a piece of writing. The skills involved in writing a clever paragraph are entirely different.

You still haven't read it out loud, have you?

Presentation or Speech?

Developing a compelling presentation involves a series of decisions and exercises to align your head with the fact that you're delivering your content directly to people. No internet. No weblog. Just you.

Your first decision: Speech or presentation? Wondering about the difference? Take a quick look at two entirely different appearances by Steve Jobs. The first is his "Three Stories" speech (*https://oreil.ly/9WaHs*) at Stanford, and the second is part of his MacWorld 2007 keynote (*https://oreil.ly/MKhNT*).

You need to watch only a few minutes of both to get a feel for the difference between a presentation and a speech. My guess is you only viewed the Stanford video, because everyone has seen Steve Jobs at MacWorld and the Stanford video is a shocker. Clearly, it's Steve Jobs. It's his voice, he's got his trademark bottle of water, but the delivery is completely anti-Jobs because he's reading his compelling stories from a piece of paper.

It freaks me out.

In Steve Martin's autobiography, *Born Standing Up*,[1] about his stand-up comedy years, he writes, "If you don't dim the lights...the audience won't laugh." This subtle, paradoxical observation is the core difference between speeches and presentations. In a speech, the audience may laugh or cry, but they are not required nor encouraged to participate because, during a speech, the spotlight never leaves the speechmaker. In a presentation, half of the art is figuring out how to create an environment where your audience can actively participate without knowing they are participating.

For a presentation or a speech, you need your audience; otherwise, it's just you in an empty room talking to no one in particular, and we already have a word for that...it's called writing.

The Unforgivable Mistake

There is one unforgivable mistake when giving a presentation. You've heard it before: don't read from your slides. As you'll see, my approach for presentation development is designed around avoiding this cardinal mistake, starting with picking the right tool.

For all my presentations during the past three years, I've created all my content inside my presentation software, which, thankfully, is Keynote (*https://www.apple.com/keynote*). In the back of my mind, I've wondered if this is the right tool to iterate a presentation. Shouldn't I follow the same process as writing and drop all my thoughts into TextEdit, where I can easily slice and dice complex ideas? No.

Start with and stick with Keynote or whatever presentation software floats your boat. First, presentation software is effectively designed to be outline software, an excellent tool for organizing and editing your thoughts without allowing them to become a book. By keeping your presentation in slide format, you're forcing your content to remain a presentation, not an article. Where each slide is a thought. Where moments of undiscovered brilliance are sitting between bullet points. We'll talk about how to find this brilliance in a bit, but for now, iterate in the slides.

Your job is to get as much of the meat as possible into outline form so that you can begin to transform it into a presentation. Don't worry about how you will say something or whether folks will get it. If you're worried that the outline doesn't allow you to capture the essential detail that you could with a

---

1 Steve Martin, *Born Standing Up* (Simon & Schuster, 2007).

blank piece of paper, start taking notes. I like the stickies in Keynote for random small thoughts. I like the speaker notes for bigger ones.

What's going to happen as you edit and re-edit is that an initial structure will emerge from your outline. Better yet, since you've stuck with presentation software, I'm guessing you're already starting to hear your voice in your head on specific slides:

- *This is a key point. I need to say this one reeeeeeeallly slowly because it needs to stick.*

- *Good data that needs to be conveyed, but...dull. Needs hip.*

Once you've got what looks like a rough presentation outline, it's time to invoke the Disaster.

The Disaster

This is the second time I'm going to ask you to do something, and this time I just want you to do it. No questions asked. I want you to go to the first slide of your presentation, stand up, and give your presentation. No questions asked.

Wait, what, whoa Rands, this is rough, and it's missing thoughts and uh...

Quiet. Give it a shot. Beginning to end of each slide. I want to hear your presentation.

Done? How'd it go? There's a reason I call it the Disaster, you know. There are three reasons you should tough out your rough presentation with zero prep:

- Get a feel for how it fits all together.

- Hear yourself speaking. This is more reinforcement that you aren't writing a book; you're writing a presentation.

- Build confidence. You now know the absolute worst-case scenario regarding this presentation. There is no way it could be worse than what you just went through.

As you stood in your office talking to no one in particular, did you notice how thoughts in your head sounded different from those on the slides? Did you discover flaws in logic? Mysterious new gaps in the content on the slides you've been staring at all morning? That's progress.

During the Disaster run-through, I take a ton of notes. I do this on a piece of paper next to the computer because, as much as possible, I want to stick with the idea that I'm giving my presentation. If I stop to edit my slides, I lose track of tempo and momentum, or worse: I end up rewriting my presentation rather than giving it. These handwritten notes look like this:

- No clue what slide #2 is trying to say.
- Segue between #4 and #5 is nonexistent.
- #10: Repeating myself.

Your first job after your Disaster is to integrate your notes as quickly as possible. For me, the post-Disaster edit is also the single most significant change I'll make to the presentation. In addition to major structural changes, I also find new content that needs to be added.

Reduction

This is an excellent time to remind yourself how not to throw up. Also, here's a quick recap of what we've learned so far:

- Practice endlessly (so that you can).
- Improvise (but never stop).
- Fret(ting).

In terms of developing your presentation, I'm going to modify bullet #1 for this chapter further. It's now, "Practice and edit endlessly." This is the largest piece of work where I have the least advice because you need to stare at your slides at 2:00 a.m. for three nights. You need to soak in your presentation. Invoke another disaster. Pitch a friend. Print your slides and pitch a tent in the woods.

My best piece of advice is a threat: an audience can smell an immature presentation on the very first slide. It has nothing to do with the quality of the content; it's you standing lamely in front of your slide and silently conveying the *OK, what I am going to talk about here?* vibe, and it's presentation death.

I have four bits of advice to help here.

First, during this endless editing and practice, you're looking for a reduction and consolidation of slides to occur. It's not that you're saying less; you're beginning to internalize the content, so you no longer need all those words to remember your point. It can be disconcerting to delete your fine ideas, so use the speaker notes or stickies if you feel you're going to forget something important. You aren't going to need them, but if it makes it emotionally easier to prune, terrific.

This consolidation is one of the reasons I usually don't send my slides to folks who ask after the presentation. My slides, standing on their own, rarely make sense without me standing in front of the room furiously waving my arms.

Second, as part of your consolidation, you'll want to start thinking about where you want to use images rather than words. If you're only going to use words to describe your fine idea, why don't you just email everyone instead of wasting an hour of their time reading the same thought plastered on the wall behind you? Remember, a presentation is a visual and auditory medium, and a slide covered with words is, well, a cop-out.

This presentation is only partially about you and what you think. Yes, you are the guiding force, but the goal is to present an idea with space around it. In this space, your audience will pour their own experience and opinions; they will make your idea their own. Pictures, charts, and graphs create structured, memorable spaces. I use them in two ways: to replace an entire thought wholesale or to augment a word slide that needs more space.

Note

A design aside: the visual design of your slides is an important topic that is outside the scope of this book, but know this—I've seen people lose their minds tweaking animations and transitions on slides. They try every single animation in the hope that just the right transition will add that specific something to their presentation, but what they don't know is that an animation fixation is usually a sign that your content blows. The same rule for typefaces applies to transitions and animations. The less your audience sees your design decisions, the more impact they'll have.

Third, you're looking for an underlying structure to your presentation that you will want to share with your audience. During this endless practice, you will develop a feel for how your presentation fits together, but this structure may not be initially obvious to your audience. For any reasonable-sized presentation, you need to design a visual system that allows audience members to know where they are instantly.

Fourth, and finally, you're looking for audience participation opportunities in the flow and tempo of your presentation. Where will you turn the lights up a little bit and remind the audience that they're sitting there, soaking in your thoughts? Let's talk a bit more about this.

Presentation Punctuation

Participation is presentation punctuation. You're going to use participation to accentuate parts of your presentation. You're going to break up complex thoughts into digestible, comfortable ideas. You have partial control of when folks will participate.

The most common participation technique is the show of hands opener. It's usually done at the beginning of the presentation as a warm-up:

"Show of hands—how many of you own a Mac?"

"Quickly, how many of you think you're paying too much for term life insurance?"

As a warm-up technique, I'm a fan of the opener. It's an up-front reminder that this is not a speech, it's just an opening salvo, and you've got another hour to fill. As you're endlessly practicing your slides, look for idea-heavy sections and give your audience a shot in the arm with a question. You don't even have to ask for a show of hands; just direct the spotlight at them for a moment:

"Tell me exactly what you do with your fingers when you read on your computer."

You're going to be able to plan only so much of your audience's participation, and therein lies the beauty of giving a presentation: you don't know when your audience will show up. Dull, wordy slides I considered deleting often got the biggest laugh. Visual slides that I've poured my heart into are often complete duds. You won't know until you're there.

Something for Their Pocket

What do you want your audience to remember? I should've asked this at the beginning, but I'm asking it now because you're almost done with your presentation, and I want to know what you're giving your audience that fits in their pocket. I want to know what part of your presentation you will leave with them.

There's a straightforward and cheap way to do this, and it's the Lessons Learned slide. The bulleted list of important points slide that, when displayed, invariably results in a slew of cameras and iPhones appearing in the audience because they know this slide fits in their pockets.

Regardless of whether or not you use it, the Lessons Learned slide is a handy one to have at the end of your deck during the entire presentation development. It defines the basic structure of your presentation and represents a goal. Could you give your entire presentation from a single slide? Fifty minutes, a room full of people, and you with your single slide with six bullet points?

That's your goal, and you can have a wildly successful presentation without achieving it, but a one-slide presentation represents the ultimate commitment to your audience. It says, "This isn't about slides. This is about me telling you a great story...out loud."

33

Bits, Features, and Truth

There's a meeting going on right now. It's a cross-functional meeting, which means that not only are multiple departments in the organization represented, but also multiple expertise types, attitudes, and agendas. The cross-functional nature of this meeting means a program manager is present, and she is likely serving in her role as translator.

See, good program managers speak all the regional dialects of the company, so when engineering says, "It's done," they jump right in and translate, "Done pending function testing, production testing, and final documentation review" so that product management doesn't tell sales, "It's done," and they start selling something that actually isn't done.

In this well-attended, multilingual meeting, a decision is on the table, and it's a decision that's happening in every single software company right this second. It's not really a decision, it's a negotiation, but it's on the table, and people are tense because this decision is under heavy scrutiny:

PRODUCT MANAGEMENT: What's it going to take to get this feature done?

PROGRAM MANAGEMENT: What he's asking is...

ENGINEERING: Quiet, I know what he's asking. The answer is, do you want to sacrifice time, quality, or features?

PROGRAM MANAGEMENT: What he's...

PRODUCT MANAGEMENT: Yeah, I've heard this before, and I still want it all.

More talking. More translating. Action items are assigned, which gives everyone the illusion that progress was made. And we all return to our respective regional offices and wait until we have the same meeting again, where we attempt to communicate intelligently with each other. But all we really do is schedule meetings...when what we need to do is figure out who makes decisions.

That Damned Triangle

Time. Quality. Features. It's usually described as a triangle, which somehow represents the state of your product or your feature. I believe the idea is that in an ideal and unattainable world, this triangle is perfect, equilateral, and seemingly at rest. There is balance among the time you have to release, the quality you are seeking to attain, and the features you want to ship.

In reality, this triangle is never at rest. It's constantly shifting, and, well, I don't think it's actually a triangle. It's simply a mental model that gives you just enough ammunition to lie. The conversation goes like this:

> PRODUCT MANAGEMENT: We need this feature to be competitive.
>
> ENGINEERING: OK. We need four extra weeks to do that feature since it's new, and you're asking late.
>
> PRODUCT MANAGEMENT: The date can't shift; we made commitments.
>
> ENGINEERING: So did we. Listen, something has to give. You're adding more work or features, which means we need more time or, if you want, less quality. Make a choice.

These black-and-white arguments don't hold water. The idea that three simple levers define a feature or a product is a passive-aggressive professional absurdity. There are myriad levers the team can adjust, but to understand them, you need to understand the people who are actually building the software.

BITS, FEATURES, AND TRUTH

Let's start with an exercise. I want you to think about the project that you're working on, or if your project is ginormous, I want you to think of the feature that you're developing. Relative to this product or feature, I want you to walk up to your nearest whiteboard and draw three large circles, as seen in Figure 33-1.

Figure 33-1. The three people you need to find or define

Now, a name belongs inside each of these circles, and it's the name of a specific role on your team. The traditional titles for these roles are engineering manager, product manager, and program manager, but I don't want you to get hung up on titles. I want you to think about the person who is best qualified to make a decision regarding the bits, the features, and the truth.

Bits

Who is the engineer who has the most influence on the bits? There are likely several influencers, but who is the engineer that everyone goes to when they have a question? Your manager's name is a good knee-jerk name to put up here, but just because they have "manager" in their title doesn't mean they know what's going on and where to go. I want the name of the person who not only gets the call in the middle of the night when there is a bit-related emergency, but also the person who makes the large bit-related decisions. I want to know the name of the person who, when they say no, the debate stops. Got it? OK, next.

Features

Who is the person who defines the content for the product or feature? This is the name of the person who is constantly asking for more without regard for cost. This person can eloquently and calmly explain the need for this feature with an argument stronger than, "Wouldn't it be cool if...?"

Truth

This might be the hardest to define because it's a role that could live anywhere in the building. While it took years to form this opinion, I believe the person who is responsible for the process is the one most likely to be the keeper of the truth.

There's a constant ebb and flow of information in any group of people. Important decisions are made in the morning that can take hours or days to move to the other side of the building. Information is tucked away for nefarious purposes. Information is laundered, adapted, and misinterpreted.

The truth is the aggregate best set of information that exists in the building, and the person who consistently has it is the keeper of the truth. You know this person; it's the person you go to when you wonder, *What the hell is going on here?* This is the person who knows the politics and the players; they know the real reason the product is late, and this is why this is usually the job of the program manager.

The complaint I hear most about program management is the same complaint I hear about managers: *What do they do all day? What do they actually own?* Practically, the most important part of the product they own is the schedule, but their larger contribution is information management.

Yeah, I know you startup folk believe you're doing just great without a semblance of program or process management. You believe that these types of folks will slow you down with their agendas and to-do lists. Here's the deal: just because no one has the title in your garage doesn't mean the role doesn't exist. In any group larger than one, someone has taken the role of keeper of the truth, and this person's key skill is information wrangling. They constantly gather the information from the group, synthesize it, translate it, and, sometimes forcibly, present this information to the folks who are busily lying to themselves:

ME: We have six weeks to ship, so we're good.

KEEPER: Feature complete was two weeks ago, and we're still writing code.

ME: But the team is fired up, working weekends, and...

KEEPER: Steve and Ryan are on vacation for two weeks starting tomorrow.

ME: Oh.

A good program manager cares about the program and the product, but they also have a calm professional ambivalence. They have to; they're always uncovering and then surviving the worst-case scenarios. These discoveries often give them the most complete picture of how the product is doing. Their ability to survive them has made them unflappable—they don't freak out because they've lived through it and know there's always a way out...somehow. All of this experience is why they usually end up owning the schedule. I'll explain why when we get to the analysis.

So, who is this calm, truth-oriented, well-informed person on your team? Who is the person who doesn't lose it? Who is the person you go to when you need to understand the intent of the other parts of the organization? They very well might not have the title of program manager, but they are there.

CIRCLE OF COMFORT

Before I analyze your circles, I need you to do one more pass where you ask yourself two questions.

Great, you've got a name in each circle. Maybe the same name is in two circles. We'll talk more about that in a moment. My first question is: For each name, what's the person's circle of comfort?

It's fine that you put Ryan in both Bits and Features, but where does his heart lie? What is his professional background? Which circle is he going to optimize for instinctively? For each circle, if you think the occupant's natural circle is different, write that name underneath their circle.

My second question is: Have you picked leaders? Look at the Bits circle. The name you put in there is the brightest engineer in the building and any time anyone needs someone to explain the architecture, he's the guy paraded across the building; but is he the leader? Does he make decisions about the direction of the product? He has incredibly strong and informed opinions about where it's going, but when it comes down to the commitment, is he the guy? No? OK, who is?

Leaders have deep experience in their circle. It's not chutzpah; it's not spin; it's the knowledge and analytical skills developed from doing the job. It's because you can walk up to them, present a hard problem, and have an immediate, informed, and comforting answer. That's the name that belongs in the circle.

Leaders make decisions. Sometimes it appears they're doing it with little data. Some decisions are great, and others are crap, but for the purpose of this circle exercise, you need to identify the three leaders relative to the bits, the features, and the truth.

CIRCLE ANALYSIS

OK, what've we got? Let's walk through different circle scenarios:

Something is empty.
> *We don't have program management, nor do we have any product managers.* Again, don't get hung up on titles. Just because your company hasn't hired these folks doesn't mean the work isn't happening. Someone is picking features. Someone is designing the schedule. In fact, if you're really small, there's a chance the same name fills all three circles. Let's talk about that.

Same name for all three circles.

Edgar is the man. He's our one-stop decision machine. It's awesome. While I appreciate your velocity and enthusiasm, I have concerns.

I believe an effective team eventually needs each of these roles clearly defined and owned by three separate people. *Rands, where's QA? What about design? Hello, Sales. These are essential parts of the business. Where are those circles?* This model is not about describing an effective business; it describes an effective product team. Sales, design, QA, marketing, customer support—the list goes on. You need all of those teams in order to build a business. Yes, design feeds essential data into product, but my assumption is that one of the reasons you wrote Mitchell's name in the Features circle is that he has a solid relationship with the design team; he knows that an essential part of his features is the design.

Three leaders. One who makes decisions regarding the bits, another who is responsible for the features, and another who cares about the truth. The theory is that these leaders are sitting in these circles because they have the ability to make good decisions relative to their expertise, and the reality is that these folks do not get along.

Program management believes engineering will never ship; product management believes the product would be nothing without them; and engineering thinks everyone else is useless because they don't know how to code. It sounds pretty hostile, except when it comes to these three leaders. See, in addition to decision-making authority, these folks have healthy tension with their circle peers. And that's a good thing.

I divide healthy tension into two equal and opposite beliefs:

- First, there's the reality-affirming belief that almost everyone in the building shares. It's the belief that *My job is the most important job in the building, and in my absence, it'll just fall apart.* It's a quiet belief that we tell no one, but it's a silent, strengthening belief that gives folks the confidence to decide *I'm an expert, I'm brilliant, and I'm right.*

- Second, and specific to our circle denizens, there's the grudging respect for the other circles and the trust in their expertise. This is a tenuous arrangement given the first belief, but part of leadership within the circle is the ability to step back from a massive decision and say, "He knows better than I."

The idea is that the ability, skills, and experience that define each of these leaders are fundamentally different. An engineer with seven years of coding experience has a vastly different perspective regarding features and products than a product manager who has transformed an MBA into a product management gig. You can fake it—an engineering leader can have a passionate opinion about a feature or a product—but there is a skill to defining, explaining, and justifying a feature that years of development won't give you.

If you're staring at your three circles and the name is the same in all three, I have two questions:

Are they all that?

Can they consistently make correct bit-related decisions along with feature decisions while realistically balancing the truth? Really? If it's just the two of you in that garage, I get it, but if it's one hundred of you and one person is responsible for all three circles, I bet they are optimizing for their circle of comfort, and that means two other circles aren't being represented.

Who do they argue with?

Without the tension between features and bits, there's no debate about feature roadmaps and technical realities. A diversity of opinions takes any idea and, hopefully, shapes it into something unpredictably better.

We can see good examples of this by examining two other circle configurations.

Bits and features are the same

So, Ryan, an engineer by training, makes engineering and feature decisions. Great. That gets rid of a lot of those pesky feature prioritization meetings, right? What other meetings aren't happening? Where else is the feature set of your product not being debated because Ryan is making unilateral decisions as the owner of the bits and the features?

Again, I'm being an alarmist, and I'm exaggerating, but I believe you cannot effectively (and don't want to) remove yourself from what you do to make a well-informed decision outside of your circle. Think of it like this: Is Ryan the customer, or does he have direct access to the customer? If the features are for engineers, there's a solid argument that he could make decisions for both the bits and the features, but if the product or features aren't targeted for engineers, why do we believe Ryan can make informed decisions about them?

I'm not saying that anyone outside of the features circle can't have an opinion about the product. You want a culture that encourages everyone to care deeply about the product you build. Still, if you're developing software for regular human beings, then you need a regular human being to speak to their needs.

Let's look at another variant.

Truth is the same as features

Tony, the business guy, owns both the features and the schedule. This is a pretty common configuration because the belief is that those who make feature decisions for the user should also make scheduling decisions. *We need feature X in May.* What's the hitch?

Well, you've got the truth bundled with the features, and I'm uncomfortable with that because the truth needs to be neutral. The truth needs to be unbiased, and with Tony's name in both circles, you've got the guy who is calling the shots for the features also making the schedule decisions. He might have solid, healthy tension with your bits circle, but how is bits going to argue with the guy who owns the levers for both content and time?

The healthy tension created by having three distinct leaders creates diverse debates about your product. Yes, this is the same debate I talked about at the beginning of this chapter, but the difference is when you have three leaders equally representing a well-defined viewpoint along with a sense of ownership, it's a balanced debate in which the needs of the technology are weighed against the desires of the customer and the realities of the schedule. When one leader represents two circles, their two votes are pushing decisions in their favor.

Let the Negotiation Begin; It's About the Debate

This is just another model. I've replaced the Time/Quality/Features triangle with circles. There are just as many ways to screw up and misrepresent this model with politics, inexperienced people, and poorly defined features. The difference here is that I believe this model not only realistically describes the forces that pull your product in different directions but that it also gives those forces a proper name.

Let's go back to the endless debate where the bits, features, and truth are equally represented:

FEATURES: *I want feature X, and I want it on the same schedule.*

TRUTH: *We need more time, and since I know all the moving parts, I know that we're ahead of schedule for one feature. I think we've got two weeks of wiggle room.*

BITS: *Two weeks isn't enough. Can we cut this one feature in half that we haven't started and no one cares about?*

FEATURES: *I can live with that.*

TRUTH: *Sold.*

Software is built by people. The best Gantt chart only tells you half the truth about the schedule, the most complete marketing requirements document can never describe why a feature is compelling, and the most detailed technical specification will never tell you what makes for beautiful code. These are only tools, and they tell little about the people who are building the software.

These people have names, and they've earned them by not only consistently making great decisions for their area of experience but also knowing when to ask someone else for advice.

34

The Reveal

You're building...something.

The whiteboards are covered with multicolored, indecipherable flowcharts; there are 16 empty coffee cups on your table; and both flat-panel monitors are covered with code. Your plant is dead. Again. It is at this moment that you discover the one thing about the thing you are building, the one feature that, when your users see it, will help them fully understand what you have been building.

This is the Reveal.

The Reveal is the other half of the Holy Shit. You, the developer, create the big idea—the Reveal—and when the idea is discovered by your users, when they recognize the magnitude, they literally say, "Holy Shit."

A Reveal is a contradiction, and it's this contradiction that gives the Holy Shit legs. The contradiction lies in the Reveal's deceptive simplicity. It's the construction of a very simple idea from previously incoherent complexity. This is how it slips so easily into the mind of the consumer. It's a single word or image that completely sums up what was only recently described by a book, an application, or an entire college degree. The amount of unspoken information contained in a good Reveal is staggering, and that is why, when we see it, we say, "Holy Shit."

In a Reveal, you have artfully and simply described the complicated; and while I know there is the taste of excitement when you discover the Reveal after that 16th cup of coffee, you haven't proven it yet. It needs testing; it needs definition...

It needs a demo.

Three Phases

As an engineer, you need to be able to construct and deliver a demo. You may not have a world-changing Holy Shit on your hands; you may just need to get feedback from a single executive or your boss. But regardless of the magnitude, a demonstration of your idea is a unique meeting with specific requirements and goals. Let's start with the ground rules:

A demo, like a magic trick, has three phases.

1. Setup. Context setting. What do you need to know before we begin?
2. Story. The arc. I will take you somewhere now, and I will explain as we go.
3. Reveal. Voilà! See where we are now? Holy Shit, am I right?

A demo is not a presentation; it's a conversation.

There are a great many demos out there being held at this very moment, maybe even in your building, but these meetings are being run by salespeople who have an entirely different motivation: they want to make a sale. There will be a time and place when you do want to sell your idea, but that's not where you're going to start. The point of your demo is to have a conversation about the idea so that you can figure out how to make it better.

Regardless of your audience, your goal is the same.

Is it your boss who asked for a demo? His boss? The business? A VC? We'll talk about different means of preparing for different motivations in a moment, but this preparation serves the same goal: you want information. The rule is: an idea only gets better with eyeballs. I know when I find a Reveal because I can barely breathe. *This is hot, and I need to tell everyone.* The problem is that the Reveal isn't just the simple, compelling idea; it's the Setup, and then it's the Story, which leads to the Reveal, and all three need refining.

Three Alphas

Let's build a demo. For the sake of this chapter, I'm assuming this is a one-hour demo where you're catering to a small group of strategic people. Where there is a single Alpha person whose opinion will carry the room; it is this Alpha person you care about. It is their opinion that is going to tell you whether you've got a Holy Shit.

There are three Alphas that you care about.

ALPHA NOTHING: "I'M SAYING ABSOLUTELY NOTHING."

Possibly the most frustrating of our three Alphas, this is a person who is going to spend the entire hour saying nothing. The entire time. Zippo. Here's what you do...

Alpha Nothing will force you to carry the entire hour, which means, yeah, this is a lot like a presentation. You need to prepare to fill the entire hour with your tap dancing, but the good news is that this work is reusable for all of the different Alpha personality types.

The core of your demo is your Reveal, and as an engineer, you'll be excited about getting to the Reveal. You know it's the shit, and your thought is that the sooner you get there, the more jumping up and down everyone will do. The problem with your enthusiasm is that it assumes and has forgotten all the endless boring work it took to find your epiphany.

The Setup and the Story leading into your demo need to document key points of your journey to the Reveal. It's not the entire journey, it's a brief summary, but it allows your audience to see and critique how you discovered the Reveal. Let's talk briefly about each:

The Setup

Likely the smallest section of your demo, the Setup provides all the background information and special knowledge the room is going to need to understand both your Story and the impact of your Reveal.

The Story

Now that the room understands the problem space, you must describe the process you went through to get to the Reveal. What did you need to learn? How did you stumble around before you discovered the Reveal? Everyone likes to think the research in R&D is a bunch of bright people in lab coats with their hands on their chins, nodding knowingly at a whiteboard. What you and I know is that research is what you do in between what you're doing, and that's a great story to tell.

Back to the problem at hand. Alpha Nothing says nothing, so you can go long on both Setup and Story. Too much of either is just the thing to break the icy stare of Alpha Nothing. Maybe not. Let's try something else.

I build each of the three parts of the demo around knowable, containable chunks of information. From a high level, there are three major chunks to start with—the Setup, Story, and Reveal—but there might be smaller chunks that you want to shape into digestible complete thoughts. The chunks serve two purposes: to allow you to structure your demo, but also to give you a place to pause during your demo and ask a simple question:

"Does what I just told you make sense?"

This check-in might seem pointless with Alpha Nothing in the room, who is just sitting there and nodding each time you ask. Still, this chunk-by-chunk check-in not only sets a comfortable information pace for your demo but it also sets the stage for you to get the information you came for in the first place.

You're thinking your Reveal is the point, it's your killer feature, and you might be right. But it's the entire story that needs constructive feedback because the Setup, Story, and Reveal are intimately tied together. You just don't know when stopping to ask for feedback might allow your audience to make a simple comment that has an immediate and lasting impact on your Reveal.

Given all the work you put into the demo for Alpha Nothing, you're going to feel a sense of sad emptiness when you finish, and it's more of the same uninformative nothing. Still, there is some reason you've decided to pitch this unreadable schmo. Let's assume your instincts are good, and this silent power-broker will do something. In my experience, you'll hear the feedback, but it will come via a back channel. It's either an email from a random person in the meeting or a request for another demo where you'll get real feedback.

I always assume that a demo will be given more than once. Since I never know how many times I'm going to demo or which Alphas I'm going to demo to, I always build my demo for Alpha Nothing because it gives me the most demo flexibility. This will make more sense as we explore the other two Alphas.

ALPHA GAME: "I'M GAME, BUT YOU DRIVE."

After the frustrating silence of Alpha Nothing, Alpha Game is a delight. She actually wants to engage in a conversation, whether it's the Setup, Story, or the Reveal. Alpha Game is also going to stay on script. She will let you drive the demo and respect the structure of the meeting, and when you get to the end of a knowable chunk, she'll constructively chime in.

Even with the collaborative nature of Alpha Game, you still want to structure this meeting around knowable chunks. Your goal with any demo is information acquisition, and, as we learned with Alpha Nothing, information often likes to hide. Your demo isn't just the script; it's the tone and tempo of the meeting. At the end of the first knowable chunk, you stop and you ask, "Any questions? Thoughts?" Perhaps there's no feedback at the first pause, but after you've done it three times, everyone in the room knows there will be ample opportunity to weigh in. However, getting them to talk is only solving half the problem.

"I don't get it."

What?

You're halfway through your Story, and a previously friendly Alpha Game says again, "I don't get it." It's the nightmare scenario. It's what you've been worrying about since this meeting was scheduled: *Am I full of shit?*

A deep breath.

Remember the rule: all ideas get better with eyeballs. The perspective you need to have isn't whether the feedback is right or wrong: What's the intent? What is she trying to say? What doesn't she get? Ask her. If you still don't understand her point, you keep asking questions. You need to ignore the fact that you're pissed that she's unintentionally invalidating your entire pitch. The question is, How is she doing it? "I don't get it" isn't a point; it's an opener. It's an attention grabber, which leads to a larger and hopefully strategic discussion.

The hope with Alpha Game is that she has a point—that you're dealing with a rational, informed, articulate person. Just as your Setup, Story, and Reveal are built around knowable chunks, so is your conversation with Alpha Game. Each observation and question is a chance for you to see your demo from a different perspective, and that's how you figure out whether you're close to a Holy Shit.

Remember, you not only have the entire picture in your head, but you also have all of the experiences that led to the construction of that picture. The confusion in the room about your demo often isn't a dismissal of your entire idea; it's where you mentally zigged when they expected you to zag, which is precisely the kind of information you're here to find out.

Managing the conversation, regardless of which Alpha you're with, is an art; you improve with practice. And you'll need all the practice you can get to deal with the last Alpha.

ALPHA DRIVE: "I'LL DRIVE."

You arrive 10 minutes early and go through the unavoidable 2.7 minutes of confusion as you connect to the smart screen and complete a test drive. You check your slides. You check your demo. Both are solid. You have two whole minutes to chat nervously with the team before the storm hits.

Alpha Drive.

You don't even get to start before she says, "Skip the slides. Show me the demo."

Wait, what?

Alpha Drive has an ego, or Alpha Drive is in a hurry. I don't know what her deal is, but she will drive the whole damned thing, and you will just go with the flow. Don't believe me? Think you're dealing with Alpha Game? OK, go ahead and try to convince her about the point of a well-structured presentation and how you're...

"That's not how I work. Show me the demo."

Told you.

You've prepared for this. You've built your presentation around this inevitable chaos. When she asks for the demo, you jump to the demo. When she gets confused because she skipped a key knowable chunk in your Story, you detect this, call an audible, and jump to that one slide: "Did you mean this?" When the hour is over, you will have likely done your entire demo...completely out of order.

Alpha Drive is an intense reminder that everyone processes in their own order and at their own pace. Just because your Setup and Story naturally lead to your Reveal in your head doesn't mean that this is how others will get there. Yes, Alpha Drive may eventually get to the Reveal and might say Holy Shit, but the journey will be entirely hers unless you take action.

Both of my favorite ways to reign in Alpha Drive involve time, and both techniques can be used effectively for any Alpha:

#1: *A perfect silence*

When you land a key knowable chunk and ask if there are any questions, wait 15 seconds before you proceed to the next chunk. 15 seconds in a meeting full of people is forever, but in the case of an out-of-control Alpha Drive, your silence can demonstrate who is actually driving the meeting.

#2: *Demo tempo*

Everyone wants to see the demo; they want to see what is real versus what is being talked about. When you get to the live demonstration, you can almost taste the Reveal; you're excited and blow right through it. Time and time again, I've watched eager engineers furiously clicking and dragging and sliding their demos all over the screen. Their enthusiasm obscures the entire reason we gathered in the first place. My rule of thumb is that when I get to the live portion of the demo, I set my head at half speed. This mental slowdown, combined with my inevitable adrenaline, balances out to a sane and consumable demo tempo.

The one guarantee with the demo to Alpha Drive is that it will not go as expected. You can pull every move out of your meeting management bag of tricks, but Alpha Drive will take you off-script and in an unusual direction.

The advice remains to remember your goal—information acquisition. Alpha Drive's annoying habit of taking you elsewhere is yet another opportunity to see your idea from a different perspective, and that's another way to learn about what you've built.

The Holy Shit Event Horizon

The perfect demo has nothing to do with you.

That's right.

Your final, often unachievable goal for your demo is your absence. The purest Holy Shit is one where a person sees your idea or application *sans* Setup and Story and, most importantly, *sans* you.

If you consistently figure out how to do this, please tell me how.

Meanwhile, the rest of us are balancing our creative bursts of energy along with a healthy dose of constructive feedback provided courtesy of a variety of Alpha personalities. Whether they're silent, helpful, or annoying, their position and their perspective will have an impact on your thinking, and that's where the real art lies.

You'll know you have a good Reveal when Alpha Nothing says something. You'll know you're onto something when Alpha Game becomes Alpha Drive in a fit of excitement. All of this feedback and perspective is relevant, but the hardest part for which I have the least advice is when to decide to ignore it all and trust that you've really built...something.

35

The Sabotage List

Imposter syndrome. It's the feeling that pure happenstance or just dumb luck is the reason you're in this current role. It's a sense you don't belong, you aren't good enough, and—real soon now—everyone will see you for who you really are.

You might have felt this before; I'm sure many of your peers feel it now. When the topic comes up among friends and coworkers, when someone asks, "How many of you have felt imposter syndrome?" I'm surprised how many confident, talented, and hardworking humans raise their hands instantly.

Where does it come from? Why does it exist in talented and experienced humans?

I don't know. I'm not a psychologist. Just another human. Trying to figure it out. A little bit at a time.

It's one of the items on a terrifyingly long list of irrational human behaviors that I don't understand. Still, where I've had success is giving the behavior a name so I can see it.

The Untitled List

There's a list on the last page of my current personal notebook. It has no title. Each time I finish a notebook, I dutifully translate the current version of this list from old to new notebooks.

This untitled list is my Sabotage List. It's a list of important projects I'm currently not doing...for reasons. I'll explain some of the reasons as best I can shortly, but the majority of the hard work is honestly building and maintaining this list.

Important projects I'm not doing. Essential projects. Doesn't make sense, right? Well, become comfortable with irrationality if you're going to finish this piece. Yes, they are important. Under self-inflicted duress and *just between you and me*, yeah, I acknowledge I'm not actively working on these projects. Why? Here are some world-class, totally reasonable excuses:

- Next thing on the list! Been super busy.
- Blocked on Person X, who needs to deliver Thing Y.
- It's on the calendar!

Do you know when someone is spinning you? Not lying, spinning. I do, and I don't need to hear a single spoken word to sense it. All I need to see is the same instant subtle physical discomfort before they answer the question. The unease accompanied by manufactured enthusiasm designed to be a cover and saccharine excitement deployed as a targeted distraction. I know because I do it too.

Why am I sabotaging myself? I don't know. I'm not a psychologist. Just another human. Trying to figure it out. A little bit at a time.

An easier question is: Why keep a list?

The Reasons

As promised, here are some obvious-to-me reasons that are woefully incomplete as to why I might not be engaging with these important projects:

- The project doesn't *deliver obvious value*. I can't see why I would execute this project when the return on investment is so low. (*Yeah, so, why is it on this list?*)
- The work is *complicated*, so complicated that I instinctively don't know how to start. When I consider the project, I'm drawing a blank. (*Yeah, so you've completed far larger and more complicated projects many, many times.*)
- There is *downstream scariness* and/or professional discomfort that will occur for one or more of my team members due to completing this project that I don't want to face. (*NooOooOOow we're getting somewhere.*)
- ...or it's something else. LALALALlalaLALLALA. I don't know. I'm not a psychologist. Just another human. Trying to figure it out. A little bit at a time.

Sabotage is a strong word. It's declarative. It accuses. That's why I picked it. The Sabotage List isn't for you; it's for me. The goal is not to resolve each item on the list. The goal is to ensure it exists as a visible artifact rather than carefully tucked away in the deep dark corners of my brain. Invisible. Hiding, but with an impressive weight.

I don't have a prescribed process when I review the list, but I am always aware it's there. Occasionally and always unplanned, I glance at the list and wonder for a moment, *Why is this here? What is the reason I choose not to act?*

Often a silent, efficient, irrational defense mechanism prevents me from thinking deeper, but sometimes...sometimes in that brief reflection, I find revelation. *Oh, I'm not working on this because...10 years ago, THIS happened, and it hurt, and I'll never forget that hurt; thank you very much.* My prior experience left a mental scar, and simply knowing it exists is immense progress. Not because I found a way forward but because now I know why I stopped.

A list carries weight. It often documents a set of things you need to do. This is a flaw in the Sabotage List. I sometimes cross an item off the list, but I'm never done. It's never empty. The Sabotage List, like imposter syndrome, is a name for a thing, but also a reminder that there is much I don't know and, no, I'll never be a psychologist, but I'll always strive to figure it out.

A little bit at a time.

36

Check Your Work,
Ask for Help,
and Slow Down

The quality of your decisions is the currency of leadership.

It starts easy. The stakes are low. There is a legion of leaders around you who understand you've just begun, so when they see the decision in front of you, they proactively offer helpful advice. If the decision appears too complicated, excessively risky, or obviously high stakes, your manager raises her hand and helpfully suggests, "I got this one."

You are thankful because you had *no idea* how to decide.

It gets harder. The stakes increase. There are more blank stares from trusted peers when these decisions appear not because they don't want to help but because they don't know. They have never seen this type of decision before. However, they can, like you, know the importance of this decision and the necessity of it being your decision. Your manager will offer to help, but she'll wait longer to offer this help because she understands the value of you learning how to make this decision.

Then it seems impossible. The stakes couldn't be higher. Trusted peers grin nervously as you walk by. They feel equal parts empathy for the difficulty of the decision and relief that it's not on their shoulders. You have zero intuition on how to make this decision. No, it's worse than that. You don't even know how to decompose the problem to start to understand how to make a decision...or decisions?

Easy, hard, or impossible. The decisions merrily show up each day unaware of your ability or availability of time. They just know you're the leader and it's your job to decide.

I have advice. Unfortunately, it's advice for once you believe you have a decision and not how to make the decision. It's the same advice repeated three times written in different ways.

Check Your Work

Let's start with the relief that accompanies the discovery of the hint of a decision. The magnitude of relief is a function of the stakes. The glimmer of potential resolution is intoxicating, but my first piece of advice is to check your work.

It's glorious, right? Your experience or intuition is providing you insight into the proper decision. It feels magical to instantly know the correct approach, and these moments blissfully increase as you accumulate years of experience.

Oh, this again. I know how to do this.

The situation may seem familiar. They might be using the exact words to describe the situation, but it behooves you as a leader to reflect on the decision and check your work.

Sure, this seems obvious, but last time it was a different set of people. How will the decision affect this set of people? Are there different potential consequences because it is a different group? Is the fact that I can see the decision so quickly because I truly know the right decision or because the stakes are high and I feel the need to decide quickly? What am I missing?

Let the decision swirl in your head a bit. Let it knock around. Let it bump into other ideas. Let it stew, simmer, and evolve. And then...

Ask for Help

I'm miserable at asking for help. It's not just the introversion thing, but also the stubborn erroneous perception that asking for help is somehow an admission of weakness. *They're looking at me to decide and if I can't (yolo) make the right decision then they won't believe I'm their leader.*

In my experience, asking for help, the clear articulation that you don't know, is a defining trust-building moment with the team. Yes, they like to see you effectively lead, they are proud when you stand in front of the team and explain how we're going to win, but they, like you, are a work in progress. When you ask your team, your peers, or your manager for help, it levels the playing field and reminds all involved that you're in this together.

Yes, it is your decision, but no one expects you to bear the entirety of its weight. Besides, you have more time than you think because my last bit of advice is to...

Slow Down

My intuition was to put this advice first, but I'm putting it last because it's the most important. The ferocity with which a high-stakes decision arrives and tells you two facts and a lie:

- Here's a big decision.
- It's 100% your responsibility.
- And you better hurry.

The urgency is often the lie. Everyone can clearly see a big decision needs to occur. It's also readily apparent that it's entirely yours to make. This combination of the decision's magnitude and obvious single ownership creates pressure. Don't confuse pressure with urgency. *Don't confuse importance with urgency* (*https://oreil.ly/gM18s*).

This last bit of advice is designed to give you the time you need to check your work. Slowing down gives you the opportunity to ask for all the help. Taking time to think on the most critical decisions, in my experience, is how you build a higher-quality decision. By slowing down, I drain the emotion, urgency, and irrationality that often arrive with these decisions, and I'm able to see what's important versus what everyone is urgently yelling.

Big decisions have a fan club. These are the humans swirling around the decision who care deeply about its outcome. They have contradicting motivations: they know enough about the decision area to call themselves experts, but they are also intimately aware (or annoyed) that it's not their decision to make.

The fan club grows annoyed when you don't move with—what they perceive as—appropriate urgency, so I'll repeat myself: *the quality of your decisions is the currency of leadership.*

It's not that you moved quickly, it's that you invested enough of your time to build a quality decision. You won't be judged on how quickly you decide; you will be judged by the consequences of your decision that appear in the hours, days, weeks, months, and years after you decide. It is these results that build your leadership reputation.

What If I'm Wrong?

That's the question that shows up in the middle of the night for me when considering a big decision. It's a good question. What if you're wrong? What will happen when you decide? Wander those pathways in your head and with your trusted peers because attempting to predict the unpredictable is a critical part of this process. You'll need to explain these potential consequences when you're presenting your decision to everyone.

That's when I know I've decided. It's not that I can explain the decision, it's that I can tell you the story of how I decided, what I expect to occur as a result, and what we'll do if I'm wrong. And you understand.

See, because I've thought it through, it's becoming a compelling, thoughtful, and defensive story. When I tell those I trust the story, they believe me.

37

OK. So, You Can't Decide

Even if you've *checked your work, asked for all the help, and are moving gingerly* (*https://oreil.ly/WJ8-4*), there will be decisions where you can't decide. You've considered and reconsidered your pro/con lists, and you've had endless debates with informed humans, but you remain mentally paralyzed.

I have an observation regarding this paralysis, and then I'll offer some advice.

First, the paralysis might mean you're subconsciously aware you've missed an essential aspect of the decision, and your brain isn't letting you decide until you mentally uncover this essential information.

In all your research, conversation, and deliberation, you've not found the obvious answer. Worse, you've discovered a whisper of a hint that there is something important yet to be discovered, and that discovery might push your decision one direction or the other.

This is a subtle slippery mindset. It's a convenient excuse for the decision impaired. It allows us to stall even longer, but in my experience, the whisper of a hint is experiencing speaking...quietly.

In this situation, I need a very long bike ride. There is no additional conversation that needs to occur. A whiteboard is not going to help. I need to push the entire situation to the very back of my brain. I need to stick it back there where the wild things are because, in this situation, they know better than I.

Maybe you don't bike. OK, what is your deep consideration activity? Where do you find random thoughts and inspiration outside of the shower? Do that for as long as is necessary and see what you discover. Don't force it; just put yourself into deep consideration and see what happens.

Or maybe...

You Just Need to Decide

Having been through a great many hard decisions, there are two distinct moods around the decision. The great debate before the decision and then the great relief after the decision.

The defining characteristic of the great relief is the sense of immediate progress. After days or weeks of careful analysis, you are suddenly moving forward again, and...it's a delightful relief. You are no longer stuck endlessly second-guessing yourself.

Remember when you accepted the job offer? Remember when you bought the new car? Remember what it felt like the moment after you said yes to the company or signed on the dotted line? A weight is immediately lifted: "OK, this is happening."

You instantly become mentally limber. What was an infinitely complicated and unmeasurable set of interrelated pros and cons has now become work. Chances are the decision is so fresh that you have no idea whether it was the right decision or not, but you don't care because you are no longer stuck. Even if unexpected consequences begin to show up, you eagerly attack them because consequences are more fun than mental paralysis.

Yeah...yeah. I am reluctantly suggesting that the move is sometimes to just yolo decide. There is a real risk here, but if you've built yourself a formidable mental block, you're wasting precious time swirling around your head and it's time to make forward progress.

A profound change of perspective follows making a decision. It's no longer theoretical; it's happening. You are doing something as opposed to talking about doing something. Even better, as potential consequences begin to arrive, you gather initial essential data on the quality of your decision. Remember that aspect of the decision you thought was critical? Yeah, now that the decision is in the wild, you see it is irrelevant. And that allegedly irrelevant detail? Yeah, now it's loudly and painfully essential. Whoops.

It's frustrating when the early reactions arrive, and you realize all your forecasting work only provided half of the essential data. Your frustration is doubled when the "I told you so" humans show up to remind you that you ignored a critical part of their counsel. Ignored is the fact that we only know the critical role of their counsel because your decision revealed the importance.

Yes, some humans are naturally talented at decision forecasting, but there is a critical difference between those critics and you. They sit at a professional, comfortable distance from the decision. They are mostly immune to the consequences, which gives them mental comfort.

Meanwhile, you are accountable for this decision, and, once again, I'll remind you that most humans believe accountability means responsibility. What it means is *required or expected to justify actions and decisions*. To give account.

The decision you made is entirely yours, and while the work preceding a hard decision can feel like an immense and endless chore, decisions and their subsequent consequences are, in fact, a privilege of leadership.

PART IV

Your Next Gig

As we near the end of *The Software Developer's Career Handbook*, you'll find yourself back at the beginning—considering your next career move. This section of the book describes scenarios both positive and negative that might influence your next gig.

Bad performance review? Time to become a manager? The company is collapsing? Just plain bored? The urgency created by each of these scenarios varies, but understanding how they actually play out is an essential part of planning your next play.

Whether the need for change is pressing or not, these chapters are worth your time because you've chosen to work in an industry that will always move faster than you. Change is a constant, and that means you constantly need to consider what is next.

38

The Screw-Me Scenario

It had all the signs of a good meeting. And I hate meetings. We were:

- Talking about a product we loved
- In great shape from a feature, quality, and schedule standpoint
- A group that historically did not kick ass
- A group that was kicking ass

The slides looked great, and the dry run was flawless, so why hadn't I slept in two nights?

I couldn't sleep because I couldn't see the Screw-Me.

You Might Be Lying

There are endless variants of meetings, but the one I want to talk about is the executive cross-pollination communication disaster. The point of this meeting is alignment. You've likely got several groups who don't usually spend much time together. You've forced them to sit in the same room so the execs can compare stories, measure reality, and figure out who is lying.

Before I explain how to get your head around this meeting, I want to talk about the intent behind this meeting. Intent starts with a question: Why does this meeting exist? If you're responsible for the presentation in this particular meeting, it exists because someone hates you.

It's not personal hate. It's professional hate, and it's exacerbated by a simple fact of organization: different groups speak different languages. Marketing speaks marketing, Legal speaks legal, and Engineering speaks engineering. There's a fundamental communication breakdown somewhere in the building, and someone feels wronged. They're feeling bullied, and since they don't speak your dialect, they're complaining up rather than across.

Normally, we deal with these Tower of Babel situations with the direct application of middle management, program managers, and other folks we pay big bucks to sit in meetings and translate between organizations. However, translation has not worked in this case. Someone high up on the org chart is hearing two very different stories and wondering which is true. Story reconciliation is on the top of your list of items to resolve in this meeting, but job #1 is to figure out who hates you.

A Rubber Stamp Affair

For these critical meetings, your goal is to make them a rubber stamp affair. The week before the meeting, you will have personally vetted your slides with each of the meeting invitees. You will have heard their concerns and made the appropriate adjustments to your deck. When the cross-pollination meeting arrives, your goal is an utter lack of drama and the finishing pronouncement of, "Yeah, we should do that, and you know how."

It never happens like this.

We're "busy," and we have "things to do," but mostly we're "looking forward to blindsiding you with a Screw-Me at the least convenient moment in front of your executive team."

It's a disappointing trait of human nature that folks who feel wronged like to exact their revenge by flaunting their knowledge and dishing out the Screw-Me at the worst possible time; but roll with it. You're already a step ahead, just expecting to be screwed. Besides, your enemy is working more with emotion than content, which will turn into their own personal Screw-Me scenario later. Right now, your job is data.

No Guilt, No Doubts, No Fear

Ideas get better with eyeballs, and before this meeting goes down, your job is to get as many eyeballs on your presentation as possible. You're not going to get everyone in the meeting, but that's not the point. The task is cross-pollination. Casting the information net as wide as possible and incessantly asking:

- Does this make sense?
- What is missing?

- How am I going to get screwed?

For vetting my strategy, I've got a Russian lit major.[1] Who do you have? I'm not talking about your boss or coworker; I'm talking about the person who can objectively look at your presentation and start poking holes. These people are rare because it's another disappointing trait of human nature that we often think we're doing each other a favor by listening well but then telling each other what we want to hear.

You lose yourself in any significant project. You've long forgotten your initial strategic assumptions, but more importantly, you've forgotten what other people need because you're furiously worrying about the daily tactical fire drills. A fresh perspective is a chance to test your entire idea and find the Screw-Me. You need someone to poke holes. You need to find and fill the gaps, and as each gap is filled, you're going to build confidence around your pitch because, well, that's one less potential Screw-Me entry point.

You're not going to find them all. That's OK because in constantly refining your pitch, you're mentally refining yourself. You're preparing yourself by seeing each perspective in your deck. That improves your chances of knowing what to do when someone starts dishing out the hate.

Game On

The meeting's on. You're walking in with a head full of data, and I hope that you are legitimately the most informed person on this particular topic in the room through your constant cross-pollination. There's still work to do:

Size the room.

Who is here? What groups do they represent? Why would they randomly show up? Who brought them? What possible Screw-Mes could they represent?

Carry the room.

Start your deck. You've got it memorized, right? They can tell this is the 32nd time you've done it. It's smooth. You've already defused two Screw-Mes by slide 12. *Amanda, you have a question?*

---

1 Michael Lopp, "Russian History" (*https://randsinrepose.com/archives/russian-history*), *Rands in Repose* (blog), September 6, 2006.

Manage the room.

> Questions aren't Screw-Mes. You can clarify and stay on track. You know that Amanda is going to ask about hard data, right? Don't let her take over the conversation. Say, "I've got your data in the appendix, but let me get through this first, OK?" Yeah, you just shut down a senior VP. Nicely done. No way you can do that without serious confidence in your preparation. *Yes, Tim?*

Tim's got the Screw-Me, and you didn't see it coming. Total left field. Completely valid strategic observation, and you don't have a clue how to answer. Oops.

You will recognize the Screw-Me by the complete silence filling the room and your head. That's the realization everyone is having that you're Screwed. First, let's not make it worse...

The Unforgivable Spin

Tim: "Rands, what about *This?*"

I'm a poker player and an experienced meeting surfer, so the room will not immediately know from the look on my face that This has Screwed me, but what I choose to do next will define my ongoing relationship with the room.

There are two options when you are cornered by This. Your animal brain, when cornered, will try to find a way out. You can taste this approach even before you begin. *I am going to spin. I am going to talk quickly and confidently about This, and I hope that in my furious verbal scurrying, they will believe I've got This handled.*

That's not what they're seeing or hearing.

This is not your staff meeting where a little verbal soft-shoe will entertain and delight. These are the execs, and no matter how many meetings you've surfed, they see straight through spin; they know this dance, and the longer you sit there spinning, the longer you allow your boss to step in, try to make the diving save, and make you look like a blithering fool.

When you feel the spin coming, it takes a little practice to make the correct move. You are going to do four things:

- Acknowledge the Screw-Me.

- Admit you don't know.

- Concretely explain the steps you're going to take to find out.
- Give yourself a reasonable deadline.

You have wholly defused Tim. See, Tim was pissed, which is why he waited until precisely the wrong moment to throw down the Screw-Me. He wanted to see you spin and make a fool of yourself in front of your management team, and what you did with the instant acknowledgment was crush emotion with structured sanity.

You can get lucky with spin sometimes. Sometimes you spin so hard that you talk yourself into a Screw-Me solution that makes sense. But this is rare and unreliable; in my experience, this frenetic verbal journey erodes confidence and wastes time.

The only question on everyone's mind during the cross-pollination disaster is, "Do you know what you're talking about?" Tim only knows what he's pissed about, and you, through your preparation, can see the entire picture. It's lame that Tim didn't speak Engineer and waited until precisely the wrong moment to Screw you, but I hope you can deliver the "I don't know" with confidence through your incessant vetting of your slides.

A Screw-Me Detection Policy

An aggressive Screw-Me detection policy is, I believe, essential to navigating groups of people. It's not just constantly knowing the potential worst-case scenario in any situation; it's that you are instinctively always looking for it. When I look at any situation, I'm always trying to figure out what sequence of events could occur that will screw me.

This strategy sounds a lot like paranoia, and yes, an unchecked Screw-Me detection policy can result in a conspiracy theory lifestyle where *they* are out to *get you*.

Yes, only the paranoid survive, but paranoia is a lot of work. You can burn many calories worrying about all possibilities, but this is not an approach I recommend. What I'm asking is that you look at specific key events strategically. Step back and look at the whole board. Ask, *What sequence of moves is going to benefit me? Can I see what is coming? And how could I get screwed?* Because teams that kick ass aren't just ones that deliver; they deliver even when they're screwed.

39

No Surprises

At the end of each fiscal year, companies take stock of their performance. *How'd we do? Better or worse?* This is a natural time to reflect upon individual performance. This is when your boss writes your review.

In my ideal management world, a review is simply a documentation of well-known facts about your performance over the year. It also contains constructive advice and insight regarding how your boss believes you can improve on that performance. My dream is that you already know all of this information because you've been getting year-round feedback from your boss.

I wish.

Whether your manager is consistently delivering this information or not, getting written feedback is entirely different from receiving it verbally. The path to your brain via the written word differs dramatically from the spoken word. Reading the highs and lows of the past year makes them permanent and real.

And then there's the surprise.

Show Me the Money

Bad news. The surprise has nothing to do with money. We're not talking about compensation here. Yes, you did a splendid job this year, and I think they should be throwing raises, bonuses, and stock your way. But it's even better if it's clear why you think you did a splendid job. Can you articulate it? And you might know, but does your boss? Can he explain to you, in detail, how well you kicked ass?

I didn't think so.

See, your boss has you and a bunch of other "yous" who all are allegedly kicking ass, and all of that ass-kickery is tricky to monitor, especially over an entire year. It gets even worse when one of your team members is not kicking ass. Legitimately or not, that's actually where a lot of your boss's attention is going. You read that right: someone else's failure is distracting from your phenomenal year.

Let's fix that.

There are three strategies I'd like you to employ when it comes to your yearly review. They are:

1. Ignore the measures and focus on the content.

2. Prepare for the fact that a review is a discussion and, sometimes, a negotiation.

3. Deconstruct the surprise.

MEASURES VERSUS CONTENT

I've experienced a lot of different review formats at different companies, but let's boil it down to three buckets. A review describes:

1. What you did

2. How you did it

3. What you need to do next

This is a massive simplification of your review. Your review has many other corporate and division focus areas, but these impressive-sounding labels are still just lenses through which you understand how you did versus what was expected.

For each bucket, there are two classes of information: the content and the measure. I want to explain how you can save yourself a lot of sleepless nights by ignoring the measures, but first, a definition.

Sprinkled across your review are measures. These are words like *needs improvement, satisfactory,* or *excellent.* These words grab you because they're easy to understand. They're effectively your grades, and you've spent many of your formative years waiting for grades to show up.

If I told you that you got an A on a piece of work, you'd internally translate that letter into a pleasant *I did about as well as I could. Go me.* Grades—measures—are efficient, and they do convey information, but they lack essential content. I'll explain via an example.

When I arrived at the University of California, Santa Cruz, in the 1990s, they had no grades. Yeah, a remnant of the '60s. At the end of the quarter, you received a written evaluation. For each student in the class, the professor or the teaching assistant would produce a written evaluation—a plain-English description of the type and quality of the work produced over the semester.

I don't know who invented the idea of ditching grades, but I hoped they wanted to ditch the measures. The intent of measures is not to derive useful information; they are designed to allow for comparison and measurement. Am I higher or lower than you? How many As? Are there more As than Bs? It's interesting data, and I'm sure if you took a classroom full of data and plotted it on a graph, you'd learn something. Look! A bell curve!

A measure doesn't help you in your career. Your performance review isn't about comparisons to others. They're about what you did and what you could do. What you're looking for is the content.

Tell me which is more helpful:

"You did well."

Or:

"You finished the work on schedule, the customer was happy with the results, but there were lingering quality issues with the code. Looking at the last two releases, you had 2x the number of bugs than in prior releases. Focus on..."

We get hung up on grades and measures because they are so gosh darned digestible. They give us the illusion that they show us where we fit, but they don't tell us what to do next. At UCSC, the point of the gradeless report card was to create a vacuum where the professor would say something worthwhile. You're not going to get rid of measures—they serve a distinct purpose—but when you're first reading your review, I want you to ignore those seductive one-word assessments of your entire year. Their simplicity, while comprehensible, is just going to obscure the complexity of your year.

Instead, look at the content behind the measures. Whatever your particular areas of focus are, does your boss effectively explain what you did, how you did it, and what you could do better? It's a simple set of requirements, but your boss will mess it up, which is why you need to be clear that...

A REVIEW IS A CONVERSATION

The written word is intimidating. An assessment of a year is a big deal, so what will you do when you sit down with your boss, and he hands you three poorly crafted paragraphs littered with the word *significant*?

No, you don't ask about the raise. You freak out about the paragraphs. *Three paragraphs? I've written more in email this morning than you just wasted on my entire year.*

Calm yourself.

Think of this pathetic piece of paper as an opening offer—a poor offer. Your job is to transform this travesty into an accurate reflection of your year, and you're not doing this just out of a sense of self-righteousness; you're doing this to set the record straight.

This piece of paper is one of the only official documents of your career at this company. If you move, if your boss leaves, or if there's a re-org, this is often the first document reviewed to understand the degree of your ass-kickery, which means you want your boss to comprehend it.

But Rands, I was just...so pissed. I spent my entire winter on the project. Three paragraphs? I was furious..

Again, your review will contain surprises, and they will rattle you, which is why you prepare with a self-review.

My move is to keep a yearlong log of significant work as a task in whatever task-tracking system I'm currently using. Whether your company asks for it or not, the moment the mail from HR alerts you to the review season, you start cobbling together your self-review. Same buckets as above. Even if you haven't been paying consistent attention, you'll be surprised by what you can dig up in a weekend, considering your year.

Take a look at your year. Was it a great year, or did you just think it was great? How'd you do? No, I'm not actually reading it so you can have an honest opinion. Yes, your boss's opinion about your year is key, he does sign the checks, but it's a key surprise-reducing technique to walk into the review with an opinion. This moment of personal honesty you're having with yourself is a big deal because that's the foundation you'll stand on when the three pathetic paragraphs appear. Having a justifiable opinion regarding your year is a powerful, defensible position.

While sending the self-review long before your boss writes his review is important, it's more important to have this well-defined opinion when sitting down to read your boss's review. Does it document what you did? Everything? Does the description of what you did match your perception? No? Why? Don't tell me, tell your boss, and make sure he gets it because it's these types of historical perception mismatches that form an unhealthy basis for emerging misunderstanding and resentment.

The point of a review is the debate—to align your perceptions with those of the person who signs the checks—but even with all this healthy structured debate, there's still going to be a...

SURPRISE!

I don't know what the surprise is. It's your review. Some of the doozies from over the years from mine include:

- The total absence of recognition for a multimonth, multiteam project that kicked ass

- A reversal of opinion regarding a piece of work I'd done, usually toward the negative

- A completely incorrect read on the impact of a significant program I'd developed

Unfortunately, the surprise is the point. A review not only forces the alignment discussion but also serves as a warning for the coming year: *What do I need to do differently to avoid being blindsided when the next review arrives?*

Fact is, you're never entirely going to get your boss on board with your year. There are opinions he has that aren't going to change, which means if you don't want another surprise next year, you have to change.

A review's value lies not only in the documentation of what was observed, but also in what was not.

The Permanence of the Written

In many years of reviews, the only consistency I've noticed is that they're getting shorter. My unsubstantiated paranoia is that lawyers apply subtle corporate pressure to retain less descriptive documentation of what actually happened in the company. But perhaps it's just a growing professional laziness.

Whatever the reason, a brief review is sad. If you're staring at three useless paragraphs, you have a couple of problems. You've got a company that allows bad reviews, and you've got a boss who is unable or unwilling to articulate the quantity or quality of your work.

That's all sorts of screwed, but a complete breakdown occurs only when you don't react.

The first review I wrote was awful. It was three paragraphs derived from scanning status reports from the past six months. I sat in the room as she read the review, and she didn't have to say a thing for me to understand that I'd be spending the weekend actually writing the review. I got an accusing, furious glare. *You didn't even try.*

So, I did.

40

A Deliberate Career

I want to hear the story of how you got your first gig in high tech. You probably did everything you were supposed to do: you went to the career center, searched the job boards, and attended career fairs.

It was all vaguely confusing. Nothing was concrete. You threw that diligently crafted résumé built on little hands-on experience at dozens of randomly smiling people and wondered, *Am I ever going to get a job?*

And then it happened. A vacation in Italy. Some bizarre, unimaginable confluence of events started with you being blind drunk and broke in Florence. You met this guy on the street who was clearly American; you hit it off. Long story short, this chance meeting on the other side of the planet resulted in you getting your first engineering gig at a fashionable startup in Silicon Valley.

Your thought as you settled into your bright 'n' shiny new gig was, *I've no control over what is happening to me. I just need to go with the flow, and I'm going to randomly meet someone who is going to randomly believe in me and then money will rain from the sky.*

As an avid fan of instinct, a frequent receiver of random career blessings, and a professional identifier of random opportunity, I understand and have lived this perspective, but hope isn't going to define your career. You need a strategy.

Three Choices

When I write the word *strategy*, I picture this thick book with a light blue cover and black binding. The title is *My Career Strategy*, and below the title in block letters, it says *TOP SECRET*. This is not, however, what I mean by having a strategy. I'm talking about a half-hour exercise in thinking about your future.

The only thing I know about your future is that you don't know what will happen or when. Opportunity will show up at the least convenient time, and the moment it arrives, whether you're ready or not, you'll have to make a decision in a moment. *Am I going to make a move?*

My thought: the more you know what you want, the better decision you'll make.

I see three big questions you can ask yourself to define a rough strategy for your career. These are questions about your next job, but combined, the answers to these questions will help you understand where you want to go, what you want to build, and how you want to build it throughout your career.

QUESTION #1: STARTUP OR ESTABLISHED?

The first and most important question is the size and maturity of the company.

Startup

There is nothing quite like a startup as an introduction to our industry. If you're looking for a fire hose with information pointed straight at your face, I highly recommend the startup. However, its ability to present you with information is only exceeded by its ability to change it randomly.

Perhaps the biggest opportunity in the startup is to build something radically new. That's why random venture capitalists throw money at this no-name group of fine people. They believe that they have a chance to build a thing that has never been built before and, hopefully, figure out how to make a lot of money from that new thing. The startup's existence is a defiant cry, "Yes, we can do something different," and that means you are guaranteed to see opportunities and gain experience early in your career that you're unlikely to see at an established company. It also means you'll experience an abundance of failure.

During the first internet bubble, there was only one measure of success. Did you IPO? If you didn't, you were considered a failure. When the first bubble burst, we discovered there were all sorts of fascinating ways to fail, varying from buyout to outright take-it-apart-and-fire-everyone failure.

Most startups are going to experience some definition of failure, but, well, failure is awesome. I mean it. There's no experience like the diving saves you'll perform in an attempt to save your job or your company. It'll be hell when it's happening, but when it's over, you're going to be the guy who attempted to pull off some amazing professional moves, and these aren't moves you'll be asked to perform at a larger company.

The single biggest asset to consider when thinking about joining a startup is the experience you'll acquire. If you choose to dream about the millions of dollars you might end up with, I ask that you equally consider the experience of watching your team dismantled as your formerly high-flying company slowly runs out of cash and scrambles to restructure itself because three college drop-outs the next town over built your idea better, faster, and cheaper.

Whether your startup fails or not, the guarantee I make is that you're going to end up with some amazing stories, and each of those stories will contain a lesson. Sure, these lessons are available at larger companies, but the velocity, intensity, and passion of the startup will make these stories uniquely yours.

Established

If your average startup is metaphorically sprinting, your average successful, established company is lumbering along at a comfortable trot. This company believes that it's running swiftly, but it's not. It ran at some point, became successful and large, and has gently slowed down thanks to its own weight.

This lumbering trot won't be obvious unless you've already experienced the pace of a startup, and that might be part of the attraction. There's nothing quite like the calm deliberation of an established company after the frenetic chaos of a startup, but it comes with a cost.

There's a constant threat in a startup, and that's the threat of failure. You can ignore it when you're busily working three weekends straight, but it's always there: "We could fail." The larger company's success has hidden this threat under the guise of predictability, domesticity, and sheer momentum. You'll have fewer responsibilities because there are more of you. The projects will take longer because what's the hurry? You won't worry if your paycheck will clear, and you'll bitch when you have to work a few weekends. It sounds kind of sleepy, but there is still much to learn.

Any job, any company, represents a wealth of experience. The risk of acquiring that experience at an established company is far less than at a startup because your larger company has hit its stride. They made it, and one would think they made it because they did something right. The questions are, What did they do right? Are they still doing it right? and How is the rightness covering up things they're doing horribly?

The risk of the established company is that they've become used to their lumbering trot. It's become stable and familiar, defining the entire company's processes and culture. *This is how we do things.* This makes their days predictable and measurable. Again, if you've been suffering through endless days of risky unpredictability at your last gig, a large company might be the perfect next move.

QUESTION #2: INDUSTRY AND BRAND

The next choice to make is what industry you want to explore. In my career, I've been a database guy, a browser guy, a web apps guy, an e-commerce guy, an operating system guy, a government guy, a social media guy, and a communications guy. If you were to map current industry trends to this career, you'd notice that my career switches followed the bleeding edge. I was at Borland when Windows application development began and made the same move at Netscape around the emergence of the internet. All of these varied experiences had a point: cross-pollination.

It's great that you've figured out how to get Ruby to scale, and I'm certain you could continue to explore the frontiers of scalable Ruby, but in doing so, there's a point of diminishing returns regarding your career. It's comforting to know what you're talking about and to be recognized by those around you as an expert in whatever it is that you do, but when I stare at a résumé where the past five years have been spent in the same gig, I wonder, *Why hasn't he gotten bored?*

Granted, your nerd attention deficiency disorder is likely to push you toward the new continually, so I'm not that worried about you moving on to tackling new technical problems. But while we're here, I want to talk briefly about brand.

The name, the reputation of a company, is a thing to consider. If you were to tell a complete stranger the name of the company you're considering, what would be their reaction? Is it well known? Is it viewed as successful? Can they name a product this company produces? This is useful information because when you eventually leave this gig, it's that name that you'll be putting on your résumé, and it's that name that will be quickly digested by future employers.

All that said, brand and reputation are not pivotal decisions in considering a new gig, especially when anonymous startups are in the mix. But if you're considering an unknown quantity in terms of company, try this: describe the opportunity you're considering. Can you? Something about web services? OK, what about web services? What excites you? What are you going to own? What are you going to build?

QUESTION #3: MANAGEMENT OR DEVELOPMENT?

There are two career tracks in engineering: development and management. That's it. As you're probably already an engineer, this decision is easy to describe but hard to understand: Do you want to be a manager?

Why would anyone want to be a manager?

Fact. There is more money to be had in management. This money results from more responsibility. By responsibility, I mean frequent moments when everyone in the room is staring at you, expecting you to make a critical decision on the spot with incomplete information.

Fact. You'll code less, you'll work more, and at the end of the day, you won't be sure you did anything.

Fact. You'll meet lots more people and be expected to get along with them.

Fact. Much of what you've done to be a good engineer isn't going to apply to being a good manager.

Chapters 41 and 42 will explore these facts further and go into more detail on the role of management. But the question remains: Is this a direction you want to head as part of your next gig? This doesn't need to be an absolute decision. There are smaller steps you can take toward management. Technical Lead is usually the title for a gig that is a primer for management. Such roles usually have larger decision-making responsibilities without all the bothersome performance reviews, so you can get a feel for wearing a management hat without fully committing.

A Complete Opportunity Move

Here's a different version of the questions:

- Where do I want to go?
- What do I want to build?
- And how do I want to build it?

As you answer these questions, other smaller questions will pop up that matter specifically to you and that you should also explore. How many people do you want to work with? How much do you want to work? How much responsibility do you want? How much stress can you handle?

Ideally, you should be able to answer these questions independently before you search for your next gig because the moment a new opportunity presents itself, you're not thinking about yourself; you're thinking about the potential new gig. You still need to be able to see how this gig fits with your personal strategic direction, as well as answer one more question: What's the opportunity to grow?

A startup is more likely to be in a state where it's hiring lots of people, aggressively attacking new problems, and having a sense of urgency. Still, you can find the same attributes in a large company in a specific group that has been tasked with the new and sexy. This hybrid might be the best of both worlds—the urgency of a startup supported by the stability of an established company—but is it the right fit for you? Does it represent an opportunity you've never seen?

At the end of this analysis is an unfortunate truth: you won't know what you're getting until you're there. The only guarantee is that it will be different from where you are now, and that means you're going to learn...something. And that's a good thing. The more you know, the fewer the surprises.

The Curse of Silicon Valley

In 30 years of engineering life in Silicon Valley, I have never heard an engineering manager tell me, "My degree in engineering management sure came in handy there." In fact, outside of company-sponsored management training, I've never heard of training specifically in engineering management. I'm certain it exists, but the fact that no coworker I've ever worked with has showered praise on an external engineering management class is intriguing.

Many of us spend years in college becoming computer scientists. So, where are the managers coming from? How are they getting trained?

The answers are both a blessing and a curse. Let's start with the good news.

Apprenticeship

You are in an industry where, for the most part, your managers used to be you.

That's right.

They have the same degrees you have. They have been through all the trials and tribulations of being an engineer. The names of the companies are different, and they probably know a few long-forgotten languages, but the core problems they faced are the same:

- The product is late.

- We have too many bugs.

- Product Marketing sure has some interesting ideas.

- No one is writing anything down.

- My manager is out of touch.

Really. Your current manager used to sit in *your chair* and think, *Who is this schmo, and how in the world did he get this gig because I'm not sure he even knows what we do.*

He does because he did.

We'll talk in Chapter 42 about the process of becoming a manager. Still, we will start by acknowledging and appreciating that ours is an industry where we choose our engineering leadership typically from among our own ranks.

Whoa, whoa, whoa, Rands. I did not pick this human; I was re-org'd under them—didn't have a hint of a choice.

First off, you choose by being there. Yes, there are quality-of-life issues if you quit right this minute, but you can quit whenever you like. Second, that's not the point. The blessing of Silicon Valley is that our engineering leaders mostly came from the trenches. They fixed bugs and shipped products, and perhaps they did it well enough that someone thought they should help make decisions and communicate about how it gets done. This leads us to the curse...

On Language

You do not work in an industry where some hotshot MBA fresh out of Harvard will pop out of nowhere and take over frontline engineering management. Why? Because any reasonably bright engineering team would eat the Ivy Leaguers alive:

Hey, Harvard, can you walk through this stack trace with me?

The benefit of an industry where our management was once us is that we have leaders who speak our language and understand our problems. This is also the beginning of the curse.

The story is this: a talented young graduate joins a startup fresh out of college. His manager pairs him with a bright senior engineer. Over the course of two years, our college grad learns software development both hands-on and by osmosis: be productive, be fantastically clever when necessary, speak truth to power, hit your dates, and don't ship crap.

Our engineer ships his product many times. Mistakes are made, lessons are learned, and suddenly six years have passed, and our college grad has become a senior engineer. The lessons he's learned have become the lessons he teaches. He has a reputation for delivering quality...no matter what. He's dependable, he wants to grow, and he wants more responsibility. So, someone decides to promote him to management.

Then the first cross-functional meeting happens. Product management, sales, and tech support, and they're asking why the team can't do a certain feature, and our freshly minted manager suddenly realizes he's totally unable to describe the technical and performance implications of their request, so he lamely says, "Well, it's hard."

Cold stares of hate cross the table, and our manager wonders, *Do they hate me?*

They do.

EVERYONE HATES ENGINEERING

Not really. That's too strong. Folks are frustrated with engineering. Here's why: Outside of engineering, no one really likes engineering. Here's why:

No one knows what we actually do to build the software, so they assume it's easy

In everyone else's head, it's really simple just to add that checkbox to that page and "just branch the code or something...use an If/Then statement or something."

How totally annoying.

What's being asked for there is the world's worst specification, but the real problem is that the person asking assumes they're describing all of the work involved. They believe that their understanding is somewhat related to the work involved in developing a product.

Worse, this misunderstanding goes both ways...

We take our work personally and believe no one else does

We take our role as owners of the bits extremely seriously. We've been staring at these bits for months. We've stayed up until 3:00 a.m. making sure they are just right. We've successfully defended these bits against our well-intentioned QA department, and they've shipped, and I'm sorry, what are you asking?

Um, it's not quite right. Could you move that field over here and that button up here because...

Do you know when this would've been good feedback? At 3:00 a.m. four months ago, after I'd given up five weekends to hit that insane date, that'd be a good time to ask me for a new feature.

Our bits are our world. We've heard of product marketing, technical support, and sales, but we erroneously and passionately believe the bits are the whole game. See...

Our relationship is with the bits

One of the defining characteristics of a career in computer science is there is little initial fortune tied to successful face-to-face interaction with human beings. In fact, ours was initially a career where social ineptitude might be a benefit.

Go back to the list:

- Be productive: generate good bits.

- Be clever: generate lots of good bits.

- Speak truth to power: defend your good bits to those who know what they're talking about.

- Hit your dates: deliver your good bit when you say you will, but...

- Don't ship crap: make sure the bits are good.

A healthy ambivalence regarding human beings goes a long way toward achieving these goals. Not busying your mind with the endless complexities of human behavior saves you precious time to focus on the bits, and our career is based on the bits. Our incentives are bit-based. At the end of the year, when our manager describes our performance, they describe it in terms of our bit-based success.

Little of what we need to be successful engineers involves interaction with those outside engineering, leading us to the Curse.

The Curse

The curse of Silicon Valley is: we're often placing our most valuable talent into a job they are utterly unequipped to handle and probably don't want.

Much of what we do as engineers on a day-to-day basis has enabled us to develop a lot of very technical and complex skills. Unfortunately, generally, they aren't skills that are valuable when dealing with people—communication, translation, soft skill mentoring, empathy, etc. Pick a management challenge:

- Communicating with a hostile room

- Writing a performance review for someone who is failing

- Firing a friend

Tell me, what experience in your eight years of writing great code has prepared you for handling any of these situations? Sure, you've had meetings where folks were going toe to toe on a hard issue, but *those were engineers*. You know how they think and how they speak, and after the meeting, you can all just return to your cubes and get back to work. Try going a few rounds with angry on-site legal counsel and tell me what that feels like and how they act the next time you have to deal with them.

Management is the art of gathering, organizing, and distributing information to the right people. Doing so means being able to quickly and effectively communicate with various personalities—engineering and nonengineering alike. A productive, clever, and reliable engineer has had little incentive to figure out human beings. In fact, we've constructed a mythical mental place called the Zone where we achieve maximum productivity, and the rule of the Zone is: no one is welcome; I am working on the bits.

The managerial leap is painful. In engineering, the truth is a clear and measurable thing. Management is a job where the truth is blurred by endless political intrigue and personality warfare.

Engineering Gone Mainstream

The generation of engineers who are currently managing teams are the ones who were used to being viewed as antisocial freaks. The managerial arrival of the millennials with a view of a world that has never been without the internet disposes of the geek-related stigma. This is a generation that will soften former hard geek social edges. Finally.

Ours is an industry that is maturing. What was an obscure career choice two decades ago is now understood by a good portion of the planet because they stare all day at the tools we build. Those tools are in their pockets, and they are part of the daily conversation.

As our industry becomes less obscure, the pool of candidates we can draw from for future software engineering managers is growing larger. And the larger the mix, the more talent and personality cross-pollination will occur. That will make software engineering no different from any other industry, and bad management won't just be a function of our generational predilections.

42

A Disclosure

My management career began with a misunderstanding.

"Rands, you're doing a great job on tools development, and I'd really like you to Lead the effort."

It sounded like your standard professional compliment. Atta boy! Go run with it! Problem was I didn't hear the capital *L*.

Lead is what my manager had said. Not *lead*, but *Lead*. He asked poorly and without definition and specifics, but he did ask. He was subsequently baffled two months later when I said, "I don't think I can finish this by next month; I need more time."

HIM: Why don't you hire another engineer?

ME: Wait, I can do that?

I see three possible situations whereby you might become a manager:

- You decide. *I believe I am going to be a better manager than engineer. I choose management.*
- You evolve. This is what happened to me. Essentially, a series of small decisions and actions where, in the end, you end up being a manager. Surprise!
- You have no choice. "You. Manage this team. Go."

Whether you get to choose or not, there are aspects of management that you need to understand.

Management Is a Total Career Restart

Now, if you're evolving into the career, this will be less obvious, but if management just landed in your lap, realize that while you're in the same game, it's a totally new game board, and you're at square one. You will use the skills that made you a great engineer, but there's an entirely new set of skills you need to acquire and refine.

This sensation will appear at the end of the day when you ask, *What did I build today?* The answer will be a troubling *Nothing.* The days of fixing three bugs before noon are gone. You're no longer going to spend the bus ride home working on code; you're going to be thinking hard about how to say something important to someone who doesn't want to hear it. There will be drama. And there will be those precious seconds when there is no one in your office wanting...something.

You Go to a Lot of Meetings

You already knew this, but managers go to meetings. Meetings are the bane of my existence, and I consider it my personal goal to kill as many as possible, but I still go to a lot of meetings. There are two useful types of meetings: alignment and creation. Briefly:

Alignment meetings sound like this.
> "It's red. Are we all in agreement it's red? OK, swell. Wait, Phil thinks it's blue. Phil, here are the 18 compelling reasons it's red. Convinced? Done now?"

Creation meetings sound like this.
> "We need more blue. How are we going to do that? Phil, you're our blue man. What should we do here?"

There are other meetings out there, but you will learn to avoid them. One is the therapy meeting. They sound like this: "Show of hands, who likes to talk about blue? Or red? I don't care. Let's explore our color feelings for the next sixty minutes."

In time you will learn which meetings to attend, but when you start, you will go to all of them because...

You Are a Communication Hub

One of your primary jobs as a manager is to be a communication hub, not only for all of those working for you but for everyone who needs something from you. This means you will spend an inordinate amount of time sitting in random conference rooms and listening. It's hard. Who are they? What do they need? Do I understand what they are saying? Should I say no now or let this fester?

Confusingly, as a manager, you often get credit just by showing up, sitting there, and nodding. As a career management strategy, the "nodding fly on the wall" approach isn't proactive or helpful. But there are critical times when all that is being asked of you is that you are the receiver of the rant. Simply by listening, by letting an idea be heard, you are helping.

However, you need to do more than listen. Whatever is being said in this meeting isn't just for you; parts of it are for your team, which means you need amazing skills of...

Abstraction and Filtering

During these endless demands for your time, you do need to communicate, but if you're relaying all the information that's being thrown at you during the day, all you'll do is relay. Your new job is one of abstraction, synthesis, and filtering. During that 30-minute status meeting, you need to develop the mental filter to listen for the 3 things you actually need to tell the team in your alignment meeting, but in a mere 3 minutes instead of 30.

Your thought is, *If there are only three things I need to know, why the hell are we spending 30 minutes in this meeting?* First, I relate to your frustration. Second, the three things you need to relay are different from the three things each of the other folks in this meeting needs to relay. Third, if you blow this, here's what will happen: more meetings.

See, your world has expanded, and now...

You Will Be a Multilingual Translator

Each group in the company has a different language they speak and a different set of needs. As a manager, you need to be able to speak all the corporate dialects of those you depend on. Think of the healthy tension between engineering and QA. Remember that flame war that went on between you and the QA guy for a week in the bug database? Engineering and QA actually speak the same language but have different goals. As a manager, you will discover an entire company of languages and goals. For example:

- Sales cares about selling and doesn't much care how hard it is to build.

- Marketing is passionate about brand, content, and voice and will argue endlessly for details you find to be irrelevant.

- Tech support talks to the customer *all day*, but still feels no one listens to what they say.

- System administrators speak many of these languages and have more power than you think.

Everyone believes their job is essential; everyone believes everyone else's job is easy, and, confusingly, everyone is right.

These roles exist for a reason. The groups each bring something unique to the corporate organism. You can giggle and make fun of their bizarre acronyms as an individual, but as a manager, you must speak their language because once you do, you'll understand better what they want.

Learning new languages is tricky, especially when you're just getting started. You'll spend 90 days being totally confused, and it gets worse because there's...

Drama Everywhere

Your manager calls you into her office first thing on a Monday morning. It's clearly urgent. She sits you down and starts, "I'm, uh, making a change in the organization. Amanda is really excelling in tools development, so I've asked her to take over Jerry's management responsibilities. I think this will make everyone more successful."

Wondering what happened to Jerry? Feel like you're getting half the story? Wrong. You're getting one-tenth of the story. People are messy, and a huge part of the management gig manages this messiness. Who knows what personal or professional issue Jerry has that forces this management change? It's really none of your business. However, it is your manager's business because the people are her job.

As an individual, you're seeing 10% of the organizational drama your manager is seeing. I know it's intriguing to get the full story, but again, it's often none of your business, and it's not your job. As a manager, you get front-row seats for all the drama in all its messy glory. This is why you now have a monthly 1:1 with the People Team. Their job is to train you how to manage the drama. This is why you need to become a great...

Context Switcher

Morning. Six 30-minute 1:1s starting at 9:00 a.m. In your fourth, your architect resigns. The human responsible for the heart of the application is leaving for a startup, and it sounds like you can't save him. Sounds grim. What's harder is after your sky-is-falling 1:1, you've got one with the quality director, who has no clue your architect resigned, and she urgently wants to talk about the bug database. That's precisely what you must do. You must effortlessly forget you're screwed and give this team member your full attention.

There will be a steady stream of curveballs headed in your managerial direction, each with its own unique velocity. One of your jobs is to not only deftly handle the pitch, however bizarre, but also shake it off and calmly expect an even stranger one.

There's a reason you'll see an inordinate amount of bizarre organizational shenanigans as a manager. See, the individuals can handle—and should handle—the regular stuff. You want a team of people who aren't bringing you every little thing, but if you successfully build this team, your reward is that what ends up in your office is uniquely kooky.

As these freakish pitches whiz by, you will be judged in two very different ways. First, what did he do about the pitch? Are we going to see more of these? Second, how was his composure as that pitch whizzed by, missing his nose by an inch? Does it look like he handled it, or is he freaked out and ready to bolt?

Leadership is not just about effectively getting stuff done but demonstrating through your composure that you aren't rattled by the freakish. Fortunately, one of the new tools you have to control the proliferation of freakishness is the ability to...

Say No

This is your second most powerful tool. Whether you're a manager, considering management, or just here for the Rands, I want you to pick the hardest problem on your plate. The one that is waking you up at 4:00 a.m. I want you to decide and to say out loud: "No."

You're not going to do that thing. QA can't test it. Engineering won't finish it. If we attempt to do it, we will fail, and we don't fail, so the answer is no.

You had this tool as an individual. You could say no, but you usually did so by cornering your manager and explaining, "Here is why no is the right move here," and then he'd say no.

As a manager, you are the caretaker of *no* for your group. When it is time to do the right thing by stopping, it's your job to bust out the no. You defend your team against organizational insanity with no.

No does not come without consequences. Saying no because you can rather than because it's right slowly transforms you into a power-hungry jerk, but again, this is your new tool to do with as you see fit. Also, it's not all no; you can also...

Say Yes

Yes is how you begin building both people and things. It's not just a positive word; it's the word that provides the structure for moving forward. "Yes. Begin." "Yes, I know he's leaving. What are we going to do?" And "Why yes, we should tackle the audacious."

There will be times when your yes needs to be unencumbered by reality, where it needs to be the inspiration that demonstrates how you perceive the unknowable.

"Yes, I think you'd be a fine manager."

Trust So You Can Scale

As a new manager, whenever the sky falls, you'll become an engineer again. You'll fall back on the familiar because those are the tools you know and trust, but it's time to trust someone else: your team.

If I could give you one word, a single, brief piece of management advice, the word would be *scale*. Your job as a manager is to scale the skills that got you the gig in the first place. You used to be the guy who did the impossible when it came to fixing bugs. OK, now you're the guy whose entire team does the impossible bug fixing.

It's time to translate and to teach what you're good at to those you work with, and that starts by trusting them to do that which you previously only asked of yourself.

Defining and maintaining this trust creates a satisfying productivity feedback loop. By trusting your team, you get to scale, and scaling means you get to do more of what you love. The more you do, the more you build, the more experience you gather, the more lessons you learn. The more lessons you learn, the more you understand, and that means when more opportunities show up, you'll have an even greater opportunity to scale...and lead.

43

Mind the Gap

Everyone is replaceable.

The first time you'll hear this rationalization is when someone valuable regrettably leaves the group. The team is off because no one wanted this person to leave, so your manager gets everyone together and lays down the departed's reasoning: "He's been here five years; he's looking for new challenges." People nod, they wonder, and then your peer, Phillip, leans over and whispers, "Everyone is replaceable."

And he's right. Nature abhors a vacuum. When someone vital walks out the door, you learn many interesting things about the remaining folks.

The Gaps

In this chapter, I'm going to walk through an analysis of some individual regrettable departures of someone on your team. You don't want this person to leave because they're adding something unique to the team, and when you learn they're leaving, you believe that something essential is permanently being lost.

There are certain situations where the departure of a single key person can lead to the collapse of a team or a company, but in this chapter, we assume the team is going to make it because although, sadly, a person you like is leaving, I believe you're underestimating everyone else.

As with any departure, there's a knee-jerk belief that this person's absence will result in immediate and irrevocable change. But the reality is that a group of people is a complex social organism, and change doesn't happen that fast. Yes, the departure will create a gap that you will worry about. I don't know what kind of gap because I don't know who is leaving, so we'll look at the obvious from the perspective of your worst fear and why you shouldn't worry, but how you should continue to pay attention.

KNOWLEDGE AND ABILITY: "ALPHA KNOWLEDGE"

The Irrational Fear: *He has knowledge about the product that no one else does. He is the only one who knows how to debug the hard problems. He is the only one who has the entire system in his head. He's the guy we call when the problem is really, really hard, and without him, we won't be able to solve really hard problems anymore.*

Don't Worry: This is clearly your Alpha when it comes to the knowledge of your team. The blessing and the curse of Alpha Knowledge aren't just that they know everything; it's that everyone else knows that they know. This is informationally convenient for the group because whenever someone has a hard question, they know exactly who to ask.

While the absence of this person is alarming, what you'll quickly discover is that all the answers to those questions everyone was asking Alpha Knowledge actually stuck in the heads of those folks. In fact, they were often asking their question as a means of confirmation rather than as a process of discovery. See, after the third time they ask, they know the answer. They know how it works, but Alpha Knowledge's presence meant they questioned themselves: *Well, I think I know, but I'd best confirm with Alpha before proceeding.*

I assume that the majority of the knowledge you believe is in Alpha's head has already been cross-pollinated to other team members. Alpha's departure will incentivize others to trust what they already know.

But Pay Attention: While it's likely that formerly quiet team members will step in to fill the knowledge gap, there *is* knowledge and ability walking out the door. But it's not the broad knowledge you're concerned about—it's the little undocumented knowledge. Why is it that variable has that particular name? What is the story behind the naming scheme for the servers? What is this cryptic note in the code that reads, "Two more of these and we're screwed"?

You can ask this person to document the state of the world as much as you like, but they're going to forget something small and something essential to the inner workings of the product. You'll discover this omission months after they're gone, and worse, when they've totally forgotten about their prior professional life. "Two more of what things? I've no idea what you're talking about."

What you need to pay attention to when Alpha Knowledge leaves is the team's ability to handle the unexpected. It's not the day-to-day operations of the team that will be impacted by the absence of Alpha. It's when it hits the fan that you're really going to miss him because it's his undocumented improvisational skills that are gone and are not coming back.

Again, essential information is walking out the door, but most of the time, the group can live without that information. Teams work around the absence because they don't have a choice, and once they've worked around it once, they've learned what is missing, and they've updated the way that works.

POWER AND INFLUENCE: "MAESTRO"

The Irrational Fear: *She's looking out for us. She's shielding us from the bullshit. She's protecting our culture. We have additional opportunities because she is here. Decisions are being made in our favor because she's sitting at the table fighting for us.*

The Reality: We're going to call her Maestro because she's conducting the business of the group. She's likely a senior manager, director, or VP, and now she's gone. Like Alpha Knowledge, the vacuum created by her absence will send those interested in her job into a frenzy. Who is going to inherit her crown? Who deserves it? What are they going to do to get it? All of these questions are interesting, but the reality is that you need to understand why she left. You're sad she's leaving, but is everyone?

Leaders define the culture that surrounds them. The reality of this culture is twofold. First, when Maestro leaves, she's permanently taking part of that culture with her. And second, the culture above and around her will seep in. Whether or not this now-intruding culture is a fit with your team is the real question. Was Maestro protecting her team from this culture? If so, why? And, most importantly, are any of the reasons for her departure a result of conflict with this external culture?

Leaders optimize reality to their favor, and the more powerful and influential they are, the more they can define a comfortable reality for themselves and their team. The more this reality conflicts with the rest of the company, the more your team will need to adapt when the Maestro leaves the building with her personal reality distortion field.

But Pay Attention: What you're going to learn in the first month after an influential leader has left the group is how much her view of the goals of your group differs from the goals set by the company. Ideally, your former leader did a fine job translating corporate vision into regionally relevant goals. Ideally, her daily direction for the group was aligned with the direction of external groups and those of whoever steps in to fill her spot.

But maybe it wasn't.

There's shielding the team from politics and nonessential crap that they don't need to know so they can focus on getting work done, but there's also shielding to an unnecessary degree. This is why, when an influential leader has left the building, I pay attention to blank stares.

There are inevitable organizational investigation meetings that occur when a person in a position of power leaves. There are questions for the remaining team, and when those questions are directed to me, I'm looking to see how my answers are being received. Nodding is the universal sign that those sitting with you are on the same page. Nodding means they understand. A blank stare means there's a disconnect, and when the blank stares come from the people your former boss interacted with, I begin to wonder what she was telling them and what she wasn't.

Whether Maestro was shielding you from crap, was creating her own reality, or was a perfect fit with the culture external to the group, a cultural gap will be created by her absence. New leaders will bring their own culture with them, and that means the team will need to adapt.

NETWORK AND COMMUNICATION: "THE INSIDER"

THE FEAR: He knows everything. He's incredibly well-connected, so we were always ahead of the game. He was the person I always went to when I wanted to know what was going down. He eliminated surprises.

THE REALITY: The Insider is the person on the team who thrives on knowing what is happening in the company. He's known for it. In staff meetings, all eyes turn to him when juicy data needs confirmation:

BOSS: And it looks like they're three months late.

[All eyes turn to the Insider]

INSIDER: [Nods]

BOSS: So, they're screwed.

The role of the Insider isn't just gossip; he's the person on the team who is the keeper of the truth (see "Bits, Features, and Truth" on page 202 in Chapter 33). Insiders are genetically compelled to know what is going on everywhere, and they hopefully use the skill as a means of keeping the folks around them equipped with the latest, greatest information, wherein lies the reality.

While the Insider is the perceived keeper of the truth, information moves in a group of people in more ways than you can imagine—especially the juicy stuff. You don't need to fear suddenly not being in the know; information will travel due to its interestingness. The Insider's absence will put a kink in your one-stop information shopping, but his absence won't leave you permanently in the dark.

But Pay Attention: Your former Insider had two roles—collector of information and conveyor of information. And it's the latter where you want to pay attention. Part of the Insider's makeup isn't just that they know what to ask whom, but also knowing who needs to know what.

What I'm looking for in the Insider's absence is who is now lost? Who was dependent on the Insider to know what was going on in the group and in the company? What essential and nonobvious communication flow has stopped with the Insider's absence? This sudden dearth of communication is likely happening in a place you don't expect. It's not a meeting the Insider no longer attends; it's that random hallway check-in he's no longer performing, and it means that someone is silently adrift. This isn't mission-critical information they're now missing; it's the comfortable information of the now.

You'd think that with the menagerie of meetings managers insist on holding, communication in a group of people would be well structured and predictable. It's not. For every useful piece of information that happens in a staff meeting, there's an equal amount of information traveling in hallways, emails, and random cube conversations. With the Insider gone, communication has stopped flowing...somewhere, and the consequences of this information standstill can vary from simple confusion to organizational chaos.

A Matter of Perspective

Again, a group of people is a complex organism, and your perspective of the organism is limited to what you can see from where you're sitting. Your perspective of this person who is leaving is just one perspective. Just as everyone's perspective about this person is different, so is their opinion about this fine person's departure.

The number one thing to pay attention to in this departure is the unexpected because there is some key relationship that no longer exists. There is someone who is utterly destroyed by this person's absence, and there are likely people who are delighted and just waiting to make their move. It's these unexpected social tertiary side effects that may affect your day-to-day, and you need to be looking for them. You need to know who these people are, and you need to understand their opinions because the organizational landscape has changed.

The vacuum created by this departure creates not only organizational confusion, but also opportunity. The jockeying to fill whatever position of power starts the moment the hint of the rumor starts wandering the hallways, and you need to figure out where you fit in this now rapidly changing landscape. Did you always want to be Alpha Knowledge? Now is a good time to fill those shoes. Do you know someone who would be a great Insider? Have you told them this?

Finally, remember that change, especially the departure of key personnel, freaks people out. They're not thinking everyone is replaceable; they're quietly wondering, *What do those people know that I don't? I'm happy here, so why aren't they? Who's next?*

The biggest risk with a key departure is that it indicates a larger movement. The biggest risk is that it's a sign that the sky has begun falling.

44

The Cello in Soho Square

This was the second time we'd heard Audrey play her cello in Soho Square. She found a bench and just started playing. We learned about the first session days after it happened and begged her to give us a warning next time, but her small smile silently said no. We mobilized. Her roommate Bruce was on cello watch. He'd message us an early warning when he saw her tuning her cello. When she left the building with her instrument, a second message was deployed, and we'd hustle across the city to the square.

Spring in Soho Square. Audrey is sitting on a random park bench, playing her cello. She had practiced alone for years and never played for anyone. The first "concert" in the Square was a shock, the second a delight, and the third the last. Sadly, Bruce, Natasha, and I sat there because we knew Audrey was a classic dabbler.

Four years ago, it was baking. Two years ago, it was architecture. The past two were the cello. Audrey would dabble in a new hobby every two years, like clockwork. Sometimes she brought us along, telling us the history of bread, generously sharing the results of her baking, and dragging us across the city to discover a rosemary ciabatta "to die for." Sometimes the dabbling was intensely private. The cello had been in her room for as long as we'd known her, but suddenly we heard it. When asked about the cello, she changed the subject. OK. New topic.

Still Playing Destiny

Yeah. Still. It was released in 2014, and here we are in 2023, and I remain an avid *Destiny* player. There've been other games during that time. Most notably: *Sea of Thieves* (I never played anything like it), *Fortnite* (I tried to get others into it but failed; still solo yolo), and *New World* (the first legitimate *World of Warcraft* competitor I've experienced in decades). Each of these games, while enjoyable, looks like a distraction compared to the total time I've put into *Destiny* and *Destiny 2*.

I would classify myself as good for most of my years spent playing *Destiny*. While I understood how the game worked, how to progress, and how to acquire epic loot, I still regularly asked fellow Clan mates many questions because I knew they knew. I had no drive to become an expert in any aspect of the game, and I could sense what was required to be an expert. I could see it in those around me. Looked like work.

In my opinion and without judgment, there are four experience classes of players within a video game:

Average

The majority of players within a game. They understand and enjoy how the game works. They will play a game until they are bored and then move on. If completing the game is an option, your Average player will likely not manage to do so. They will become competent and build a good feel for the game but will probably not cross the finish line.

In a multiplayer game, your Average player will briefly wonder how Good or Better players perform that skill, acquire that fancy armor, or achieve that thing. Still, they won't wonder long because their commitment to this game is minimal. They don't take the time to understand the intricacies of the game. They enjoy gently being led along a well-designed path.

They are...most players. If I had to guess, Average players represent 50–60% of the player base.

Good

Still a double-digit percentage of the player base. Your Good players have committed to the game. These humans will complete the game and then be looking for more. Video game designers build more challenging modes and difficult achievements for these Good players because they want to give Good players a reason to keep coming back.

Because Good players are likely to play the same content over and over again, they are more versed in the intricacies of the game, where complexities could mean in-game economy, weapon dynamics, lore, play styles, or numerous other aspects of a given game.

Your Good players understand multiple aspects of the game and, as a result, have developed an aptitude for playing the game. They have developed skills. When Good players see other players perform exceptionally, they ask themselves, *How did she do that?* When Good players see better players sporting unique outfits and other heretofore unseen loot, they wonder, *How do I acquire that flying dragon?*

While not the majority of the players within the game, Good players are a sizable chunk, the Dabblers. If Average players are 60% of the player base, I'd say Good players are 30%.

Great

A single-digit percentage population. Great players are measured by their demonstrated high aptitude for the game. These players don't play the game; they live the game. When changes come to the game, they can explain why the changes are occurring and how they'll affect gameplay. They know new game features before anyone else because they comb all news sources for any snippet of credible information to continue to piece together a complete picture. When Good players see and compete with these Great players, the Good player is good enough to know, *Whoa, she is one of those...the great ones.* Great players are less than 10% of the players in a game.

S-Tier

Someone explained S-Tier to me a few years back. We were discussing scout rifles in *Destiny*, and someone in Discord said, "But, Mida (a gun), right now, Mida is S-Tier." *S-Tier?* S-Tier is the top tier. It may mean "Superb" or "Super" and may originate from academic grading in Japan. In video game culture, S-Tier means "the best."

I've never been S-Tier at any video game, but having watched many humans work at becoming great, I can tell you the difference between Great and S-Tier is...a second faster. It's a subsecond judgment call based on endless experience where you are almost imperceptibly better than your peers. The seconds add up.

As a Good player, all I can tell you about them is, "I know when I see them." I have never been great at video games, so how could I possibly explain what it means to be S-Tier? What is the difference between Great and S-Tier? It's microscopic. Acquisition of this skill is exponentially more complex than Good, and only a handful can tell the difference. Consistently a smidge better...forever.

I'll never be S-Tier, so am I just another Dabbler? Wait, that's not the question.

Are You Willing to Do the Work?

You might read between the lines and believe I'm suggesting the label *Dabbler* has a negative connotation. Like a Dabbler isn't genuinely committed to the effort, they're just there because it's interesting...right now. Briefly.

Here's what the Dabbler knows. There is an infinite list of exciting things to learn, but the Dabbler knows they have finite time, so they dabble. They get 80% of the juice, and they move on. Respect.

S-Tier knows the last 10% of the challenge is the hardest, but it also teaches you the most. S-Tier sticks with it because they contradictorily and confidently believe two things:

- This puzzle, project, or challenge task can be conquered.
- There is always 1% more to learn.

Some humans have a natural predisposition for a skill. The cost of getting from Good to Great appears lower, but it is the story we tell ourselves because we instinctively know the real cost. Do you know what it takes to be Great? Endless stubborn effort. It's not that you are unlucky in the genetic sweepstakes; you know being Great means never giving up.

It's inspiring to see someone be Great. You see them do their thing and tell yourself, *I could never do that.* What you don't see is the practice. It's the invisible years they spent working on getting better. The incessant failure. The friends and family who innocently and deflatingly asked, "Why are you working so hard?"

To Inspire

One of my favorite quotes is from Penn Jillette (*https://oreil.ly/mB3n_*), magician: "The only secret of magic is that I'm willing to work harder on it than you think it's worth." This applies to *any* craft.

Whether striving for S-Tier or a Dabbler, the work is the same. Spending the time to understand. S-Tier focuses on impressive depth, whereas the Dabbler appreciates the variety and complexity of breadth.

The magic you produce is twofold. First, it's the immense joy and sense of accomplishment of discovering understanding. It's reaping the rewards for curiosity, whether it's one thing or everything.

Second, it's the unintentional inspiration. Here I am, years later, telling you about Audrey in Soho Square. Three unannounced concerts.

She still inspires me. I wonder what she is learning...right now.

45

The Exodus

It's a day like any other. Two morning meetings with nothing unusual. The usual lunch followed by your staff meeting where...Andy shows up late. Andy is never, ever late for anything. *Odd...well, whatever.*

Staff finishes, still, nothing notable, except Andy says nothing the entire time, which is also odd. You're now officially wondering what is up with Andy, so you grab him and pull him to the closest office:

YOU: Dude, what's up?

ANDY: I'm leaving.

In a fraction of an instant, you can do all the political and social math regarding Andy's departure. You can see the complete set of unchangeable reasons he's leaving; you can predict who will follow, and you know that there isn't a damn thing you can do about it.

This is the Moment, and you can see how it will all crumble down at that moment.

This Sucks

At some point in your career, hopefully, through no fault of your own, an organization will start collapsing around you. It's a horrific experience that I hope you can avoid, but one you nonetheless need to understand.

Sorry about the collapse. That sucks. Everything that follows is a dispassionate and judgment-free review of the awful things that will occur, but before I start, I'd like to point out the singular upside to this collapse: you'll learn to see it coming.

Having been through three of these organizational disasters, you'd think I would have learned my lesson. Well, I have. I've learned that often there is no way to prevent organizational breakdowns of this magnitude, and sometimes the best you can do is either get out or find a comfortable place to hide.

Second, nothing in this chapter will help you prevent this cataclysm. In fact, this chapter assumes your disaster is in progress, guaranteed to be as bad as possible, and you're in it for the whole thing. Again, sorry.

TWO THREADS

To understand how this exodus begins, you must understand how information moves around your company. There are always two ongoing types of conversations in the building. One is tactical, and one is strategic. Each of these conversations or threads drives a specific part of your company and, consequently, a particular piece of your organizational collapse.

Let's talk about the tactical first.

Tactical

This is the daily conversation of the company. It includes the thoughts and opinions of everyone on the team. Content varies wildly by team and group, but these are the public topics associated with the team's work. We all care about our local scenery and whatever might eventually affect that scenery.

When everything is normal in the group, the tactical thread is kind of boring, but as we'll see, it changes when the sky falls.

Strategic

The easiest way to start thinking about the strategic conversation is, *This is what managers are talking about all day.* When I say *managers*, I mean from your boss all the way up to the CEO. The strategic conversation is the constantly evolving plan of action for the company. How are we doing? What's next? What's not working? How can we do better? Who is screwing up?

If you're reading that paragraph and filled with inner rage about the secrecy of managers and not being included in this conversation, I want to remind you that the sky is falling, and you need to chill out so you can figure out what to do next. Your being included in these strategic conversations very well might have prevented this worst-case scenario; your knowing might have given you insight that may have changed your course of action. But the collapse is happening, and all we're doing here is understanding how it might play out.

These participants in the strategic thread usually comprise the first wave of folks walking out the door. Whatever the underlying reasons are for this organizational collapse, they will first travel the strategic thread, as this is where early detection and triage will occur. If you're viewing the tactical thread as content provided by a bunch of docile sheep waiting to see when the next wolf will show up, you're a manager, and judging. Remind yourself of the world where your daily work was blissfully ignorant of the strategic shenanigans of the management caste.

THE FIRST WAVE

The first wave of departures consists of folks privy to the strategic conversational thread. They've heard what's coming and done the political and social math, so they're out. A few things to pay attention to here.

Where does this exodus begin?

Without a single conversation, you can infer a lot simply from the starting location of the exodus. If sales is bleeding people, one might assume something is wrong in sales, and if sales are bad, well, everything's bad. A mass departure from engineering says the same thing: something is wrong in engineering, which means something is wrong with the product, which means you may not have anything to sell.

Why are they leaving?

Now is an excellent time to figure out why. There will be a well-crafted message traveling the hallways explaining these departures, but the message has been created to spin whatever it is that this wave of departures is fleeing. You need the truth.

If you want to understand why a bright strategic person is gone, you need to get them behind a door in a safe place where you can ask: "OK, WTF?" This is how you're going to get the real story.

Why are they letting them go?

In any exodus, there's a linchpin departure in the first wave. This person is perceived in the group or organization as essential to the business. *If they leave, we're dead.*

And they're leaving.

The troubling part of the linchpin departure is that everyone knows this person is essential. Worse, everyone in the strategic conversation knows this, *and* they understand why this person wants to leave and is still going.

If this person is essential, that means everything has been done to retain them, and they're still merrily getting the hell out of the building. Whether you've successfully uncovered the root cause of the exodus or not, the linchpin departure is an excellent leading indicator of what's about to happen: the second wave.

THE SECOND WAVE

If the first wave is the departure of strategic resources, the second wave is tactical, and for each person in this wave, it starts with the Moment.

While randomness is part of doing business on planet Earth, most folks spend a lot of time insulating themselves from this randomness. They go to school to learn what randomness might occur so they can try to predict it, they get married to reduce the randomness of the heart, and they get a job so their day is full of predictable things to do.

Injections of randomness freak people out. They see these events as assaults on the foundation they've built against the randomness, and in this attack, there are two typical responses: fight or flight. This is the Moment. It's the instant recognition that your world has been forever changed by the uncontrollable random, and there's likely not a damned thing you can do about it, so you either decide to dig in or make a run for it.

Now, the first wave is already in progress, so why am I talking about the Moment relative to the second wave? The Moment occurs for everyone in the first wave, too, but the Moment has much more potential for organizational damage in the second wave.

The scary potential of the second wave is that the legitimate strategic reasons behind the first wave transform into crazy conspiracy theories based on people's core discomfort with a random world. The tactical conversation thread drives the second wave, and once the exodus has begun, the tactical thread mutates from the daily dish to the formidable grapevine. See, in an absence of actual information, people make stuff up (think back to Chapter 16).

The one thing to pay attention to in your role as an observer of this hypothetical disaster is: What is being done to inform the second wave? Management has two approaches.

Approach #1: Wait it out

Remember, we're in the middle of the first wave and the beginning of the second wave. The time to prevent this disaster has passed, and now we're into damage control. The question is, When do they start? I suppose your management team has already screwed up by not reacting during the first wave because I'm assuming a worst-case scenario. It's the second wave now—are they still waiting?

Management sees acknowledgment of the disaster as a disaster in itself. They believe that if the world knows this disaster was allowed to occur, there would be a significant downstream impact, which is ironic because the downstream impact is already happening. They're making it worse by ignoring it.

Sigh.

Approach #2: Stem the tide

Hopefully, a conversation will begin. Someone will stand up in front of the room and project a list of bullet items directly targeted at explaining this disaster. This will be a well-shaped message geared to answer one question: "What are we doing to stop this randomness from happening?"

The good news is that management has decided to do something. Given the bizarre theories traveling the tactical channel, any message is better than the destructive silence.

The specific managerial repairs that need to be made are a function of the disaster, and I don't know what disaster that is. Still, if you see the disaster's true nature, my questions are: Do they talk about it? Are they doing something to stem the tide, or are these crafted messages just different versions of waiting it out?

Never underestimate the ability of a management team to interpret reality to their benefit. Managers at all levels are incentivized to observe and report on a world that supports a business's view of progress. These reports vary from subtle adjustments to the truth to outright lies.

As an aside and in defense of managers who are doing their best, this optimization for the self is natural human behavior. It's not that you believe that the world revolves around you; it's just from where you're sitting, it seems like it might. The problem with this self-optimization relative to management is that they have the unique responsibility to optimize for themselves and you. There are situations where those separate goals conflict. Think of it like this. Your manager is going to have their world-altering Moment just like you, and the question is: Are they going to look out for their interests or yours?

The second wave is when things just get weird. Half-true stories are being told in the hallways, and personalities have altered as people are shoved out of their comfort zones. The normal workday is full of drama and intrigue, and that's the other problem with the second wave: its existence is a reason to leave.

Whether they're doing something about it or not, management's hope is a quick end to the second wave because they're under the false impression that completing the second wave is the end of the exodus.

Again, wrong.

THE THIRD WAVE

In this hypothetical disaster, you're still here. You needed front-row seats to understand the exodus's mechanics fully, and you've got one more wave.

The third wave is the devious wave.

The first wave is gone, the second is gone or about to be gone, and one morning you have a brief glimpse of normality. No one walks into your office with their Moment on their face. It's been a couple of days since anyone has resigned. It almost feels normal.

And you want it to be normal. All of this wave bullshit has been exhausting, and during all of these waves, productivity is shot along with morale, so when a day has just a glimmer of normality, you mentally leap on it: *Hey, do I actually get to work today?*

Not so fast.

During the first two waves, a pile of people has been cast to the wind. Maybe they landed inside of the company, perhaps they landed elsewhere. One of the things they took with them is an intimate knowledge of the inner workings of your group. This means that every talented person who hasn't left in the first two waves will be recruited by these annoying, happy former coworkers who dangle just one thing: *You know where I am; there's no disaster, right?*

The folks who have survived the multiple wave exoduses are tired, demoralized, and adrift, so they are susceptible when a familiar face shows up with good news about a bright future. If they're talented and situationally aware, I've no idea what they're still doing on the sinking ship, but they're still there...for now.

The third wave isn't of the same magnitude as the first two waves. It's aftershocks, but anyone who has been through a natural disaster knows it's the aftershocks that drive you crazy. The third wave wears on the folks who have weathered the storm; the third wave might be why they choose to leave.

Which Wave?

This wave model is inevitable. It's how groups of people react when their home becomes professionally treacherous. Horrible news leads to noteworthy departures. All those departures lead to larger departures.

I'm sorry to have hypothetically kept you in the building for this entire event, but knowing how it's going to play out gives you context so you can figure out your move. Are you the first one out? Or will you wait for your friends to throw you a lifesaver?

Here's the good news: you've just been through hell. You've just acquired years of professional experience watching the intricacies of your organization slowly collapse around you. You've made three new lifelong friends with now-former coworkers who took you aside before they left and said, "The best part of working on this project was working with you." And unless this disaster kills your company, this rapid restructuring of your group will result in opportunities you would have never seen.

Surviving the collapse of an organization is like surfing big waves. You only know the wave is significant when it gets close; surfing it scares the hell out of you and screwing up during the ride results in an additional beatdown, but when you're done, you're better equipped to handle the next wave.

46

Bad News About Your Bright Future

You...are kicking ass.

A wealth of experience makes decisions appear to be easy. Experience gives you confidence, and you use that confidence to deliver your wise decisions with moxie. Those watching you think, *Boy, he's got it figured out.* The rub is this: confidence is a delicious answer to uncertainty, but confidence is a feeling, a perception. What you're really banking on is your experience and your history of hard knocks, which have given you a useful and valuable perspective on which to base your decisions.

And experience has a half-life.

Confidence works well with experience and creates success, and when you're successful, everyone says, "Way to go!" and you believe those compliments and turn them into additional confidence that turns into more success and then more confidence, and the cycle repeats.

Again, you are kicking ass.

Success. Fame. These are a type of experience, but they aren't what got you the compliment in the first place. It's that you did something significant; you worked and did something significant. Not that you said you did something with confidence.

Like any industry, high tech is full of people confusing success and fame with experience. They're thinking that showing up at conferences, giving interviews, and writing books about things they did in the past is experience. It's not. It's storytelling, and while it might be valuable storytelling, these people are slowly becoming echoes of who they were and moving further from the work they did that matters. They're confusing compliments for experience.

You may not be one of these people, but it doesn't mean you're not exhibiting the same behavior. My question is, Each day, are you struggling to build something new or just easily repeating the success of your past? Success feels good, but you're not actually doing anything.

Building stuff every day exercises all the muscles necessary to remain vital. Experience fades and becomes irrelevant without a constant flow of the new.

I'm happy you are kicking ass. It's ass that needs kicking, and you are doing it well. I believe the success-based environment can be deliciously deceiving. I think that much of what created that environment was blood, sweat, and tears, and who wants more tears? Look deeply at your favorite success story, and you'll find a bit of misery. It's a great motivator, but who wants to do that again?

You do.

What's Next

This book began with a mantra:

> We seek *definition* to understand
>
> the *system* so that we can discern
>
> the *rules* so that we
>
> know what to do next so that
>
> we *win*.

Each person on the planet has a small set of rules they silently repeat to themselves when they find themselves at a crossroads, and it's these core beliefs that structure their thinking and give them the impetus to choose.

No trait is more important to the engineer than their structure. The specific type of structural obsession varies from engineer to engineer. Some are fixated on time constraints, others carefully observe and enforce rules, but for each engineer, I believe the quest is, *Learn enough about my world to predict what's next.*

Surprises disrupt structure, which means when the unexpected occurs, the nerd or the geek panics. *Wait, I had a definition, I understood the system that dictated the rules...WTF?*

Chapter 1 laid out two goals for this book:

- Improve your improvisation skills of the moment.
- Define your career strategy.

You'll notice that *Learn enough about my world to predict what's next* is not included as a goal for this book because whether you've been wildly successful or not, you'll never know what's going to happen next, and embracing that idea is a strategic career advantage.

More bad news: not only can you not predict what's going to happen, but I'm pretty sure you're not even fully appreciating what's happening right now.

Biased by the Now

The traditional reason to leave a gig is that something has gone wrong or is no longer to your liking. The degree of wrongness varies from simple boredom to complex hatred, but whatever the story is, it's clear it's time to make a change. If this is the case, go back to Chapter 2 and get started. Here at the end, I want to talk about nonobvious reasons to make a change and some of the ways your brain is deceiving you. I want to explain why you'd leave your job when everything's swell and you believe you're kicking ass. I want you to consider why you'd leave a job you love.

You are biased by the now. I suggest that you cannot imagine what your professional life would be like if you were no longer doing it.

It's not that you're not bright or aware of your surroundings; it's that there's too much data. There are the intricate personalities of the people you work with who compose an entirely unique culture of the team, the organization, and the company. There's the politics that change the professional mood of the building every day. There's everything you're living and breathing right now, and while I believe you could explain to me over a beer what it's like to work at the company, it would be a description of the moment. You would carefully and descriptively explain to me what it was like to work there for the past two weeks, but it would not be a complete description because there's far too much data to organize and describe.

You have an opinion and impressions about your gig. Still, these are based on your brain gathering together all the data it sees as important and carefully fitting that data into your view of the world. After that, the data is thrown away because it's too much. It's not that you shouldn't trust your opinion about your gig, but I suggest that just because you think you've figured it out and are happy doesn't mean you're growing.

I'll ask the same questions I touched on in Chapter 2:

- Have you failed recently?
- Is there someone within throwing distance who challenges you daily?

- Can you tell me the story of something significant you learned in the last week?

The intent behind these questions is disruption: When has something occurred that you did not predict? It is these disruptive and decidedly non-geek-friendly moments that engage your brain in interesting ways. I'm of the opinion that your brain's reasonable and healthy quest for happiness isn't always aligned with your professional growth because your brain does not seek conflict.

An Uncomfortable Ending

You should be uncomfortable with this chapter. I'm uncomfortable writing it. I am suggesting:

- Just because you're kicking ass doesn't mean you're successful.
- Misery is productive.
- Conflict is learning.

I hope that at the end of this book, you're better equipped to deal with misery, change, and conflict. Perhaps you understand your boss better, and the reorganization may make more sense. Your professional improvisation skills may have improved by reading the stories of how I've navigated Werewolves and Leapers. Finally, and hopefully, you have a better idea of where you want to head in your career because having that structure can help when your career is not going according to plan.

Knowing all of this helps, but misery, change, and conflict are still going to show up randomly, and sometimes you should create them in a professionally healthy sense. Without reason, with no big plan, just a leap in a strange direction for no other reason than to see what it teaches you.

You're in a hurry.

Epilogue: Hurry

Most interesting ideas come to me between 8:00 and 10:00 a.m. This is sacred time. I spend most of this time in the car driving to work. I create two or three startups during the average drive to work. The music from the car speakers and constant hum of traffic provides a creative, catalyzing ambiance.

And then I get to work, and I Google my ideas. "How about a replacement for Twitter?"

It's called Mastodon. Crap.

"Wait, wait, wait, what we need is people feeds. An RSS-type thing that shows me the relevant events for the people I care about."

FriendFeed. Right. Someone already did that and nothing became of it. Goddammit.

You're in a hurry.

Do the math. We are all staring at the same set of data. Yes, there is a lot of data, and there is a very low probability that you can surf it all, but here's the rub: there are many of us. In fact, there are a lot of us. When you combine all of us with the equally huge amount of data, you understand that when I arrive at work and Google my great ideas, I'm no longer surprised when my precisely designed drive-to-work business model is already a business.

You're in a Hurry

The epiphany I want to discuss is this: What are you waiting for? Seriously. I know you've got a mortgage and 1.5 kids, but during your sacred time, when you discover that bright idea, and subsequently discover that no established competitor exists...why aren't you making the leap?

I know what you're waiting for.

See, you've been doing the same comfortable thing I did for 20 years. You're obeying the organizational structure, where charts describe who owns what and who owns whom. I am intimately familiar with the mindset that reads:

"We will complete our work by following the rules of mediocrity."

Do just enough. Don't rock the boat. Make yourself indispensable without being noticeable.

And it works. There is absolutely no way to argue that following the rules doesn't result in a comfortable life, but...

You're in a hurry.

Maybe you're waiting for validation. You're waiting for that someone you respect to say, "Yes, you bright person, you should do that thing." It was your parents when you were a kid, and then it was your first boss, but now it simply needs to be you.

What you need to understand about these people who support you is that they're not here to slow you down; they're here to get the hell out of your way so you can be brilliant. You need to discover the moment when you know better than everyone around you—when you make the first move without asking permission.

You don't need to quit your job and build the next Twitter. Try it. Try it with something small. A thing where you'd ordinarily preflight it with your boss, bounce the idea around the hallway, and move forward. Skip the hallway and move on with your idea.

Don't worry if someone else is already working on your idea. I'm confident they are, but they are decidedly not you, and it's the *you* that makes your idea unique.

Whether successful or not, it's a terrific way to get into a lot of trouble. There's a long list of established rules and regulations that you violate with your creative impertinence, but it feels great, right?

Trusting your gut and charging forward. It can be addictive.

It's not your only operating procedure. There are teams to communicate with and strategic corporate alignment that needs to be maintained, but then there's you, on the subway to work, drinking a Starbucks when inspiration strikes, and rather than just soaking in that brief moment of illumination, I want you to do something about it because...

You're in a hurry.

The Rules of Back Alley Bridge

Back Alley is a simple version of bridge with some strong similarities to Spades and Hearts. A quick search of the web reveals a version of Back Alley Bridge that was popular during the Vietnam War. I learned this version during my college career at University of California, Santa Cruz.

A full game is a relatively long experience, running roughly one to two hours, depending on speed of play. Don't play drunk; it's not fun.

Preparing for Back Alley Bridge

You will need:

- 1 deck of 52 standard playing cards (plus the 2 jokers).
- The 2 jokers need to be marked to make them distinguishable from each other. I recommend using a felt-tip pen to mark one joker with the word *BIG* and mark one with the word *LITTLE* (see the next section, "Rules of Play").
- 1 pad of paper and a writing utensil used to keep score.
- 4 players (2 teams).

Rules of Play

1. Players and cards
   a. The players form 2 teams. Players on the same team sit facing each other.

   b. The game is played clockwise.

   c. The trump in Back Alley is always Spades.

   d. The BIG joker used in Back Alley is the highest trump card. The LITTLE joker is the second-highest trump card.

   e. The cards in each suit rank from highest to lowest:

   A K Q J 10 9 8 7 6 5 4 3 2.

   For the trump, or Spades, the BIG and LITTLE jokers would come before the ace.

2. Deal

   a. Initial dealer is determined at random.

   b. The dealer shuffles and deals out all cards so that each player has 13 cards. This will leave 2 cards left over.

   c. Turn to deal rotates clockwise.

   d. Each subsequent hand is dealt with 1 less card (i.e., 13, 12, 11, etc.). Two hands are dealt with a single card, followed by dealing with 1 more card (i.e., 2, 3, 4, etc.) for a total of 26 hands. (Variation: deal every *other* hand, i.e., 13, 11, 9, etc. This allows the game to be completed in roughly 1 hour.)

3. Bidding

   a. Starting with the player to the left of the dealer, each player bids as to how many tricks they can take, and each team's bids are totaled. If the player does not bid any tricks, they "pass."

   For example: Player 1 bids 5, Player 2 bids 2, Player 3 bids 3, and Player 4 bids 2. That totals 12 out of a possible 13 tricks.

   b. There are two special bids in Back Alley called BOARD and BOSTON.

   If a player bids BOARD, they are saying that their team will take *every single* trick in the hand (see item 6, Scoring).

   If a player bids BOSTON, they are saying that their team will take the *first* 6 tricks in the hand (see item 6, Scoring).

   — Unlike the BOARD bid, a player may not declare BOSTON when there are 6 or fewer tricks being played.

Players may double, triple, or quadruple any of these bids.

— This occurs very often when there are only a few cards in the hand. For example, Player 1 bids BOARD, Player 2 passes, Player 3 bids DOUBLE BOARD, Player 4 passes (see item 6, Scoring). In this case, DOUBLE BOARD would be the highest bid and would lead.

— A player may not bid a double, triple, or quadruple bid unless the appropriate single, double, or triple has already been bid. Example: The first bid cannot be DOUBLE BOSTON.

4. Redeal

a. There are two situations where a hand can be redealt:

If *all* players pass during the bidding process, or

If, at 7 or more cards, a player's hand contains no aces, spades, or face cards.

5. The play

a. Highest bidder leads with anything they want, except trump, unless:

If the team has bid either BOARD or BOSTON, they may lead with trump.

b. Each player *must* follow suit if possible. If they can't, they can trump and thereby normally take the trick. Or they can throw another card (usually low) of another suit because that way they cannot take the trick.

c. Once trump is broken, anyone can lead with trump or another suit.

d. The BIG joker is the most powerful card (i.e., the *highest spade*). When the BIG is led, both players on the other team must follow with their largest trump card while the partner may lead any spade (if they have one). The LITTLE joker is the second-highest trump card (i.e., below the BIG joker but above the Ace) and has no other special characteristics.

e. In the following play, the person that took the prior trick leads the next trick.

6. Scoring

   a. Team scoring is 5 points per trick bid and taken, with 1 additional point for any tricks taken over the bid. −5 points per trick bid if the team does not take the number of tricks they bid, which is referred to as being SET. Examples:

   Bid 5 and get 5: the team receives 25 points. (5 tricks bid × 5 points)

   Bid 7 and get 8: the team receives 36 points. (7 tricks bid × 5 points + 1 point for the extra trick)

   Bid 4 and get 2: the team receives −20 points. (4 tricks × −5 points)

   Bid 4 and get none: the team receives −20 points. (4 tricks × −5 points)

   b. If a team bids BOARD, the points per trick are adjusted to 10 points per trick. −10 points per total tricks if the team does not achieve the number of tricks they bid. If a board is doubled, tripled, or quadrupled, the points are multiplied accordingly.

   Bid BOARD on a 2-card hand and get both tricks. Team receives 20 points. (2 total tricks × 10 points)

   Bid BOARD on a 3-card hand and get 2 tricks. Team receives −30 points. (3 total tricks × −10 points)

   Bid DOUBLE BOARD on a 3-card hand and get all tricks. Team receives 60 points. (3 total tricks × 10 points × DOUBLE)

   c. If a team bids BOSTON, a flat bonus of 100 points is awarded to the team that successfully takes the first 6 tricks, plus 1 point per extra trick. A flat bonus of −100 points is awarded to the team that declares, but fails to take, the first 6 tricks.

   Bid BOSTON on a 10-card hand and get the first 6 cards plus 1 additional trick. Team receives 101 points. (BOSTON + 1 extra trick)

   Bid BOSTON on a 7-card hand and get only get 3 tricks. Team receives −100 points.

   Bid DOUBLE BOSTON (this does not happen very often and usually only as a last-ditch effort on the final hand) and get only 4 tricks. Team receives −200 points. (−100 points × DOUBLE)

   d. At the end of 26 hands, the team with the highest score wins.

Index

About the Author

Michael Lopp is a veteran Silicon Valley–based engineering leader who builds both people and products at historic companies such as Slack, Borland, Netscape, Palantir, Pinterest, and Apple. When he's not deeply concerned with staying relevant, he writes about leadership, bridges, superheroes, and humans at the popular weblog *Rands in Repose*. This is the way.

Michael also rides bikes that each have names (Sia, Isabelle, Shasta, Maeve), wonders about semicolons, drinks red wine, and tries to understand how forests work among the redwoods of Northern California because curiosity is how you grow.

Colophon

The cover illustration is by Susan Thompson. The cover fonts are Guardian Sans and Gilroy. The text font is Scala Pro, and the heading font is Benton Sans.